EDUCATION
IN
MEDIEVAL INDIA

Compiled & Edited
by
Dr. R.K. Pruthi

SONALI PUBLICATIONS
NEW DELHI-110002

Edition : 2025

ISBN 81-88836-65-6

Published by

SONALI PUBLICATIONS
4228/1, Ansari Road,
New Delhi-110 002 (India)
Phone: 23266109, 23279245 • Fax: 91-11-23253475

Printed by:
Navya Digital, Delhi - 110092

Preface

Education during medieval period underwent cross-cultural experiences. At the same time both Islamic and Hindu educational systems remained in practice throughout the medieval age. Philosophy, principles and methods of education were mainly based upon the religions of the two communities.

Aim of this book is to make available to our readers, various perspectives of the education during the period with the background of the Hindu and Muslim cultures. This will enable our readers to understand the evolution of education during the medieval age.

We record our acknowledgments to the authorities and institutions for excellent work on the subject.

Librarians, institutions and their staff members have been kind and helpful, we thank them all.

Last but not the least my publisher and his staff members at different levels have worked hard. They deserve love and also patronage of my readers.

R.K. Pruthi

Contents

1

Introduction

Muslims attached great importance to education. Their Prophet said "It is better to educate one's child than to give gold in charity". To him the acquirement of knowledge was an act of piety. According to him, "one who speaks of (knowledge), praises the Lord; who seeks it adores God; who dispenses instruction in it, bestows alms; who imparts it to fitting objects, performs an act of devotion to God. Knowledge enables its possessor to distinguish what is forbidden from what is not; it lights the way to heaven, it is our friend in the desert, our society in solitude, our companion when bereft of friends; it guides us to happiness it sustains us in misery; it is our ornament in the company of friends; it serves as an armour against our enemies. With knowledge the servant of God rises to the heights of goodness and to a noble position, associates with sovereigns in this world, and attains to the perfection of happiness in the next". A little reflection of what we said about the Hindu ideals of education would show the both Hindus and Muslims have prized education as the greatest gift in this world. Hazrat Mohammed, like the Hindus believed in perpetual learning, when he said that knowledge should be sought, "from the cradle to the grave" and should be acquired, "even if it be in China".

There is no doubt, that most of the Muslim kings were well known as lovers of letters. They were themselves learned and patronised the learned. Their courts were full of scholars and they always appointed very highly educated personages on responsible jobs. There is evidence to show that some of the kings had a separate department, which looked after religious and educational institutions. These kings provided educational facilities by opening schools, colleges and libraries. There were great centres of learning where thousands thronged to acquire knowledge. Stipends and scholarships were granted by the state to those students who were poor. The state would set up orphanages for the free education of poor and orphan children. In the state schools and colleges teachers and professors were paid by the Government. Endowments were created and large estates set apart to maintain educational institutions.

According to the injunctions of Hazrat Mohammed the acquisition of learning was compulsory for all—boys and girls. He enjoined upon the parents that, "no present or a gift of a parent to a child is superior to a good liberal education". The school, therefore, catered both for girls and boys. Of course, for girls there were separate schools as the Muslims believe in purdah system. The females of aristocratic families engaged private tutors, who taught them at home. Men of advanced age or women were employed to teach girls. Many widows considered it their sacred duty to impart religious education to girls.

From this patronage of education Hindus were not excluded. Although the Hindus maintained their own schools, several of them studied in Maktabs and Madrisas in, order to equip themselves for government service under the Muslim rulers. The language and literature of the Hindus was encouraged. Some of the Kings and chiefs got several books of Sanskrit translated into Persian and Arabic. Many a Muslim scholar learned Sanskrit and Hindi. Some of them became well-known poets in these languages. Likewise, several Hindus made a mark in the language and literature of Persian and Arabic. It was due to the impact of Hindu-Muslim culture and literature and social intercourse that Urdu language got its birth in India.

Aims and Objectives

The aims and objectives of education of the Muslims were similar to those of the Hindus. The basis was religion and the ideal was to produce religious-minded and pious persons. Every Maktab and Madrisa, therefore, had a mosque attached to it. Their education was a blend of religious and secular instruction. Character formation was also a great objective of education. They wanted to discipline the intellect of the young and inculcate in them the essentials which should promote their moral and material improvement. 'Education should prepare for this life and life after death' was also not ignored. The youths under the Muslims were given training in several practical skills of life.

Initiation Ceremony

The initiation ceremony for commencing education was as picturesque in the Muslim period and among the Muslims as was the case in the Brahmanical and Buddhist system of education. This ceremony was called "Bismillah-Khani" or Maktab ceremony (putting a boy in school for the first time). When a child attained the age of 4 years, 4 months and 4 days, an auspicious hour was fixed, in consultation with an expert astrologer to perform this ceremony. The child was dressed in the best clothes, seated on the cushion in the presence of a gathering of friends and relatives and was entrusted to the care of the tutor. There was a shower of good wishes on the novice by all concerned.

This Maktab ceremony in the case of girls was a little different. When a girl commenced her studies, a blessing was written for her on a coloured paper known as Zarfishani. Rich presents were given to her tutor in the presence of many people gathered for the purpose. Her tutor was entertained frequently and was given presents whenever the girl began a new lesson of a new book.

Educational Institutions

Elementary Education: This type of education was provided in primary schools and private houses. Every mosque had a Maktab or a Primary school. On the religious side certain portions of the Quran, essential for saying daily prayers and devotions, were taught. On the secular side instruction in 3 R's was given.

There were teachers who would hold their classes in their houses. The teachers imparted free education, except that they expected personal service on the part of pupils and help in kind from the parents. Sometimes a rich man would engage a tutor to teach his sons and daughters on a small remuneration. Generally, he allowed the children of his less affluent neighbours to study along with his children. The tutors engaged at home were drawn both from the Hindus and the Muslims.

The novice was at first introduced to alphabet. He was taught correct pronunciation, punctuation and signs of accents. Then he was taught to combine these letters into words and phrases. Writing was practised on "takhti" with reed pens. After teaching him reading and writing elementary arithmetic was taught. Such village schools were found almost everywhere, wherever there was a mosque.

Secondary Education: All the mosques, Khanqahs (monasteries) and dargahs (shrines) provided religious as well as secular education. In the latter were included subjects like grammar, literature, Persian, and Arabic, geometry, some science, economics and history. These schools were either supported by State grants in cash or land or by the philanthropy of some big persons.

In fact in the Muslim period we find no distinction between a secondary school and a college because both of them were called Madrisas.

Higher Education: In some of the big towns like Gopamau and Khariabad in Oudh, Jaunpur in Agra, Lahore, Multan, Delhi, Ajmer, Lucknow, Murshadabad, etc. there was arrangement for higher studies. In these centres of education, students came from inside the country and from Afghanistan and Bukhara. The subjects taught were of advanced type. Subjects like Grammar, Literature, Persian, Arabic, Geometry, Science, Economics and History, which were taught at the secondary stage, were taken up again for more critical study. Other subjects at the higher stage were rhetoric, logic, theology, metaphysics, jurisprudence, astronomy, the art of administration, arithmetic, algebra, physics, medicine, natural philosophy, etc. The medium of instruction was Persian, because this was the court language of the times. Arabic was compulsory for Musalmans. Hindus could read their own national books. All these great centres of education did not teach all the subjects mentioned above. Every great centre of learning had specialised in teaching some subjects. The selection of subjects was made by students according to their future aims and ambitions. When some of these centres of higher learning rose to the status of Universities, provision was made for almost all the subjects mentioned above.

Educational Assemblies and Symposia: In order to create love for learning and respect for scholars there used to be held educational assemblies and symposia. Learned people would often collect together.

They initiated a discussion and enlightened the gathering, collected for the purpose. If educated people expressed their opinions on account of having read many books, the illiterate people expressed their opinions on various subjects by virtue of their accumulated experiences. In this way their outlook was broadened and they got knowledge from scholars. Lectures for the common folk were common and thus the people at large were kept in touch with topical subjects. Similarly poetical symposia also widened the mental horizon of the people and created in them love for learning. Kings and princes offered rich rewards and precious presents for intellectual tournaments. This gave great stimulus to scholars to excel each other in composing poems or other literary pieces. The best poet of the day received the title of Malak-us-shaura (Poet-laureate).

Vocational Education: Besides the scholastic studies there was ample provision for vocational, professional and technical education. The Industrial Commission in 1918 said, "At a time when the West of Europe, the birthplace of modern industrial system, was inhabited by uncivilised tribes, India was famous for the wealth of .... high artistic skill of her craftsmen. And even at a much later period, when merchant adventurers from the West made their first appearance in India, the industrial development of the country was, at any rate, not inferior to that of the more advanced European nations". This view of the Commission is supported by four eminent economists. Professor Weber says, "the skill of the Indians in the production of delicate woven fabrics, in the mixing of colours, the working of metals and precious stones and in all manner of technical arts.... enjoyed a world wide celebrity." Mr. Ranade believed that, "industry not only supplied all local wants, but also enabled India to export its finished products to foreign countries". Professors Jathar and Beri and of the opinion that the trade and prosperity of India attracted European traders. They came not for raw materials but because they valued the manufactures and crafts of India. All these encomiums of Indian arts and skills cannot be without any reason. There is evidence to show that there was a good deal of artistic, vocational and technical education, otherwise the fine fabrics, the beautiful shawls, the painted-wares and the gold and silver ornaments of India would not have been known throughout the world. There were many 'karkhanas' or manufacturing centres which gave technical training to those who had aptitude for it. Besides, the experts in various useful and fine arts accepted apprentices. The teachers charged no regular fees. Presents, however, were given to them frequently by their pupils. There was not much emphasis on the theoretical side of arts and crafts. Artisans and craftsmen, instead of developing their mental powers, were given practical training. Inventors of new things and markers of important mechanical works were encouraged by the kings who gave them rewards and munificent allowances. Feroze Shah Taughlak maintained a regular department of industries. He placed all his slaves under master craftsmen to learn different arts. Learning of fine arts, painting and music was especially encouraged by the monarchs and principal chiefs, who kept a number of artists in their courts and in their houses to teach Art to their children. The presence of so many magnificent buildings shows that the art of stone-cutting had reached in zenith. There were many trade guilds, providing education for various professions and trades. For commercial education the trading classes had their own schools, where this type of education was imparted to their children in business management and accounts.

State Patronage of Education

Education by the State was altogether non-existent under the Brahmanical and Buddhist system of education. At that time it was exclusively a private enterprise. The kings and rulers did endow educational institutions with liberal grants. They patronised scholars and respected them, but never opened educational institutions directly under their own management. The position altered during the Muslim rule. The Muslim rulers not only patronised scholars by giving them scholarships and responsible job in their courts and encouraged private effort in education, but they also opened State schools and colleges.

Muhammed Ghori was the first Muslim king of India who set up many schools and seminaries in the province of Ajmer for spreading Islamic culture and learning. His successor Qutub-ud-din Aibak was a learned person and encouraged secular learning in the several mosques that had come into being on account of the Muslim conquest. Altamash and Razzia who followed Aibak founded a college each. The latter planned sucessfully the Muizzi college in Delhi. The courts of Nasir-ud-din and Balban were frequented by learned and talented people. The former is reported to have founded two colleges, one of them at Jullundur. Under the Khilijis, Delhi became a great centre of learning. All the Tughlak kings were scholars and attracted learned personages from far and wide. For the diffusion of knowledge and imparting instruction to people. Feroze Shah appointed learned teachers in different parts of his dominions. He repaired all the Madrisas, which were in a decadent condition and founded 30 new colleges. The description of Feroz-Shahi Madrisa is a sufficient testimony to the fact that the colleges were all well equipped in every respect. For example, this Madrasa had a magnificent building with gardens and separate apartments for foreign scholars. It was a residential institution, where poor students enjoyed the same facilities as the rich.

Sayad kings, sucessors to Tughlaks, brought educational eminence to the two cities of Badaon and Cuttair. They compared favourably with Delhi as educational centres. Lodhis founded many schools and colleges and made education compulsory for military officers. It was during Sikandar Lodhi's time that Agra competed in learning and culture with Delhi. Not only the Imperial kings of Delhi encouraged the spread of learning, even the provincial Governors did their best in this direction. Cities like Multan, Jaunpore and Malwa possessed a superior standard of education.

The best attention given to education was under the Mughals. Babar entrusted his Public Works Department the duty of looking after the schools and colleges. Most propitious time for education was that of Akbar and Aurangzeb. Although himself an unread person, Akbar had scholars around him. Agra, Lahore and Fatehpur Sikri became great centres of literary activity. Nurmerous Maktabs and Madrisas were founded and richly endowed. Akbar was not only concerned with the multiplication of Maktabs and Madrasas, but he also wanted that the quality and content of education should be improved. During his reign the curriculum was modified to enable the students to acquire education acording to their particular aims and ambitions. According to Ain-I-Akbari "every boy ought to read books on morals, arithmetic, agriculture, mensuration, geometry, astronomy, physiognomy, household methods, the rules of government, medicine, logic, the physical sciences and history". He thought that too much time was being wasted in learning, reading and writing and, therefore, gave the logical methods of learning these two skills. He wished to reduce the time spent on them. Of course, he wanted that whatever was taught should be taught thoroughly. He said, "are was to be taken that he (the pupil learns to understand everything himself, but the teacher may assist him a little". Thus he advocated self-study with a proper guidance by the teacher. To him sound education depended upon intelligent co-operation between the pupil and the teacher. The curriculum advocated by Akbar shows that the subject of practical utility were not neglected. His main emphasis was on the teaching of morals. The work of Akbar was not undone by his sucessors—Jahangir and Shahjahan. All the educational institutions, with their rich endowments, continued in unabated propersity.

Aurangzeb was himself well versed in Arabic, Persian, as mother tongue, Chugtai Turkish, in several arts and science, in theology and the mysteries of Arabic grammar. He founded numerous schools and colleges. Imperial Firmans were issued to Provincial Governments to look to the education of their subjects. But his attitude towards Hindu educational institutions was not worthy of an emperor. In 1669 he ordered the Hindu schools and temples to be destroyed, though all other Muslim rulers tolerated them. He, however, had very progressive views on education. To him the prevailing methods and content of education was utterly useless. About the education of princes, for example, he wanted that they should be "acquainted with the distinguishing features of every nation of the earth; its resources and strength; its mode of warfare, its manners, religions, form of government and where in its interests principally consist". "Origin of states; their progress and decline" according to him, must be studied. He considered the subject of history as most vital study for princes. He hated verbalism and wasting too much time on grammar, language and law. Comprehensive knowledge, elevating the individual and rendering him capable of glorious deeds, was his ideal. He preferred sciences to philosophy. The latter he wanted to train the intellect for reasoning power, instead of stuffing the intellect with foolish propositions. To him mother-tongue, rather than Arabic, was a convenient medium of instruction.

Extent of Education

There was a good deal of education in India under the Muslims. We have, however, no statistics to prove that, except that in every village, however small, there was a mosque and in a town and in a city there were several mosques. Every mosque had a school attached to it. It can be safely gathered that there must have been a large number of young people attending the schools. Again. there could not have been a rich crop of poets and philosophers, historians and others without popular education. The percentage of literacy must have been quite high to be able to impress scholars in those days.

Teacher-pupil Relationship

In the Muslim period the teacher was as much respected as during the early period of Indian history. There was intimate relationship between the teacher and the pupil, although the practice of living with the teacher was not as common with the Muslims as it was in the case of Brahmans and Buddhists. Pupils were expected to serve their teacher and in return got sometimes free food and always free knowledge from him.

Although one teacher did not have many pupils to teach, yet if there were many, the teacher would take the help of senior and advanced students to teach the younger or the junior ones. Punishments were quite severe. Truants and delinquents were caned on their palms and slapped on their faces. A strange mode of punishment was to make the children "hold their ears by taking their hands from under their thighs while sitting on their tip toes." Korah or whip was also quite common. Any form of punishment devised and thought of by the ingenuity of teacher was permissible.

The system of education prevalent under the Muslims was suited to the times. It catered to the religious, cultural, intellectual and vocational needs of the people. This system produced great scholars, savants and seekers after truth. Hindi as well as Urdu got their birth during these times. It, however, cannot be denied that inherent defects in the system of education were not removed in spite of the progressive views of Akbar and Aurangzeb. When the British came they found the indigenous system in a decadent condition.

2

Education when the Muslims Invaded

At the time when the Muslims had invaded India, education was flourishing well qualitatively here. The current of Indian education flowed on incessantly in spite of the vandalism perpetrated by the invaders and Muslim rulers with regard to the destruction of educational centres of the country. Hindu society was founded on solid and fundamentally invulnerable principles and as such the Mohammedan efforts could not prevail in destroying Indian culture entirely so much so that their influence on education was insignificant. Political agitations remained confined mainly to the towns. The tradition of religious, social, economic, democratic and decentralised system of education prevailing in villages remote from the towns could not adversely be affected. Well-established and organised educational institutions had fallen prey to the Mohammedan vandalims, but the *Ashrams* of preceptors of ancient pattern functioned uninterrupted in the forests and country-side. Moreover, there were some saints, philosophers and warriors who safeguarded the interests of Indian education and culture and raised their voice against the foreign atrocities and tyranny. The Hindus produced vast literature of high standard even during the period of political disturbances and anarchy and continued their own educational system.

The pattern of education was nearly the same that had existed for long traditionally. The preceptors still taught their disciples the *Vedas, Puranas, Smaritis,* the *Upanishadas*, Philosophy, Logic and Bhishag or Medicine in their own Asharams. Owing to the destruction of organised educational centres by the invaders, the form of education did not remain collective; it became decentralised and education was imparted individually. Students still led a life of severe discipline and served their preceptors, remaining in close contact with them. It is, however, true that discipline was followed not so strictly as it was done in ancient times.

One special feature of Hindu education of this period was that regional languages made appreciable progress. Hindi which had originated from *Prakrat,* had become the *lingua franca* of the masses. A sense of nationalism was engendered among the Hindus by the considerations of sheer self-preservation. The religious and social leaders directed their attention towards the Hindu religion. This is clearly reflected in the poetic productions of contemporary poets. Some philosopher-poets such as Kabir, Dadu, Nanak and Tulsidas etc. sang of the essential unity and equality of all religious creeds and preached to the people to honour all the religions, which helped the fusion of various creeds anti faiths.

Thus it is clear that from the viewpoints of curriculum, method of teaching and aims of education, the Hindu system of education remained during the medieval period mainly the same as it had existed through ages. By the way, it should be noted that Buddhist religion had become extinct entirely during this period. This was naturally followed by the downfall of Buddhist system of education and its place had been taken by the Brahmanical education. Education, in spite of being secular, was religious essentially. This period witnessed unique progress of literature. Centres of education could be established only at those places which were remote from the Mohammedan influence.

Though Hindu education during this period did not enjoy State patronage, yet it would be nothing short of mistake to think that the standard of Hindu education had declined or literature of higher order was not produced. The Hindus were not outpaced by the Mohammedans in the field of literary production and they bequeathed to the posterity commedndable literature in Sanskrit and regional languages. They did never acknowledge the supremacy of the Mohammedans in the sphere of literature and arts though they were greatly influenced by the Islamic culture and education. Consequently, religious and philosophic literatures made marked progress during the medieval period.

Several commentaries were written upon different branches of philosophy i.e. the *Yoga, Veshaisika* and the *Nyaya.* The Buddhist and Jain logicians wrote many books on logic. Devasuri was the most famous of Jain logicians of the period. The Raj-Tarangini written by

Kalhan—the only historical treatise of the period—was produced during the middle of twelfth century. The entire literature illumines the contemporary educational system of that period. The creation of standard literature on different subjects is an eloquent proof of the superiority of contemporary Hindu system of education.

Evolution of Hindi and other regional Vernaculars had begun to take place. These languages were used as the media of Hindu education. Students learnt Sanskrit in order to read religious and theological works. *Pali* and *Prakrat* were developing themselves into the form of Hindi, languages as Rajasthani, Marathi, Gujerati and Bengali had also begun to be used as media of education. Many eminent works were produced in these languages during the medieval period. Hindu education was not confined to northern India but it was prevalent in the southern parts of the country as well. Vijayanagar was an important educational centre of that period. Raja Krishnadev Rai of Vijayanagar made admirable efforts for the growth of education and literature, and patronised eminent artists and poets.

During the reign of the afore-mentioned king, many volumes were produced on music, dance, drama, grammar, logic, philosophy and other branches of learning. Painting and sculpture and other fine arts were vouchsafed liberal patronage. During the inceptive stage of medieval period, the Jain authors produced compositions in Tamil and Kanarese. During the 13th and 14th centuries, the Shaiva movement raged fiercely in southern India and it gave birth to ample literary production. Works in Sanskrit and Telugu were also written. The Vedic lecturer Sayan and his brother Madhav Vidyaranya made appreciable contributions to Sanskrit literature. The two brothers wrote commentaries on the Vedas and also produced other philosophic treatises.

Thus we see that when Islam was proceeding on triumphant career during medieval age in India and a foreign culture and civilization was artificially being imposed upon Indian culture by trampling it underfoot, still at that time the Hindu educational system was advancing with sure though slow strides. In the absence of State patronage, it not only survived but also produced immortal literature owing to meagre patronage of some wealthy citizens and mainly to its unique social organization. The system of education was essentially Vedic in pattern and ancient aims and ideals predominated. This time honoured system of education in course of time collapsed eventually owning to certain important and unavoidable factors such as the advent of the Britishers in India, their new system of education, compulsory study of English language, political slavery of India and her social anarchy etc. The abject slavery and economic exploitation of the Indians made them lose all faith in spiritualism and religion and seek refuge in absolute materialism.

The natural result of it all was that the utility and importance of Sanskrit and ancient subjects dwindled considerably. Scientific inventions annihilated time and space and thus internationalism took hold of educational sphere. This new system quite overshadowed the ancient system of education. Some attempts were made by Daya Nand and Ravindra Nath Tagore for the revival of ancient system by harmonising the Oriental and Occidental systems of education; but it was entirely metamorphosed so much so that essential attributes of ancient system were becoming extinct gradually from day to day.

3

Education and Social Life

The conquest of the major parts of North India by the Muslism Turks is the dominant historical event of the thirteenth century A.D., but its full effects were felt for the first time during the period under review. The conquest was attended by extensive settlements of the foreigners whose number was being increased by constant migrations from the Islamic lands as well as by occasional mass conversions of the indigenous people. Because of the inflexibility of their religious creed, which permitted no compromise with other faiths, the settlers remained (as their co-religionists still remain) a distinct social unit, thus introducing a permanent cleavage of the Indian population along religious lines. The impact of militant Islām had as yet but little effect upon the age-old social life of the older inhabitants. Even the teachings of the saints and mystics of the fourteenth and later centuries, which formed one of the most characteristic developments of the time, left the Hindu society as yet practically unchanged. Indirectly, however, the new menace to the existence of the indigenous culture led to the production of a large number of *Smṛiti* Digests and Commentaries tending towards systematization of the old social and religious law. The somewhat different pattern of the social structure, envisaged in the historical records of the indigenous people of different regions of the time, bear the impress of this teaching.[1]

In so far as the social life of the vast majority of the Indian population following the indigenous faiths is concerned, the *Smṛiti* authorities therefore constitute, for the centuries of our survey, our basic authority. What distinguishes this period from the preceding one is the paucity of inscriptions such as those which helped previously to check the *Smṛiti* evidence in the precise context of its application to specific regions and dates. This defect is somewhat compensated by the rise of regional schools of *Smṛitis* with their respective authoritative Digests. Such, in the first place, is the school of Mithilā of which the principal authorities for our period are the *Gṛihastharatnākara* and other works of Chaṇdeśvara (1300-70), the *Vivādachintāmaṇi* and other works of Vāchaspati Miśra (1425-90), and the *Vivādachandra* of Misarumiśra (*flor*, c. 1450). Such, again, is the school of Banaras of which the *Madana-ratna-pradīpa,* attributed to a chieftain in Gorakhpur area called Madanasiṁha and consisting of *Vyavahāravivekoddyota* and other sections (composed between A.D. 1425 and 1450), and the *Madanapārijāta* of Viśveśvarabhaṭṭa (composed between A.D. 1360 and 1390) are our authorities. Such is also the school of Bengal with the celebrated commentary, *Dīpakalikā,* on *Yājnavalkya-Smṛti* and other works of Sūlapāṇi (1375-1440) as our authority. Such finally, is the Southern school having as its principal authorities, *Parāśara-Smṛiti,* with the gloss of the celebrated Mādhavāchārya (hereafter referred to as *Parāśara, Mādhava*) and other works of the same Mādhavāchārya, otherwise called Vidyāraṇya (1300-1380), the Nṛisiṁhprasāda consisting of the *Vyavahārasāra* and other sections (composed between A.D. 1490 and 1515) of Dalapati, and the *Saravativilāsa* (comprising *Vyavahārakāṇḍa* and other sections) of Pratāparudra (1497-c. 1540).[2] More indefinite in their application are the *Smṛiti* sections belonging to the late *Purāṇas* like the *Bṛihaddharma Purāṇa.* The picture which emerges from our survey of this vast and scattered material is that of conformity to the general pattern of the old *Smṛitis* with some importnt developments which will principally form the subject-matter of this chapter.

Social Divisions and Sub-divisions

The social structure in the *Smṛitis* consists, as is well known, of four primary castes (the Brāhmaṇas, the Kshatriyas, the Vaiśyas and the Sūdras) with diminishing rank and status, an indefinite number of the so-called mixed castes of varying status, and finally, of a group of despised castes coming at the bottom of the scale. The duties and occupations of these castes (specially of the Brāhmaṇas and the Kashatriyas) are described at great length in these works. The *Smṛtis* likewise describe, under the head *āhṇika,* the daily routine of the householder (*grihastha*) and the would-be householder (*snātaka*) belonging to the three upper classes. The picture is that of incessant toil devoted to religious practices and acts of piety. As a *Smṛiti* authority (Daksha quoted in the *Gṛihastharatnākara,* 134) observes: "From sunrise to sunset the Brāhmaṇa should not remain idle for an instant, and he should devote himself to his compulsory, occasional and optional duties, as well as other blameless occupations."

The above rules are repeated in the *Smṛti* commentaries and Digests of our period with ocasional comments which will be briefly noticed here. As regards the Brāhmaṇa's ocupations the *Parāśara-Mādhava* (I, 425-26) first declares agriculture and so forth to be of the nature of duties prescribed in the scriptures, on the ground that officiating at sacrifies and the like are of too rare an occurrence to furnish means of susistence for householders in the Kali Age. Quoting in the next place a number of mutually contradictory texts about the lawfulness of the Brāhmaṇa's occupation of agricultue, and author adjusts the difference in two alternative ways; they refer, we are told, to different degrees of distress (the Brāhmaṇa being held to be entitled to pursue agriculture through others in a time of slight distress, and in person at a time of grave distress), or else to different *yugas* or Age-cycles (the Brāhmaṇa's pursuit of agriculture through others being declared to be his duty in times of distress in the other Ages and his principal duty in the Kali Age). The professions of trade and crafts, like that of agriculture, we are told elsewhere by the same authority (I, 435), belong to all castes, and the Brāhmaṇas in particular are entitled to practise agricutlure. In view of this clear and authoritative exposition of the normal occupations of Brāhmanas, the ban on the modes of subsistence previoulsy conceded to them in times of distress, which occurs in a list of forbidden practices of the Kali Age (*Kalivarjyas*) quoted with approval by the author in another context (I, 123-27), seems to be somewhat unreal. On the other hand, the prohibition in the same list of *Kalivariyas* of the Brāhmaṇa's living by non-accumulation of grain for the next day—a practice which is extolled in some of the *Smṛitis* as the most praiseworthy for a Brāhmaṇa—appears to be thoroughly in accord with the spirit of the age. The high eulogy of Brāhmaṇas is accompanied in our present works, as in the *Smṛitis,* with strong denunciation of unworthy members of this order (*Parāśara-Mādhava.* III, 158 ff.; *Bṛihaddharma Purāṇa,* III, 2. ff).

As for the duties of the next two castes in the order of social precedence, it will be sufficient for our purpose to quote the observations in the *Parāśara-Mādhava* (I, 390-97). Describing the duties of the king, after the *Smṛti* standards, under the heads, 'punishing the wicked' and 'cherishing the good', the author takes great pains to justify the orthodox position that these constitute the distinctive duty of the Kshatriya. The title of king, it is argued after quoted texts, appertains to the Kshatriya, and the right to wield weapons for the purpose of protecting the people likewise belongs to him alone.

In so far as the *Smṛiti* routine of the daily duties of the householder is concerned, a few comments of our authors call for notice. One who has studied the whole Veda, we are told in the *Gṛihastha-ratnākara* (249), should repeat the same from the beginning, one who has studied only a portion of the Vedas is to repeat the *Purushasūkta* (Rv., X, 90) and similar texts, while one who has studied only the *Gāyatri* hymn is to repeat the *Purāṇas*. The *Parāśara-Mādhava* (I 292-93) similarly explains that one who is capable of performance of the Vedic rites should not be content with the rites prescribed in the *Smṛitis,* but one incapable of performance of the Vedic rites should perform those of the *Smṛitis* and one unable to perform even the latter should follow good custom. These extracts, while illustrating the characteristic tendency of the *Smṛitis* to adjust their rules to the varying capacities and inclinations of the people at different periods, are a reminder of the decline of Vedic learning and rites among the upper classes at this period. Of equal importance is the explanation in the *Parāśara-Mādhava* of the householder's daily obligation of hospitable reception of guests. The praise of feeding friends along with condemnation of feeding enemies, as well as the prohibition of feeding the ignorant along with the injunction of feeding the learned which we find in the *Smṛiti* texts, we are told (I, 349-50), does not apply to guests arriving at the end of the *Vaiśvadeva* offering (presenting to the fire before meals). In fact the mark of a guest is not his learning and so forth, but simply his arrival within the prescribed time-limit after that offering. The term 'guest', it is further explained (I. 352), excludes one of the same village arriving regularly on selected days, and is confined to an unknown man arriving on a sudden and suffering from the pangs of hunger. Furthermore, the reception of the guest with words of welcome, the customary offering for a respectable person, a seat and so forth is the due of the Brāhamana alone, while the Kshatriya and the rest are simply to be given food at the Brāhmaṇa's residence (I, 353). These extracts illustrate the cotinuance of the old

Smṛiti rule inculcating universal, though not indiscriminate, charity, some-what limited by the exigencies of caste. It remains to mention that the householder's duty of hospitality to guests is impressively set forth in the *Smṛti* sections of the late *Purāṇas* (*Bṛihaddharma Purāṇa,* II. 5. 34-36, 15, 26-30; *Brahmavaivartta Purāṇa,* 84.1.ff.).

As regards the duties and occupations of the Sūdras our authors betray a twofold attitude. The complete dependence of the Sūdra upon the Brāhmaṇa is reflected in such works as the *Parāśara-Mādhava* (I, 418-20), where we are told that the Sūdra's highest duty is the service of the Brāhmaṇa, as it ensures for him supreme bliss, along with his distinctive occupation, while, by constrast, the service of the Kshatriya and the Vaiśya is his subordinate duty, as it secures for him merely his occupation. It is emphasized still more in the *Bṛihaddharma Purāṇa* (III, 4-5; 24-25; 31-32). On the other hand, our authors tend to relax the strict *Smṛiti* rule forbidding dealings in certain classes of commodities by a Sūdra engaged in trade in default of service, and they justify this by reference to different occasions as well as different grades of Śūdras. The prohibition of the sale of five specified classes of commodities, we are told in the *Gṛihastharatnākara* (479-80), applies to the Śūdra in normal times, but not in times of distress; the parallel set of prohibitions, the author further observes, refers to good Śūdras and not to condemned ones; the Śūdra does not become an outcaste even by selling meat, and so forth. The prohibition of the sale of salt and the like, we are told more briefly in the *Parāśara-Mādhava* (I, 422-23), applies to Brāhmaṇas engaged in trade in times of distress, but the Śūdras incur no blame on that account, although they are forbidden in other texts to deal with liquors and meat.

The older religious disabilities of the Śūdras are repeated by our authors with a certain tendency to relax them within the narrow canonical limits. The Śūdras, according to the *Bṛihaddharma Purāṇa* (III, 4. 15-32), must not practise the Vedic or the ordinary religious exercises, and he must not study the Vedas or the Purānas nor explain the sacred texts, but he may listen to recitations of the Purāṇas and study as much of the Āgamas (Tantras) as is permitted to him by his *guru:* he must not utter *mantras* with the words *svāhā* and *om.* Discussing a hypothetical argument which questions the Śūdra's right to enter upon the householder's life, the *Parāśara-Mādhava* (I, 537) concludes that the Śūdra is so entitled on the ground of reference to him in the section on marriage and to his rights in the section on householder's duties of the type of the five great sacrifices. Similarly discussing an argument which disqualifies the Śūdra for rites capable of being performed only by offering to the sacred fires, the *Madanapārijāta* (231) concludes that whenever the Śūdra is allowed to offer oblations to the fire, he should perform the same in the ordinary fire, and that he should use only the *mantra* consisting of the single word *namaskāra*, as he is not entitled to use any other.

As regards the Śūdra's social disabilities our authors' views vary from comparative laxity to extreme rigidity. In the face of strong condemnation of eating food from a Śūdra in a *Smṛiti,* the *Gṛihastharatnākara* (334) explains that the prohibition refers to the food of condemned Śūdras, while the food of good Śūdras may be eaten (the author slyly adds) for the purpose of gaining cows, lands, and so forth, but not otherwise. Referring to the permission even for Brāhmaṇas to take the food of five specified classes of Śūdras, the author further explains (337) that their uncooked food may be eaten in normal times and even their cooked food may be taken in times of distress. This explanation is repeated by Śūlapāṇi (on Yājnavalkya, I, 166). By contrast, the *Parāśara-Mādhava* (III, 305) mentions the penances of different grades which a Brāhmaṇa, eating a Śūdra's food, must undertake according as he does it intentionally, or in a time of distress, or else unintentionally. The author expands this statement in another context (III, 379-80), where he explains that not only eating the Śūdra's food, but living in the same house with him sitting in the same cart with Śūdras engaged as agricultural labourers, and receiving religious instructions from a learned Śūdra whose sense of right and wrong has been developed by listening to the recitations of the Purāṇas and so forth, are to be avoided. The author likewise (III, 325) qualifies the *Smṛiti* permission to eat four varieties of the Śūdra's food by explaining that it applies to the Kshatriyas and the Vaiśyas at a time when they are tired by the toils of journey, and are unable to procure food from other castes, and that the food in any case should be limited to just what is sufficient to save one's life in times of distress. This is further qualified by the statement (III, 327) that for the above purpose the food of condemned Śūdras, like that of Chandālas, should not be taken, while the food of good Śūdras may not be avoided. The author concludes (III, 337) with clarification of the *Smṛiti* rule admitting the lawfulness of the food of certain specified classes of Śūdras, although, somewhat inconsistently, he elsewhere (I, 123-27) quotes with approval the *Kalivarjya* text including the acceptance of food of five classes of Śūdras in the list. The extreme limit of the Śūdra's social disability is reached in the *Madanapārijāta* (133) justifying by argument a quotation which requires purification by bathing with clothes on, for touching a Śūdra. The divergence of our authors' views is reflected in two contradictory interpretations of Manu's celebrated dictum about the natural as well as the divinely ordained servitude of the Śūdra. On the one hand the *Vivādaratnākara* (146), applying the dictum to the general clause of law permitting four specified classes of Śūdras to be released by the master's favour, observes that the clause does not apply to the Śūdra. Applying the same dictum to the clause which makes a Brāhmaṇa liable to punishment for enslaving men of the three upper classes out of greed, the author states that he who forcibly reduces a Śūdra to slavery is exempt from punishment. On the other hand, the *Vivādachintāmaṇi* (68), quoting the same dictum, observes that it is meant simply to deprecate the condition of the Śūdra, for otherwise there would be no such dealings as the sale of Śūdras and so forth (which are laid down in the *Smṛitis*).

At the end of this brief survey of the status of the four castes after our authors, we may notice their references to the discriminatory clauses, caste-wise, of the *Smriti* penal law. These clauses, which provide for punishment for the same offence committed by a Brāhmaṇa, a Kshatriya, a Vaiśya and a Śūdra on an ascending scale, are repeated often at great length in the *Smṛiti* Digests and Commentaries of our period. Not only, however, was their operation necessarily restricted by the occupation of large tracts of the country by the arms of Islāam, but our authors occasionally drop hints about the disuse of the old discriminatory clauses, as when the *Vyavahāravivekoddyota,* concluding its chapter on defamation and assault, observes that although many other varieties of punishment have been laid down in the *Smṛitis* according to the differences of subject-matter under these heads, kings in these times are unable to put them into effect for fear of rousing popular discontent.

Of more practical applciation than the above are our author's references to the discriminatory clauses in the *Smṛiti* law of penances. The *Madanapārijāta* (791-92), in the context of its statement of the penances for Brāhmaṇa-murder, upholds a *Smṛiti* rule fixing the penances in the ratio of 1:2:3:4 for Brāhmaṇas, Kshatriyas, Vaiśyas and Śūdras, so as to make an inconvenient text (Śaṅkha) yield the forced interpretation that the diminishing scale of penance 1:3/4:1/2:1/4 according to the order of the castes refers to the diminishing capacity of the individual sinner irrespective of caste. This is followed by the author's clear and emphatic statement, on the authority of Vijnāneśvara, that the rule fixing the penances for the Brāhmaṇa, the Kshatriya, the Vaiśya and the Śūdra in the diminishing proportions, as mentioned above; applies to other matters than the four specified crimes of violence. The ascending scale of penances, is likewise applied in respect of various sins in the *Prāaśchittasāra* (30 and 36) and in Śūlapāṇi's commentary on Yājnavalkya (II. 250). This is justified by the argument just stated that the descending scale of penances applies to matters other than the four crimes of violence (which are specified in the *Prāyaśchittasāra* (36) as comprising homicide, theft, criminal assault on other men's wives, and assault in general). Elsewhere (121), however, the *Prāyaśchittasāra* prescribes the same penances for Brāhmaṇa, Kshatriya and Vaiśya on the ground of silence of the texts about the descending scale of the same. The *Madanapārijāta* (869) neatly sums up its view by stating that the descending scale of penances applies to the minor sins, and the ascending scale to the mortal sins.

In so far as the group of mixed castes is concerned, we may notice a short discussion in the *Parāśara-Mādhava* (I, 512-13) about the status of the *anuloma* castes, meaning those supposed to have sprung from the unions of Brāhmaṇa, Kshatriyas and Vaiśyas with girls of inferior castes. Repeating the view of Manu, the author observes that the issue of a Brāhmaṇa by his married Kshatriyā wife is similar to, but not quite the same as, a Brāhmaṇa, because of connection with his low-caste mother, and that the same is the case with the issue of such other unions. The view of Vishṇu and Śaṅkha, assigning to the issue of *anuloma* marriages the caste of the mother, we are further told, refers to their acquisition of the duties of the mother's caste, while they are proved on the contrary to form a separate caste by the fact that otherwise the superiority of the father would have no application. The above discussion proves the author's position to be midway between the exceptional *Smṛiti* view elevating the issues of *anuloma* marriages to their father's caste, and the ordinary view degrading them to the caste of their mother.[3]

As regards the despised castes our authors recapitulate the Smṛiti rules about their degraded status. The *Parāśara-Mādhava* (I, 257-58) explains after quoted texts that one touching a Chaṇḍāla at the first, the second and the third remove, should purify himself by bathing with his clothes on, while one doing so at the fourth remove should merely touch the water. Purification by bathing should be undertaken in both cases, when the touch is intentional. The Chaṇḍāla, we are elsewhere (III, 387-88) told in amplification of the original text, should be kept at a distance of four *yugas* (the length being understood in the light of popular usage): one coming nearer without touching him should bathe with his clothes on: one touching him unintentionally should bathe and look at the Sun (by way of purification), and one doing so intentionally should perform double this penance or some other act of purification. Explaining the detailed description in the original, the author elsewhere (III, 81-94) mentions the different penances to be undertaken by a Brāhmaṇa for conversing or sleeping on the same bed, or going in company with a Chaṇḍāla, for looking at or touching a Chaṇḍāla, for drawing water from a pond owned by a Chaṇḍāla, for drinking water from a well wherefrom water has been drawn in a Chaṇḍāla's vessel, for unwittingly eating a Chaṇḍāla's food or living for some time in the same house with him, for association with a Chaṇḍāla on a journey to a field or garden or another village, and lastly in the event of a Chaṇḍāla's entrance into the house even once. The author likewise mentions the similar but less severe penances for drinking water from the vessels of other despised classes such as washermen and so forth, and for association with them.

A pattern of social structure, somewhat different from the above, prevailed in the different regions of the country according to the realistic accounts of this period. In the Hindu kingdom of Vijayanagara, for instance, there were, next to the Brāhmaṇas, such important caste-groups as Cheṭṭis (merchants), Vira Panchālas (artisans), Kaikkolas (weavers), and barbers. There were besides immigrant castes from the north like the Tottiyars, the Saurāshṭras and the Reḍḍis, whose influx resulted in degradation of certain indigenous castes like the Kurumbars. The lowest caste consisted of the Dombaras (jugglers and soothsayers), Jogis, Maravaras, and so forth. The disputes between the various middle castes above mentioned (and specially between the two great divisions of the righthand and left-hand castes) made up much of the social history of those times. In so far as the Brāhmaṇas were concerned, they were treated with the traditional high respect by kings and nobles alike. In agreement with the *Smṛiti* stanards of the south, as mentioned above, the Brāhmaṇas were employed on a variety of occupations, namely, as merchants and agriculturists, ministers and provincial governors, generals and commanders of fortresses.[4] A cross section of the social structure in the Vijayanagara Empire, which is but very imperfectly noticed in the *Smṛitis*, consisted of the great ministers and other officials, as well as the feudatories (*amaranāyakas*) holding charge of districts on condition of furnishing financial contributions and military contingents, on the one side, and the mass of the people on the other side.[5]

Slavery

Slavery was fairly common, and the matter-of-fact was in which Ibn Batūtah refers to the acquisition of slave-girls in lots, and their distribution as ordinary gifts or presents, throws a lurid light on the moral ideas of the time. A sort of communal spirit seems to have prevailed in this matter. The Muslims took delight in enslaving Hindu women *en masse* from the highest to the lowest rank, and many of them, including even those who once were princesses, were forced to entertain the Muslim court and the nobility with dance and music. Sultān Mahammad bin Tughlaq made free gifts of them to his relations and the nobility, and sent as presents to the Chinese Emperor "one hundred male slaves and one hundred slave songstresses and dancers from among the Indian infidels". On the other hand, according to Nizām-ud-din, "even Musalmāns and Sayyid women were taken by the Rājputs and were turned into slave girls. They were taught the art of dancing and were made to join the *akharās*."[5a]

The *Smṛiti* authorities of this period repeat the clauses of law relating to slavery in the older texts under the familiar head of law called 'non-rendition of service after making a contract to serve or obey.'[5b] It will suffice to quote here their comments on the rules for the emancipation of slaves. Expanding the *Smṛiti* clause on this point the *Prāśara-Mādhava*, the *Vivādachandra*, the *Vivāda-chintāmaṇi* and the *Vyavahārakāṇḍa* observe that not only the four classes of slaves (one born in the household, one purchased, one acquired, and one inherited), but one who has sold himself to slavery, are released by the master's favour, the privilege being extended still further in the *Vyavahāravivekoddyota* so as to apply to all classes other than those who have fallen off from the monastic order. According to the *Vyavahāravivekoddyota* and the *Vyavahārakaṇḍa,* five other specified classes of slaves are released simply by saving the master from imminent danger of his life, the *Parāśara-Mādhava* extending this privilege to all classes of slaves. On the other hand, the *Vivādaratnākara, Vivādachandra* and the *Vivādachintāmaṇi* limit the application of the equitable *Smṛiti* rule, requiring the master begetting a son on his female slave to release them both, by stating that this should be done when the master has no other son. Coming to the historical records we may state that slavery, to judge from the combined evidence of the contemporary inscriptions as well as foreign acounts, was a recognized institution in the Hindu Empire of Vijayanagara.[6]

A word may be said here about a disreputable class of women whom we had occasion to notice in the course of our survey of the preceding periods. From the combined testimony of a number of foreign observers (Abdur Razzak, Barbosa and Paes) and a Kanarese poem, we can estiamte the large numbers and the affluence of the courtesans at the capital of the Vijayanagara Empire. The combined evidence of inscriptions and foreign notices in the same area likewise points to continuance of the institutions of dancing girls in the service of temples.[7]

Marriage

The elaborate rules, relating to marriage, in the *Smṛiti* are repeated, often at great length, by our authors with occasional comments, which will chiefly concern us here. Thus, in the first place, inter-caste marriages among the three upper classes are included in the list of forbidden practices of the Kali Age, quoted with approval in the *Parāśara-Mādhava,* (I, 123-27) and the *Madanapārijāta* (15-16). This would tend towards the creation of strictly endogamous castes. In fact, however, our authors repeat and amplify the old *Smṛiti* rules of hypergamy. Summing up its explanation on this point after the canonical standards, the *Gṛihastharatnākara* (38) observes that girls of other castes (*jātis*) may be married (by a Brāhmaṇa) one after another in the regular (*anuloma*) order, that he becomes liable to censure by doing otherwise, and that the *Smṛiti* prohibition against marriage with a Śūdra girl refers to a marriage where another wife (of a superior caste) is available, just as the *Smṛiti* condemnation of begetting a child on a Śūdra wife is applicable when the same can be done on another wife. The hypergamous rule in the *Smṛiti* is justified by other authors on more worldly grounds. Referring to the texts which recommend a Brāhmaṇa to marry Kshatriya and other girls in the *anuloma* order after his marriage with a girl of his own caste, the *Madanapārijāta* (133-34) declares the latter type of marriage to be of the principal kind, and the former type to be the less desirable course. For it is a *Smṛiti* rule that among the two duties laid down for the married man, the first (namely, the sacrifices) can be performed only with a wife of the same caste, while the second (namely, sexual pleasure) can be enjoyed with any married wife. We have a more complete explanation in the *Parāśara-Mādhava* (I, 493-98). While girls both of the same and of different castes are suitable for marriage (with a Brāhmaṇa), we are there told, the former are praiseworthy, but if the Brāhmaṇa, after first marrying a girl of the same caste for the purpose of his religious exercises, feels sexual desire, he may marry girls of inferior castes in the respective (prescribed) order. The author next adjusts two contradictory views, one condoning the Brāhmaṇa's uion with a Śūdra girl, and the other requiring a Brāhmaṇa and a Kshatriya to avoid her, by observing that they reflect the opinions of different authorities (as is illustrated by a text of Yājnavalkya), or else refer to different Age-cycles (as is proved by a text including inter-caste marriages of the three upper classes in the list of forbidden practices of the Kali Age).

The *Smṛiti* authorities of our period repeat the old exogamous rules forbidding marriages on the ground of sameness of *gotra* and *pravara* as well as of *sapiṇḍa* relationship between the parties to the match, and they extend the last relationship, after the great majority of the older authors, to seven degree on the father's side and five degrees on the side of the mother. As regards the term *sapiṇḍa,* both the *Madanapārijāta* (129-133) and the *Parāśara-Mādhava* (I. 465-66) refer to its double interpretation signifying, after the school of the *Mitāksharā*, those who are connected together by having particles of the same body, and after the school of the *Dāyabhāga,* those who are connected because of the ball of rice or its leavigns offered to the common ancestor at the *Śrāddha* ceremony. But while the *Madnapārijāta* quotes the former explanation, only for its rejection in favour of the latter, the *Parāśara-Mādhava,* combining the two explanations, observes that one should marry a girl who is not a *sapiṇḍa* in both senses of the term. The *Gṛihastharatnākara* (8), by contrast, contents itself with quoting in part the classical exposition of Vijnāneśvara (on Yājñavalkya, I, 52-53) in favour of the former interpretation. To complete our acount, the *Madanapārijāta* (139-40) and the *Parāśara-Mādhava* (I, 467-68), as well as the commentary of Śūlapāṇi (on Yājñavalkya. I, 56), explain away the texts narrowing down the *sapiṇḍa* relationship still further to the third and the fifth degrees on the mother's and the father's side respectively. This is justified by the argument that the said texts apply to the issue of an adopted mother or father or of step-mothers of different castes, or of *āsura* and similar disapproved types of marriage, or else to Kshatriyas, and so forth.

On the question of validity of the ancient South-Indian custom of marriage with the daughter of the maternal uncle (*mātula-sutā*),—which by the way disregards the *Smṛiti* rule of prohibited degrees of marriages as between cognates—our authors like their predecessors, are sharply divided in their opinions. On the one hand, the *Gṛihastharatnākara* (8 and 10), while pointedly condemning marriage with the *mātula-sutā* in the course of its explanation of a verse of Manu, quotes the text requiring one to perform a penance for marrying such a girl and to maintain her after separation. On the other hand, Dalapati, the author of the *Saṁskārasāra,*[7a] justifies the above custom on the ground of its mention in the Vedas. The strongest defence of this custom, mostly after the arguments in the *Smṛitichandrikā* (I, 70-74), is found in the *Parāśara-Mādhava* (I, 469-73), where the author, in the course of a long and learned discussion, observes that the custom is justified by the combined authority of the Vedas, the *Smṛitis* and the customs of cultured men, and he concludes that it is lawful within its particular region, even in respect of *āsura* and similar forms of marriage.[8]

The *Smṛiti* authorities of this period repeat the arguments of their predecessors for explaining the relative importance of the prohibitory rules about marriage. Where (as in the texts prescribing marriage with a girl who is not *sapiṇḍa* of the mother), we are told in the *Madanapārijāta* (140-42), the injunctions and prohibitions have no visible merits and demerits, these can be deduced from the scriptures alone. and when a man disregards the same, the girl does not become a wife at all; where, however, the injunctions and prohibitions are laid down in view of their visible merits and demerits (such as auspicious names of girls), their violation does not prevent the girl from becoming a wife, but it merely entails a penance. The same explanation is found in the *Gṛihastharatnākara* (28-29). It is, however, remarkable that the *Madanapārijāta,* after quoting a few exceptions to the general rule given above, winds up with the remarks that the final decision should be made in accordance with regional usage—a statement which is in complete accord with the spirit of elasticity of the *Smṛiti* rules in these matters.

Long before this period, the *Smṛitis* had enjoined upon guardians of girls, under severe moral and spiritual sanctions, the obligation of giving them away in marriage before puberty, the age of the girl being specifically stated to extend to seven, ten, or, at the most, twelve years. The clear and emphatic repetition of this rule is found in the *Parāśara-Mādhava.* The author, in one place (I, 474), quotes the texts fixing the relative ages of the bridegroom and the bride as 30 and 12, 28 and 8, 30 and 10, 21 and 7, and more generally in the proportion of 3:1. Elsewhere (I, 481-82) the author, while commending, after the older writers, the guardian's bestowal of a girl not yet of a marriageable age and in fact of an age without any sense of shame, explains away a text permitting a girl even after puberty to stay in her father's house till her death rather than be given away to an unworthy husband. In yet another context (III, 120-21) the author quotes the appropriate texts so as to emphasize the impurity of the girl reaching puberty in her father's house, as well as that of the guardians failing to give her away before that time. Only at the end, he grudgingly allows, that the giving away and acceptance of a girl even at twelve years of age is not prohibited, if she has not attained puberty at that time. Equally emphatic is the view of the *Madanapārijāta* (149-50). The author enjoins upon guardians, after quoted texts, the bestowal of a *nagnikā* (explained alternatively as one too young to have any sense of shame in the presence of males, and as one who has not attained the age of puberty) even upon a worthless husband, rather than keeping the girl unmarried beyond her puberty. In accordance with other quoted texts the guardians are required, under strict social and religious sanctions, to give away the girl at eight, nine or ten years of age when she has not reached puberty.

In contrast with the above clear statements, those of the *Gṛihastharatnākara* are singularly rambling and confused. Quoting the older *Smṛitis* the author explains (39) that the marriage of a girl, twelve or sixteen years old, with a bridegroom of thirty years of age is commendable, but that of a young girl with a bridegroom thrice her age is still more praiseworthy. Modifying the above statement in another context (47), the author observes that unlike the marriage of a sixteen-year-old girl with a thirty-year-old bridegroom, which, though justified by the superior qualities of the husband, is still to be condemned, the marriage of a *nagnikā* (meaning a girl of ten years not knowing as yet how to wear clothes properly) is praiseworthy. The author ends, characteristically enough, with the forced interpretation of a *Mahābhārata* text so as to make it mean that a thirty-year-old bridegroom should marry a sixteen-year-old girl or else a *nagnikā*. In yet another context (83), the author quotes, without comment, a Purāṇa text which prescribes diminishing periods of continence immediately after marriage according as the ages of the bride and the bridegroom are in the proportion of 8:24, 12:30, 16:32, and as the bride's age is 20 or more.

In the event of a girl failing from various causes to get herself married before puberty, the *Smṛitis* permit her the privilege of self-choice (*svayamvara*) of her husband after a short or long period of probation. These rules are quoted by our authors with some slight explanations. Reconciling the older references to two distinct time-periods, the *Gṛihastharatnākara* (42-43) states that the girl should wait for three years if her father or other guaradians, in spite of their efforts, fail for some reasons to give her away, but she should wait only for the expiry of her three monthly illnesses in the contrary case. A girl without guardians, we are told in the *Parāśara-Mādhava* (I, 483-84), may select a husband with the necessary qualifications before reaching puberty: even where there is the father or other guardian, the girl on reaching puberty should await their decision for a little while, and in case they are indifferent she should herself select her husband. Referring to the different time-periods prescribed by the authorities, the author further observes, that while normally waiting for three years, she need wait only for the three months, as stated above, if a sufficiently qualified bridegroom is available. In the absence of other corroborative evidence it is not possible to ascertain how far these radical rules were still observed in actual practice.

The eight forms of marriage known to the ancient *Smṛitis*, along with their estimate of the comparative merits and demerits of the same, are quoted with pedantic thoroughness by our authors.[8a] It will be enough to mention here a striking defence of the disapproved forms of marriage in the *Parāśara-Mādhava* (I, 489-90) and the *Madanapārijāta* (157). Replying to a hypothetical objection that *āsura* and the like marriages, in the absence of the ceremony of taking the seven steps (*saptapadi*) together, do not produce the relationship of husband and wife, the authors state that this ceremony can be performed after the union, and therefore, the girl certainly becomes a wedded wife.

The old *Smṛiti* rules, permitting the revocation of marriage in certain special circumstances, are repeated by our authors. A girl, says the *Madanapārijāta* (150-53), may be given away to another bridegroom after the ceremony of selection (*varaṇa*), but before that of *saptapadi,* in the event of detection of defects on either side, since the relationship of husband arises only after the last-named ceremony. The same rule applies in the case of a bridegroom dying before the *saptapadi* (the girl in this case being asked to be given away to the bridegroom's younger brother or a man of the same *gotra* or any other man in the order of sequence), of a girl carried away by force but not married with the utterance of the sacred texts, of a bridegroom going away to another country after selection of the bride and payment of the nuptial fee (the bride in this case being required to wait for a specific period of time), and lastly, of a bridegroom wanting in the qualifications of family, character and so forth. The author, however, qualifies his approval by stating that the practice of giving away the girl to the younger brother of the deceased husband, and so forth, like the one immediately mentioned before, is hateful to the people and as such should be followed in accordance with the regional usage. Referring to the same *Smriti* rules the *Gṛihastharatnākara* (48) explains that while the girl given away in any one of the first five forms of marriage can be given only once, one taken in marriage in accordance with the three other forms can be given away afresh to a worthier bridegroom. The ceremony of selection, we are further told (54), is not sufficient for the creation of wifehood in the event of a fault being found in the bridegroom. We may quote, lastly, the author's neat summary of Nārada's celebrated text enumerating fourteen classes of eunuchs, and permitting revocation of marriage with them after short or long periods. When the defects of any one of these classes, we are told (33), are known beforehand, the girl should not be married to him: when the girl is married in ignorance of these defects, the man should be medically treated and the result should be awaited: when the man is proved to be beyond cure, the girl should be married to another, even though she had been given in marriage to the former.

The lead of the canonists of the preceding period forbidding remarriage of widows is followed by our authors. The re-marriage of girls, whether the marriage has been consummated or not, occurs in the list of forbidden practices of the Kali Age quoted with approval in the *Parāśara-Mādhava* (I, 123-27), and that of girls whose marriages has not been consummated is found in the similar list of the *Madanapārijāta* (15-16). Consistently with this attitude the *Parāśara-Mādhava* (I, 492-93, III, 44). interprets a number of texts clearly in favour of widow re-marriage, as referring to another Age-cycle.

On the subject of the mutual duties of the husband and the wife, our authors repeat the old *Smṛiti* view with occasional comments. According to the *Parāśara-Mādhava* (I, 506) it is the husband's duty properly to maintain his wives, irrespectively of their youth or old age, provided they are of good behaviour. The *Gṛihastharatnākara* (86) quotes a text making the husband liable to heavy punishment for abandoning his chaste and gentle wife, and compelling him to take her back. By neglecting to maintain his wife who has been given to him by the gods, we are told in the *Vyavahāravivekoddyota* (318), the husband becomes guilty of injuring them: even the wicked wife should be given maintenance in the shape of bad food and so forth. The husband deserting his faithful wife, it is further declared (319), should be fined and compelled by the king to take her back, failing which the husband should be made to pay her one-third of his property if he is rich, and what is sufficient for her maintenance, if he is poor. On the wife's part, she has, we are told in the *Madanapārijāta* (190-96), the obligation of leading a life of studied dependence (she should not act independently even in domestic affairs), of sobriety (she should be restrained in her dress and behaviour in the presence of superiors and she should avoid bad company), and above all of absolute devotion and loyalty to her husband: she should adopt a life of ascetic restraint during her husband's absence abroad. The wife despising her husband on any acount, such as poverty, explains the *Parāśara-Mādhava* (III, 30 and 34), commits great sin and, as such, is liable to the prescribed penance, while the wife, undertaking vows and so forth in disregard of service to her husband, should propitiate him and perform a penance at his dictation: the wife, undertaking a vow without the husband's permission, is purified by the fact of fruitlessness of her endeavour and is not liable to a separate penance.

The specific moral as well as physical defects of the wife justifying her supersession by the husband, along with the time-lags for certain varieties of these defects, are repeated by our authors after the old *Smṛiti* law. The *Parāśara-Mādhava* (I, 508) somewhat relaxes the strict *Smṛitis* rule on this point by stating expressly that out of the two kinds of supersession, the one meant for fulfilling the law in the shape of begetting a legitimate son and so forth is justified by the occasions mentioned, but the other which is intended for gratifying sexual passion needs no such occasion. Nevertheless we are told (509), that the husband, in the latter case, must propitiate the wife, failing which he should be compelled by the king to pay her one-third of his property, or to maintain her with food and clothing, according as he is rich or poor. The superseded wife, if she has not been given *striādhana* before, should get as much as is given to the newly married wife, and in the contrary case, she should get half of the same[8b] or as much as would make their shares equal.[8c]

The old *Smṛiti* rule, relating to the abandonment of women in special circumstances, is relaxed in one respect, and intensified on another point, in the *Kalivarjya* text quoted with approval in the *Parāśara-Mādhava* (I, 123-27). On the one hand, it prohibits the abandonment of women of honoured relationship on the ground of sexual connection with men of low castes, although it is a fact that some *Smṛiti* texts (Vaśishṭha and Bṛihaspati) had expressly required women guilty of such connection to be abandoned. On the other hand, the above-mentioned text forbids social intercourse with women who have been polluted by rape and so forth, even after their performance of the prescribed penance, such women having been held previously (Vaśishṭha, Atri and Parāśara) to become pure after penance and their own monthly illness. A complete explanation of the occasions justifying the abandonment of women is given in the *Parāśara-Mādhava*. While a couple, belonging to the despised caste and incapable of performance of the ceremony of marriage, incur no blame by mutual separation on acount of disagreement (II, 324-25), a wife, taken in accordance with the ceremony of marriage can be abandoned only for unchastity, for wanton character, and for other specified serious crimes. While the act of hating her kinsmen, to the point of applying poison or black magic and so forth against them, as well as of procuring abortion, makes the women equally liable to be cut off from conversation (III, 32) the latter act is incapable of expiation, and the guilty woman must certainly be abandoned. On the treatment of the abandoned women, our authors explain and expand the older views. Fallen women, equally with men, we read in the *Madanapārijāta* (968), are to be abandoned in the event of their not performing the (appropriate) penance, and to be taken back after its performance, but there is this special rule that the women in the former case are to be allowed residence near the house as well as food and clothing. Neither death nor mutilation, according to the *Vivādaratnākara* (426) and the *Parāśara-Mādhava* (II, 325), is to be the lot of the abandoned woman. A woman abandoned for specified crimes, we read in the *Parāśara-Mādhava* (II, 325-25), in the context just quoted, should be denied conjugal relations and participition in Vedic and *Smriti* rites as well as conversation and so fourth, while one abandoned for disease and the like should be conjugal relations alone. A woman guilty of proved unchastity, as when she becomes pregnant by her paramour in the event of her husband's death or prolonged residence abroad, it is further observed (III, 284-90) by the same author, shall be banished to a foreign land; a woman of suspected unchastity, as when a Brāhmaṇa women goes out to another village or country to live with a man who is not her guardian and to whom she has made advances of love, cannot be allowed to reurn to her residence; a woman going out wilfully to live in another village cannot be permitted to return to her kinsmen even after performing a penance, for the *Smṛiti* ban against the abandonment of women applies (only) to one who is repentant for her act and is entitled to penance for the same; a woman, angrily leaving her house herself and alone for being assaulted by her guarandians for her faults, may return home within ten days without being liable to a penance, but a Brāhmaṇa woman returning home after these days of grace is incapable of penance and is to be abandoned, and even the house where she is given shelter becomes impure like that of the Chaṇḍālas.

The *Smṛitis,* from the time of Bṛihaspati onwards inculcate upon the widow, the obligation of self-immolation on the funeral pyre of her husband (*sahamarana, anumarana,* or *anugamana,* commonly known as *sati*) as her alternative or else as her exclusive duty. The former view is repeated in the *Madanapārijāta* (196-203). The former view is repeated in the *Madanapārijāta* (196-203). The author, it is true, explains that the injunction (after Hārita) to perform *sahamarana* is the general duty of all chaste wives, other than those who are pregnant or have infant children, down to the Chaṇḍālas. Where the husband has died abroad, it is further explained, the Brāhmaṇa widow may certainly burn herself along with his bones, while a widow of another caste, failing to procure the bones, may burn herself with or even without any of his symbols. The author, again, offers a double defence of self-immolation after the Digests of the preceding period, namely, that the ban on Brāhmaṇa women (Paiṭhīnasi, Aṅgiras and others) refers to their mounting a separate pyre, and that the Vedic passage forbidding unapproved suicide in general terms does not conflict with the *Smṛiti* text specially prescribing suicide (to the widow) by entering the fire on her husband's death. On the other hand, the author, after stating that self-immolation is an optional rite as being attended with the reward of heaven and the like, emphatically rejects the contrary view declaring it to be a compulsory rite, by pointing to Manu's silence in this matter. This is followed, significantly enough, by a long quotation tending to show that the observance of the vows of widowhood likewise procures (for the woman) the reward of heaven and so forth. The view declaring self-immolation to be the widow's exclusive duty finds its emphatic support in the *Parāśara-Mādhava* (III, 45-49). While great bliss, we are told by the author after the original text, attends the widow adopting a vow of chastity instead of contracting a second marriage, she earns still greater merit by following her husband on the funeral pyre; in fact while the chaste wife, performing the ceremony, brings bliss both on herself and on her husband, the sinful wife is released from her sins by this act. This statement is accompanied by the double defence of the rite as above mentioned. The author concludes with the remark that subject to the usual restrictions all women are eligible for *sahamaraṇa*. That the above discussions, involving the qualified or absolute sanction of self-immolation by the widow, must be interpreted in a limited sense, is proved by the fact that the same authors elsewhere (as we shall presently see) vindicate the widow's right as the foremost heir of her sonless and divided husband, the author of *Parāśara-Mādhava* taking the lead in this respect.

The most authentic evidence of the prevalence of *sati* in different areas is furnished by the contemporary historical records. It is noticed as a peculiar custom of the Indians of Quilon on the Malabar coast by Friar Odoric (c. A.D. 1321-22), and of 'India the Less' (meaning Sind and the western coast as far as the north of Malabar) by Friar Jordanus (A.D. 1323-1330). We have eyewitnesses' acounts of the performance of *sati* near Dhar in Mālwa by Ibn Batūtah (1342), and in the Vijayanagara Empire by Nicolo Conti and Duarte Barbosa in the beginning of the fifteenth and sixteenth centuries respectively. The two last-named writers testify to the large numbers of wives and female slaves who burnt themselves along with their deceased husbands and masters in the Hindu empire. We have a striking reminiscence of the *Smṛiti* doctrine on this point in the statement of Odoric that women, with sons, were exempted from the performance of *sati,* and of Ibn Batūtah that the custom was not obligatory, although highly esteemed. Ibn Batutah further adds that permission had to be obtained from the Sultān to burn the widow.[9]

Position of Women

The *Smṛiti* authorities of this period extensively quote the old doctrine of perpetual subjection of women as well as that of their lifelong tutelage under their male relations at sucessive stages of their lives. They quote likewise the corollary of these doctrines in the shape of the duty of the husband to guard his wife well by keeping her engaged in household work and so forth in the interest of the families of both and of their progeny.[9a] Our authors repeat in particular the religious disabilities of women (such as their disqualification for Vedic study and sacrament in accordance with Vedic *mantras*) after the older texts. We may quote in this connection the very characteristic explanation of the *Parāśara-Mādhava* (I, 484) and the *Madanapārijāta* (37), that the division of women into two classes (after Hārita), namely *brahmavādinīs* or 'students of sacred lore' (who go through the ceremonies of *upanayana* or investiture with the sacred thread, keeping the sacred fire, begging for alms within their own household) and *sadyovadhūs* or 'those who are married straightway' (for whom, as the time for marriage draws near, the *upanayana* is performed somehow), belongs to a different time-cycle (*Kalpa*).

The penalties for women under the *Smṛiti* criminal law, which include capital punishment with revolting cruelty for a number of serious crimes under the heads of violence (*sāhasa*) and adultery (*strīsaṁgrahaṇa*), are repeated by our authors. References are made simultaneously by them to the remarkably humane rule of Kātyayana that women are liable to half the fine payable by men, and that they are to lose a limb where the men are punished with death. In view of the fact that the operation of the *Smṛiti* penal law was necessarily restricted by the occupation of large tracts of the country by Muslim rulers, and that the above penalties are repeated by our authors without any serious comment, it may be surmised that their application at this period was largely a matter of academic interest.

Of more practical importance than the above are our authors' references (with a distinct tendency towards their lenient interpretation) to the penance for women in the *Smṛitis*. Thus the special rule, prescribing half the penance for women as compared with men, is applied to particular types of sins in the *Parāśara-Mādhava* (III, 29 and 34) and the *Prāyaśchittasāra* (32, 56, 64 and 75), although the *Madanapārijāta* (891-92), by way of exception, makes the women liable to the very same penances as men for one of the mortal sins. Women are exempted from tonsuring the head according to a quotation in the *Prāyaśchittasāra* (22), and from a longer list of such penances after a quotation in the *Madanapārijāta* (870). Although women (of the three upper classes), conceiving as a result of illicit intercourse with a Śūdra paramour, we are told in the *Parāśara-Mādhava* (III, 115-16), cannot be purified and must be abanoned, a woman doing so by connection with a man of another caste is purified by penance; a woman guilty of unchastity, not resulting in conception, is purified by the appropriate penance, or even by her monthly illness, according as the sin is physical, mental or verbal. Elsewhere (280), the author, meeting the objection that a woman having connection with a Chaṇḍāla cannot be purified by the observance of vows but must be abanoned, argues that like land contaminated by the residence of Chaṇḍālas and so forth which is reclaimed by the operations of digging (the soil), applying colourwash (to the wall), and so forth, a woman in the above situation can be reclaimed by the performance of vows. To this the only qualification is that Brāhmaṇa women are purified by special penances.

The most considerable development of our authors' ideas on the present subject relates to the women's property rights. Thus, in the first place, they amplify Yājñavalkya's clause of law (I, 115) about partition of property by a father among his sons and wives. The father, says the *Vivādaratnākara* (65), should make his wives equal or unequal sharers, according as he gives equal or unequal shares to his sons. This is subject to the explanation that a wife, not receiving wealth from her husband or father-in-law (as *strīdhana*), should receive as much wealth as would make her share equal to that of her son, and in the contrary case, a half share. Where the sons, born of the Brāhmaṇa and other wives, we are told more fully in the *Madanapārijāta* (662-63), take equal shares, their mothers likewise receive the same, and where the sons by a Kshatriyā, a Vaiśyā and a Śūdra wife take their shares in the proportion of ¾, ½ and ¼ respectively, their mothers also follow suit. According to the *Vyavahāravivekoddyota* (331), the mother takes equal share with her sons at partition after the father's death if she has no *strīdhana,* but she takes a half share at partition during as well as after the father's lifetime, if she has the same. The author, in the same context, rejects the view of an anonymous authority, permitting the mother and the rest to take what is necessary for their bare existence, as well as the view of *Smṛitichandrikā,* allowing them to take what suffices for their subsistence where the property to be divided is large, and an equal share where it is small. Expanding Yājñavalkya's clause (I, 117) about partition of property by a father among his sons, Śulapāṇi observes that the daughters should divde their mother's property equally among themselves after payment of her debts.

The widow's right as the foremost heir of a deceased sonless male divided from his family, which was first conceded by Yājñavalkya and Vishnu, is repeatedly vindicated by our authors against adverse criticisms. The wife, it is explained, is the first heir if she is chaste, but not otherwise (*Vyavahāravivekoddyota,* 359); the order of sucession, with the wife coming first in the list of heirs, applies to all castes, meaning those born of marriages in the *anuloma* and the *pratiloma* orders, as well as the Brāhmaṇa and the rest.[9b] The wife, following the vow of widowhood, takes the property of a man without principal or subsidiary sons, while one who had fallen off from her vow is to get only her maintenance;[9c] the wife of a man dying without son, grandson, and great-grandson takes his property.[9d]

The widow's right is supported with discussions by the other authorities. The reference to widows, even of divided and not reunited husbands, getting a maintenance alone, says the *Vyavahāra-vivekoddyota* (360), applies to exclusively kept concubines. Similarly Śūlapāṇi (on Yājñavalkya, I, 135-36), explaining the references to brothers and daughters taking the property, observes that the former text applied to an unchaste and adulterous wife, while the latter passage refers to an appointed daughter. In the next palce the *Vyavahārakāṇḍa* (405-08) justifies the widow's right to take the property before the father on the ground of her greater propinquity; the wife (*patnī*), it is argued, confers greater seen and unseen benefits after the Vedic and *Smṛiti* standards (upon the deceased)—the *patni* being explained to mean a wife who is married according to *brāhma* and other approved forms—and is entitled as such to perform the sacrifices, and not a wife who is acquired by purchase. According to the *Vivādaratnākara* (589-93), the reference (Manu) to the mother and the father as the heirs of a son dying without issue applies to one who has left no principal or subsidiary sons and no wife. The clause of law (Paiṭhīnasi) declaring the wife of a sonless man to be the heir after the brother and so forth, the author continues, refers to one who is other than a chaste wife, and who slightly fulfils the duties of widowhood. Giving another explanation of the above clause, the author observes that it refers to property other than that which has been earned by the father, the grandfather and so forth (or in other words, to self-acquired property).

The fullest vindication of the widow's right as her husand's foremost heir occurs in the *Parāśara-Mādhava* (II, 355-60). The clause of law (Nārada), making the other brothers the heirs in case a brother dies without issue, and giving his widow a life-long maintenance, the author observes, applies to one who has been re-united with his family, or has not been divided at all. Again the clause (Manu), mentioning the father or the brother as the heir of a sonless man, does not lay down the order of succession, while the rule (Kātyāyana), making the father, the brother, the mother and the paternal grandmother, the heirs as above, refers to the case of an adulterous wife. The interpretation (Dhāreśvara and the author of *Smṛitisaṁgraha*) that the widow inherits the property provided she submits to *niyoga* (appointment for raising issue to her deceased husband), is disproved by the argument *inter alia* that the vow of chastity is imposed upon the widow by a number of *Smṛitis* in the present context. Other texts giving the widow a bare maintenance during her lifetime refer to an exclusively kept concubine, or else to a wife guilty of proved or suspected adultery. The author finally argues that a Vedic text held in disqualify women for a share in the property, which, by the way, led even such an advanced legist as the author of *Smṛitichandrikā* to exclude such women as are not expressly declared to be heirs in the Smṛitis, simply means that the wife of the sacrificer is not entitled to her share of the *Soma* juice taken in a particular (*pātnīvata*) cup.

Besides justifying the postion of the widow as the next heir of a sonless man divided from his family, our authors vindicate the extent and nature of her interest in her husband's property. The clause (Bṛihaspati) denying to the wives the right to inheriting immovable property, we are told in the *Parāśara-Mādhava* (II, 360), means simply that they are forbidden to sell the same without the consent of the other heirs. The widow, says the *Vyavahārasāra* (250) after a *Smṛiti* clause, takes the whole property comprising movables as well as immovables. According to the *Vivādachintimani* (237), the widow should perform the first as well as the yearly funeral offerings for her husband and take his whole property. When the property is divided, we are told more fully in the *Vyavahārakāṇḍa* (408-10), the *patnī* (as distinguished from a wife procured for enjoyment) should take the whole property (along with immovables) of her husband, and perform, to the measure of this wealth, various pious acts for her own and her husband's spiritual benefit. Adjusting a few contradictory texts after the *Smṛitichandrikā*, and author further observes that where there are wives with the without daughters, the former takes the immovables and the latter the movables, and where there are only wives without daughters, they take both immovables and movables to the exclusion of the mother, and so forth.

The widow's interest in her husband's property is most fully vindicated in the *Vyavahāravivekoddyota* (359-63). The clause of Bṛihaspati quoted in the *Smṛitichandrikā* as denying immovable property to women, we are told, is not found in many other Digests and authors of Digests, namely, Vijñāneśvara, *Kṛityakalpataru*, *Ratnākaṇa*, *Pārijātc*, Halāyudha and others, and it appears, as such, to be unacceptable. Even if we are to accept it on the authority of the *Smṛitichandrikā*, it should be taken to refer to a wife married according to the *āsura* and other disapproved forms, unlike the *patni*, who is married in accordance with *brāhmā* and other approved forms. The adjustment of contradictory texts in the *Smṛitichandrika*, the author continues, in the sense that the wife without daughters does not take the immovable property while the wife with daughters takes the same, seems to be a guess and nothing more. Adjusting a few other texts, the author further observes that where the husband has died undivided or reunited with his family, his wife gets only food and clothing during her lifetime, if she is other than a *patnī,* but if she is a *patnī*, she gets as much share out of her husband's wealth as will enable her to live in comfort and to perform her compulsory and occasional duties, as well as her optional duties of the kind within women's capacity. The clause (Kātyāyana) denying to the *patnī* the freedom of gift and so forth, we are further told, means that she cannot spend the money on actors, dancers and such-like visible objectives, but she is certainly entitled to gift, pledge or sale of the same for "invisible" purposes. The author's final conclusion is that where the husband has died divided and not reunited, the wife is entitled to his entire property, both movable and immovable.

We may briefly notice in this connection our authors' references to other female heirs of a sonless man as described above. Justifying the order of sucession after Yājñavalkya, *Vyavahārakāṇḍa* (413-14) observes that while the daughter's propinquity to the deceased arises from the invisible benefit conferred through her son, the mother's greater propinquity is derived from the benefit conferred through her direct participation in the fire-offering (*agnihotra*) and other rites (performed by the father). On the other hand, although the father himself confers spiritual benefit upon the deceased by the performance of his *śrāddha,* the daughter is physically inseparable from the latter. The author next rejects the narrow interpretation of the daughter in the present context in a number of specified and unspecified Digests, as one who was appointed to raise male issue for her father having no son of his own. Coming to another point, we find that the father is preferred to the mother in the order of succession is the *Vivādachandra* (93) and the *Vyavahāravivekoddyota* (364), and the mother to the father in the *Vivādaratnākara* (595), the *Vyavahārasāra* (251) and the *Vivādachintāmaṇi* (241). The mother, it is argued in the *Vyavahārasāra* after Vijñāneśvara, comes before the father in the dissolution of the copulative word (pitarau) for parents in the original, while the mother's propinquity is greater than the father's. Lastly, we have to observe that the paternal grandmother is placed after the brother and the brother's son in the *Vyavahāravivekoddyota* (365) and the

Vyavahārasāra (252) on the ground that the contrary text of Manu does not lay down the order of sucession.

We now come to our authors' treatment of the *Smṛiti* law of *strīdhana* (which term is used in the technical sense of certain special kinds of property acquired by a woman on specified occasions and at different stages of her life). These authorities, namely the *Parāśara-Mādhava* (II, 368), the *Madanapārijāta* (671) and the *Vyavahārakāṇḍa* (379), give us a comprehensive view of the scope of *stridhana* so as to include under this head, according to the fullest interpretation, what is inherited, acquired by partition, received as gift, or obtained as treasure tove, and so forth, as well as the ṇuputial fee. A similarly comprehensive definiton of *saudāyika* (dowry) is given in the *Vivādaratnākara* (511) and the *Vivādachintāmaṇi* (217), so as to make it comprise what a girl receives either before or after marriage at her father's or her husband's residence from her father or mother, or their respective families. The remarkable clause (Kātyāyana and Vyāsa), limiting the amount of *stridhana,* is interpreted in different ways by our authors. It is taken in its narrow literal sense, so as to disqualify the wife for receiving *stridhana* beyond the limit of the prescribed 2000 *paṇas* as well as immṇovable property[9e] in a slightly wider sense so as to disqualify the wife for disposing at her will of property exceeding this limit although given by her husband[9f], and in its widest sense so as to mean that the limit applies to property given only once during many years for the girls livelihood and in this case it does not exclude immovable property.[9g]

The woman's dominion over her *strīdhana* is completely recognized by our authors[9h] after the older texts. The wife, we read, is free to dispose of her *saudāyika* property (and of *strīdhana* in general), comprising both movables and immovables, by gift or sale at her will; she can dispose of her property acquired from her husband, other than immovables, which she is entitled to enjoy during her lifetime and which devolve upon the other heirs thereafter; the husband is civilly and criminally liable (in the sense of being forced to pay back the principal with interest and to pay a fine) for appropriation of his wife's *strīḍhana* otherwise than on a number of specified occasions. Referring to a clause under which the husband is liable to pay the value of the *strīdhana* appropriated by him even with his wife's consent, the author of the *Vyavahārakāṇḍa* explains that the husband is not dependent upon another, but has no independence in respect of his wife's *strīdhana,* while by contrast the lawfully married wife is constantly dependent, though entitled to ownership thereafter in respect of her husband's wealth. Finally we may mention that our authors repeat after the older texts the special rule of sucession for the *strīdhana* of the mother as as to make full brothers along with full sisters or the unmarried sisters alone, or the full brothers alone, or else the mother and the father the first heirs according to the particular class of such property.[10] Following the equitable interpretation of the *Mitāksharā* and the *Smṛitichandrikā* our authors further declare that unmarried sisters take the property in preference to the married sisters, and among married sisters those who are unsettled (i.e. without children or with poor husbands or unfortunate) take the same in preference to those who are settled.

Food and Drink

The *Smṛiti* rules relating to lawful and forbidden food and drink, along with the penances for violation of the same, are repeated, sometimes at great length, by our authors. The rules about meat-eating, in particular, follow the old pattern, with a distinct tendency towards abstention from the same. The *Madanapārijāta* (338) and the *Grihastharatnākara* (380-81) explain the occasion justifying meat-eating in the *Smṛitis,* which include, according to the former's interpretation, the preparation of meat for feeding Brāhmaṇas at the honourable reception of guests and so forth, and, according to the interpretation of the latter, partaking of the same when this is commended by the Brāhmanas. Other occasions, explained in the *Grihastharatnākara,* are those when the meat is purified with *mantras* for the purpose of sacrifice, when there is the risk of a man losing his life otherwise, when the meat is procured by the man himself (in the case of Kshatriyas engaged in hunting animals), and when the meat is purchased and eaten after worship of the gods. The ban against meat-eating at *śrāddhas* in the Kali Age, we are further told by these authors, applies to the Brāhmaṇa alone, since a *Smṛiti* (text) (Pulastya) prescribes the offering of herimit's food by Brāhmaṇas, of meat by Kshatriyas and Vaiśyas, and of honey by Śūdras respectively. Going further than the above the *Gṛihastharatnākara* observes that the merit of abstention from meat-eating applies likewise to the occasions above mentioned, while the *Madanapārijāta* states that there is no obligation to eat the remnants (of meat) offered in honour of the Brāhmaṇas, the gods, the fathers and so forth, and that meat-eating on other occasions is attended with considerable demerit. According to the *Śrāddhasāra* (57-58), the decision of Pulastya, quoted above is to be followed, in spite of the general reference to meat, honey and the like, as fit offerings at *śrāddhas* by all castes, while the provision for meat-offering at *śrāddhas* and so forth in numerous (*Smṛiti*) works should be understood to apply not to all and sundry (this being hateful to the people), but only to those (such as the Kshatriyas and so forth) who are inclined towards meat-eating.

The *Smriti* rules forbidding or restricting the drink of intoxicants, caste-wise, are repeated and amplified by our authors. The *Gṛihastharatṇākara* (393-95), referring to three kinds of wines (*surā*),—namely, those prepared from rice-flour (*paishṭī*), from molasses (*gauḍī*), and from honey or from *madhuka* flowers (*mādhvī*),—repeats the older view that all these are forbidden to the Brāhmaṇa, while the Kshatriyas and the Vaiśyas incur no blame by drinking the last two kinds. Intoxicants (*madya*), we are further told, are forbidden only to Brāhmaṇas. The point is stated more fully by the other authors. The *Madanapārijāta* (813-24), while identifying *paishtī* with *surā*, and declaring *gauḍī* and *mādhvī* to be equivalent to the same in respect of Brāhmaṇas alone, observes that the Brāhmaṇa, from his very birth, is forbidden to drink all *madyas* with *surā* at their head, that the Kshatriya and the Vaiśya are forbidden to drink *surā* but not *gauḍī* and other kinds of *madya*, and that neither *surā* nor *madya* is forbidden to the Śūdra. The *Parāśara-Mādhava* (III, 409-13), after distinguishing in the first instance between eleven kinds of *madya*, osberves that *madya* is forbidden to the Brāhmaṇas but permitted to Kshatriyas and Vaiśyas. Further it explains the grounds (according as the act is intentional or not, is done once or repeatedly, is performed for the treatment of a disease, otherwise incurable) for the application of different types of penances to Brāhmaṇas. The *Prāyaśchittasāra* (39-45), after first quoting the above-mentioned division of *madya* into eleven kinds and of *surā* into three varieties, and after observing that *madya* is a generic designation of which *surā* is a species, concludes at the end of a short discussion that all *madyas* are forbidden to the Brāhmaṇas, but not to Kshatriyas and Vaiśas, who are in fact expressly permitted to drink *gauḍī* and *mādhvī*. In accordance with the old *Smṛiti* estimate of different varieties of intoxicants, the *Madanapārijāta*, the *Parāśara-Mādhava* and the *Prāyaśchittasāra* apply the extreme penance of suicide by drinking red-hot *surā* to a Brāhmaṇa who has drunk *surā* (meaning *paishṭī*) intentionally once, or the other two kinds of *madyas* repeatedly. In so far as the Śūdra is concerned, it is significant that the *Bṛihaddharma Purāna* (III, 4, 27) and the *Prāyaśchittaviveka* (37) substitute the act of illicit connection with a Brāhmaṇa woman, in place of drinking wine, in the list of five mortal sins for Śūdras.

The *Smṛiti* ban on drinking intoxicants by women is applied with different degrees of intensity by our authors. Strictly applying the rule, the *Parāśra-Mādhava* (I, 507) requires that wives of the three upper classes drinking *surā* (identified with *madya*) are not only to be superseded, but abandoned. The *Gṛihastharatnāīkara* (84) more leniently explains that wives of the three upper classes drinking *madya* are to be superseded. Going further than this, the *Madanapārijāta* (188) observes that the wife is to be superseded if she drinks *madya* forbidden to her proper caste. We have a further explanation, though of a somewhat academic character, in the *Madanapārijāta* (824) where we are told that wives of the three upper classes, belonging to all castes down to the Śūdras, are forbidden to drink *surā* on pain of suffering half the penance for men, and that even the Śūdra wife of a Brāhmaṇa is forbidden to drink any kind of *madya* on pain of bringing sin upon her husband and blame upon her offspring, though not loss of caste either for herself or her husband.

The contemporary historical records partly confirm and partly supplement the evidence of the *Smṛitis* The Brāhmaṇas and the Kshatriyas among the Marāṭhā people, we are told by Ibn Batūtah, while living on a diet of rice, vegetables and sesame oil, forbore to drink wine which was regarded by them as one of the worst vices. From the evidence of Barbosa we learn that Brāhmaṇas and Lingāyats in the Vijayanagara Empire abstained from eating fish or flesh, while the king and the nobles were used to eating fish and all kinds of meat except beef. The daily slaughter of countless sheep as well as of pigs of excellent quality for food at the capital city of Vijayanagara is noticed by Paes.[10a]

Standard of Living

The high standard of living known to the either times seems to have prevailed at least at the upper levels of society during this period. Leaving aside for the present the reference to the conditions prevailing in the contemporary Delhi Sultanate, we may quote here the authentic evidence relating to the Vijayanagara Empire. Speaking of this territory, 'Abd-ur-Razzāq observes that "all inhabitants, high or low, down to the artificers of the Bazar" wear "jewels and gilt ornaments in their ears and around their necks, arms, wrists and fingers". The male costume, according to Barbosa, consisted of clothes with girdles along with short shirts of cotton (or silk or coarse brocade) and small turbans (or silk or brocade caps). The people, we are told by the same observer, wore "rings set with precious stones as well as many ear-rings set with fine pearls", and they anointed themselves after bath with "white sandal wood, aloes, camphor, musk and saffron all ground fine and kneaded with rose water." The women, according to the same traveller, wore garments of very thin cotton or silk, while their ornaments consisted of "nose-screws made of fine gold wire, sapphire or ruby pendant, ear-rings set with many jewels, necklaces of gold and jewels of very fine coral beads, bracelets of gold and precious stones and many coral beads fitted to their arms." The height of luxury was reached, as in the preceding period, at the royal courts. The splendours of the royal palace at Vijayanagara, the display of pomp and magnificence by the kings at their ceremonial public receptions as well as on festive occasions like the annual *Mahānavamī* festival, their huge female establishments including their nunerous queens with their eunuchs and other attendants, their costly dress and furniture, are vividly described by a number of contemporary observers, namely, Nicolo Conti (1421), 'Abd-ur-Razzāq (1443), Varthema (1502), Barbosa (1514) and Paes (1522).[11]

Trends in General Manners and Character

Some important references, after the *Smṛiti* authorities of this period, to the manners and general character of the great majority of the Indian people who were followers of the indigenous faiths, have been given in the foregoing pages. But the point is sufficiently important to deserve a more detailed treatment. Firstly, as regards the question of rigidity of caste distinctions our authors' attitude indicates some contradictory or at least divergent tendencies. On the one hand, they continue to condone (as we have seen above) *anuloma* marriages (even of Brāhmaṇas with Śūdra girls under special circumstances), while simultaneously condemning, in the *Kalivariya* text, quoted with approval in the *Parāśara-Mādhava* (I, 123-27), inter-caste marriages of the three upper classes in general terms. On the other hand, they emphasize the immense difference between the status of the Brāhmaṇa and the Śūdra in such passages as the *Parāśara-Mādhava* (III, 171-76), explaining the qualifications for membership of the learned assembly (*parishat*) for adjudging penances.[12] In the second place our authors, while discussing the eligibility of the three upper castes for the order of ascetics, arrive at different conclusions: the *Madanapārijāta* (365-73) confines these privileges to the Brāhmaṇa alone to the exclusion of the Kshatriya as well as the Vaiśya, and the *Parāśara-Mādhava* (I, 536-38) extends it to all the three castes, with the qualification that the Kashatriya and the Vaiśya are not to wear the red robe and not to carry the (ascetic's) staff. The opinion of the *Madanapārijāta* is followed by Śūlapāṇi (on Yājñavalkya III, 56-57). Thirdly, the *Madanapārijāta* (785-86), discussing the vexed question of the validity of killing a desperado (*ātatāyī*) Brāhmaṇa, seeks to reconcile the contradictory texts condemning and exonerating the act, by taking the former to mean that killing an *ātatāyī* Brāhmaṇa is inherently blamable, and the latter to signify that the blame for this act is less than that incurred by killing a Brāhmaṇa who is not an *ātatāyī*. On the other hand, killing an *ātatāyī* Brāhmaṇa is included in the *Kalivarjya* text quoted as above in the *Parāśara-Mādhava*. Again, the *Madanapārijāta* (827), explaining Manu's text (which prescribes the penance of courting death by a Brāhmaṇa guilty of stealing gold), observes that the injunction not to kill Brāhmaṇas and the prohibition against killing them for any offence whatever apply to matters other than penances. Similarly, while our authors treat the penance for suicide in various ways by Brāhmaṇas guilty of one or other of the mortal sins, the *Kalivarjya* text quoted as above in the *Parāśara-Mādhava* as well as the shorter passage cited in the *Madanapārijāta* (16-17) includes prescription of the penance of death in the list of forbidden practices of the Kali Age. In the fourth and the last place, we have seen how our authors tend on the one hand to emphasize the Śūdra's duty of serving the Brāhmaṇa, and on the other hand seek to relax the rules relating to dealings in forbidden commodities in the case of Śūdras engaged in trade. We have further seen how the same authors differ on the point of lawfulness of the Śūdra's food as well as that of interpretation of Manu's celebrated dictum about the Śūdra's natural servitude. An extreme view of the Śūdra's social disabilities is taken in the *Kalivarjya* list, quoted in the *Parāśara-Mādhava*, which includes partaking of food of five specified classes of Śūdras by the Brāhmaṇa householder, and engaging Śūdras as cooks in householder's residences among the prohibited practices of the Kali Age. The furthest limit in this direction is the *Smṛiti* passage quoted in the *Parāśara-Mādhava* which requires (as we have seen) penance by bathing for touching a Śūdra. For the rest, our authors agree in combining, as before, the eulogy of deserving Brāhmaṇas with condemnation of unworthy members of this order, as well as in continuing the old restrictions on the Brāhmaṇa's food and drink. Only in the *Parāśara-Mādhava* we have a striking relaxation of the strict rule requiring the Brāhmaṇa to engage in the occupation of agriculture, trade and crafts only in time of extreme distress. Lastly, it may be mentioned that our authors tend to relax, as mentioned above, the old religious disabilities of the Śūdras within strictly canonical limits. On the other hand, they agree in perpetuating the extreme disabilities of the Chaṇḍālas and other despised castes.

On the question of rigidity of social behaviour, the attitude of our authors is marked by similar contradictory tendencies. On the one hand the *Parāśara-Mādhava* (I, 112), following the original text of Parāśara, explains that there is no degradation from caste for conversation and so forth with one fallen from caste (*patita*) in the Kali Age in contrast with former Ages. With this may be compared the inclusion of pollution, by contact with a *patita*, in the *Kalivarjya* text quoted in the same work. This invovles relaxation of the strict *Smṛiti* rule (Manu and Vishṇu) prescribing degradation from caste for close association with one guilty of the mortal sins. On the other hand, social intercourse with individuals of the three upper castes making a sea-voyage, even after their performance of the prescribed penance, is included in the above-quoted *Kalivarjya* text. This implies an intensification of the old *Smṛiti* rule, which merely includes (in Baudhāyana and Bṛihaspati) sea-voyage among the mortal sins, and declares (in Manu) a Brāhmaṇa undertaking sea-voyage to be unfit for a *śrāddha* invitation.

The position of women was not made worse, but was actually strengthened and consolidated on some points by our authors. To begin with, they continue, but do not add to, the social and religious disabilities of women. Again they repeat the old rules enjoining upon the guardians early marriage of girls along with those giving the girl the right of self-choice of her husband, and permitting the revocation of her marriage with an unworthy bridegroom under special circumstances. They reproduce likewise the old rules of penance relating to sinful women with a distinct tendency towards relaxation of the old severity. Similarly they repeat the old rules relating, on the one hand, to the wife's supreme duty of service and devotion to her husband and, on the other hand, to the husband's reciprocal obligation of maintaining the faithful wife together with its legal sanctions. The husband is held, as before, to be liable to pay compensation extending to one-third of his property to his superseded wife. Again, while it is agreed that the abandonment of sinful women means that expulsion from the household in extreme cases, it is usually taken to involve their temporary disgrace and penance, followed by restoration to their old position. On the subject of the widow's obligation of self-immolation on the funeral pyre of her husband, our authors' opinions vary (as we have seen) from its emphatic approval to its qualified recommendation. To their great credit, it must finally be said, that they completely vindicate the widow's right as the foremost heir of her sonless and 'divided' husband, as well as the woman's complete dominion over her special kind of property (*strīdhana*).

The old custom of religious suicide was continued during our period. The *Tirthachintāmaṇi* (47-52) and the *Gaṅgāvākyāvalī* (305-10) contain a high eulogy (after the Puranic texts) of suicide (by starvation and even by cutting off limbs from the body for being devoured by birds and so forth) as well as of natural death at various selected spots in Prayāga and its environs. We have a similar approval of suicide at Vārāṇāsī by entering the fire and so forth in the *Tīrthachintāmaṇi* (347) as well as suicide by starvation in the waters of the Gangā in the *Tirthachintamaṇi* (263) and the *Gangāvākuāvalī* (267-92). The prohibition of suicide by starting on the 'Great Journey' (till one falls dead), as well as of suicide of very old people by entering the fire, or falling down from the precipice, in the *Kalivarjya* text above mentioned, is negatived by other references. For the *Smṛiti* authorities of this period not only continue to prescribe suicide in the above and other forms as a penance for the mortal sins, but the *Madanapārijāta* (801) explains that the penance of entering the fire belongs to the Kashatriyas alone, and that of falling down from the precipice belongs to the other castes as well, while it deliberately extends (844) the penance of starting on the 'Great Journey' to Brāhmaṇa women guilty of illicit intercoruse with Śūdras, and so forth, in the *pratiloma* order.

While on this subject, however, we may notice the tendency of our authorities, namely, the *Parāśara-Mādhava* (III, 393) and specially the *Prāyaśchittasāra* (203-06), to amplify the principle of substitutes (*pratyāmnāyas*) for penances according to the diminishing capacity of the sinners.

The custom of religious suicide, noticed above, is corroborated by the evidence of the contemporary foreign observers. How Hindu devotees used to cut off their limbs with sharp knives or their necks with sharp swords in fulfilment of their vows before their deities in Ma'bar (Coromandel coast) and in "Greater India" (meaning the tract extending from Malabar indefinitely towardss the east), is told by the Friars Odoric and Jordanus respectively. According to Ibn Batūtah, the Indian people (meaning the Hindus) had the custom of drowning themselves voluntarily in the Gaṅgā as an act of spiritual merit.[13]

The statements of our authors testify to the continuance of the ancient custom of pilgrimages to the scared places (*tīrthas*). The ritual of pilgrimages to Prayāga, Purushottama (Puri), Konārka, the Gaṅgā, Gayā, Vārāṇasī and so forth, is given at great length in the *Tirthachintāmaṇi,* just as that of the pilgrimages to Dvārakā and along the Gaṅgā is described in the works *Dvārakīpattala* of Binābāi and the *Gaṅgāvākyāvalī* of Viśvāsadevi (or perhaps of the poet Vidyāpati) respectively. The sacred legends (*māhātmyas*) of Setubandha-Rāmeśvara, Āmardaka, Gayā, the Godāvarī, the Kṛishṇavenī, the Narmadā and other *tīrthas* are enumerated in the *Tirthasāra* of Dalapati. The *Prāyaśchittasāra* of the last named author mentions (206-11) pilgrimages to various *tīrthas* as *pratyāmnāyas* for a number of penances. Among the foreign observers Ibn Batūtah noticed pigrimage to the Gaṅgā as a peculiar Indian custom.

From the statements of our authors we may conclude that the old sentiment of veneration for the cow was continued during this period. A long list of penances for killing or maiming a cow is given in the *Madanapārijāta* (856-59), and a much shorter list in Śūlapāṇi's commentary on Yājñavalkya (III, 263-64). We have a high eulogy of the cow in the *Bṛihaddharma Purāṇa* (II, 6.31f). No wonder, therefore, that Śūlapāṇi (on Yājñavalkya, I, 109) and the *Gṛihastharatnākara* (294) specifically forbid the killing of cows in honour of guests (as laid down by Yājñavalkya and Vaśishṭha) on the ground of its inclusion in the *Kalivarjya* list of *Brahma Purāṇa*. The worship of the bull is mentioned as a peculiar Indian custom by Odoric and Jordanus in their accounts of Quilon and 'India the Less' respectively. The high respect paid to the cow by the inhabitants of Calicut is noticed by 'Abd-ur-Razzāq.[14]

The sentiment of veneration for the cow is extended by the *Smṛiti* authorities to other animals as well. Sacrificing animals with recitations of the Vedic texts in honour of the bridegroom, the guests and the ancestors is included in the *Kalivarjya* texts which are quoted in the *Parāśara-Mādhava* and the *Madnapārijāta*. A long list of penances for killing different species of birds, rodents and quadrupeds is given in the *Parāśara-Mādhava* (III 61-72).

Muslim Religion and Society

The early history of Sūfiism in India has been discussed above.[1] The Khalji period (1290-1320) saw a further intensification of the activities of this school, thanks mainly to the three great saints of the period, Hazrat Nizām-ud-dīn Auliyā of Delhi, his spiritual preceptor, Shaikh Farid-ud-din Mas'ūd Ganj-i-Shakar of Ajodhan, and the latter's nephew and disciple, 'Alā-ud-dīn Sābir of Piran Kalyar. The memory of these saintly personages and their sucessors is as fresh today as it was centuries ago, and their anniversaries (*'urs, d'rās*) are celebrated with as great eclat today as ever, when musicians and poets gather in thousands to pay the tribute of glowing praise to their miraculous lives and to enliven the huge concourses of the pilgrims to their shrines. The unbounded influence of the saints on the masses often roused the jealousy and suspicion of the rulers, but they carried on their mission quietly and peacefully, unruffled alike by the glamour of the royal court and the hostility of the kings. None of the latter, indeed, had the courage to molest them or to persecute their followers openly, though some of them tried, ineffectively, to alienate popular sympathy from them, accusing them of disseminating heretical ideas and sheltering criminals in their monasteries.[2] It is possible that occasionally these saints encouraged certain public risings and demonstrations against tyrannical rulers, but that they ever did so with any selfish motive can hardly be proved. On the other hand, their sole purpose in blessing such movements was the welfare of the common people.

Besides these spiritual teachers, mention may also be made of another class of ascetics, the *qalandars*, who did not usually found any orders or establish any spiritual centres, but wandered about, leading lives of seclusion, renunciation, and poverty, striving not so much for the spiritual and moral uplift of the common people, as for their own individual salvation. This attitude of aloofness, however, did not protect them against popular curiosity, and they were generally held in high esteem and surrounded by admirers and devotees. They were usually clean-shaved, went about clad in woollen robes of coarse texture, and were not so particular about the observance of religious duties enjoined by Islām. Of these *qalandars,* the most celebrated was Bū ‘Alī of Pānipat, a brother of Shaikh Jamāl-ud-dīn Hanswī who died about A.D. 1333. The cumulative effect of the presence in large number of such saints and ascetics was the transformation of Islām in India from a simple and puritanic religion, with emphasis on the performance of outward legal duties (*takālīf-I-shar'īya*) to a complex, devotional creed in which miracles and superstitions, combined, of course, with saint-worship, played an important role. It became a common practice now to get oneself attached to a spiritual preceptor, who alone, according to the popular belief, could guarantee bliss and happiness in this life and the life hereafter. Dates of the anniversaries of the more famous saints used to be memorized with assiduous care, and in course of time the months of the lunar calendar, in which these dates fell, came to be known by the names.[3] A pious Muslim, especially among the uneducated classes, would rather miss the five ritual daily prayers and the obligatory fast of Ramazān than fail to make a suitable offering (*nayāz*) on any of the important dates consecrated to the memory of a saint.

The dissemination of Sūfi ideas in India was continued during the Tughluq period by the disciples of Hazrat Nizām-ud-dīn Auliyā, the most notable of whom was Shaikh Nasīr-ud-din of Awadh known as Raushan Charāgh (the Bright Lamp), who was killed by a *qalandar* in A.D. 1356 and lies buried near Delhi.

As noted above, the *Bhakti* movement was very popular among the Hindus during the period when the Sūfi movement gained strength in India. The two parallel movements, based upon doctrines of love and selfless devotion, helped a lot in bringing the two communities closer together, in spite of occasional reactionary movements, such as that started by the fanatical Sayyid Muhammad who claimed to be the Mahdi[4]. Sultān Sikandar Lodī apparently came under the influence of the orthodox *'ulamā* and is said to have committed certain acts of intolerance, to which reference has been made above.[5]

The Muslim society in the meantime was fast becoming Indianized. Below the Sultān, who was a despotic ruler with no limit or restraint on his powers except such as was dictated by considerations of a peaceful and stable government, there stood certain privileged classes, namely the *umarā* or nobels and the *'ulamā* or scholars, holding fiefs and estates. The slaves of the royal household may also be regarded as a privileged class, for in spite of their morally degraded position, they were usually well cared for and often exercised considerable influence on their royal masters. This is clearly shown by the examples of Malik Kāfūr, the lieutenant of Sultān 'Alā-ud-dīn Khaljī, and Malik Khusrav, the favourite of that monarch's son, Qutb-ud-dīn Mubārak Shāh. There does not appear to have been any strong and prosperous middle class in those days, so that the wealth and splendour of the upper strata of society formed a strange contrast with the poverty and squalor of the masses, both Muslim and Hindu. The Muslim nobles were usually of foreign origin,—Persians, Turks, Afghāns and Sayyids or Arabs,—and mostly kept themsleves aloof from their Indian subjects and dependants. The arrogant aristocratic classes gradually developed a sort of caste system which was alien to the spirit of Islām and was certainly the product of Indian influences. Thus a Turk (or Mughul), a Pathān, a Sayyid, or even a Shaikh,[6] would never think of a matrimonial alliance with a person of a lower rank, that is one outside these four *dhāts* or *qaums,* or even outside his own particular denomiantion. The *purdāh* or seclusion of women had already become a common practice. This is evident from the remarks made by conemporary historians and poets on the bold step taken by Sultāna Raziyya in discarding the veil and dressing herself up in male attire. Khusrav, in the *Matla 'al Anwār* and elsewhere, has addressed his "paradise daughter" in the most loving words, but it is obvious from the bits of fatherly advice which he gives her, that he considers the woman's right place to be her home, and her most sacred duty, obedience to her father or brother. This naturally led to the institution of the *harem* in the case of the more prosperous and respectable classes of society. It must not, however, be supposed that polygamy or the keeping of concubines was a common practice. This sort of luxury could be afforded only by a privileged few. In most cases the harem was no more than a separate living quarter for the women-folk of the family, corresponding to the *zanānkhāna,* as opposed to the *dīwānkhāna* or the male quarters of a later period. *Purdāh* was, however, unknown among the lower classes, specially in rural society. How far the adoption of the *purdāh* of a rigid type by the Muslims in India was due to Rājput influence, it is difficult to determine. What is certain is that the peculiar social conditions in India were largely responsible for the development of this system which was unknown in other. Muslim countries in medieval times.

Right from the kings and the nobles at the top down to the humblest citizens, the Muslims had become thoroughly Indianized. The costly royal dresses, the gilded and studded swords and daggers,[7] the umbrellas (*chhatra*) of various colours, the richly caparisoned elephants which, as an emblem of royalty, were stationed in the durbār-hall and accompanied the state cavalcades, were all typically Indian paraphernalia of royal pomp and splendour. The old Indian practice of chewing the betel-leaf had become very popular among the Muslims.[8] Khusrav, in his account of his maternal grandfather 'Imād-ul-Mulk, speaks of continuous relays of this delicacy being brought to his assemblies in the *dīwān-i-'arz,* and distributed among those present there. The seasoning of food with rich spices and chillies, almost unknown in the Muslim lands, had also become widely prevalent; the culinary art brought by the Muslims to India had already absorbed several Indian elements. Standard dishes which, from their names, would appear to be of foreign origin, such as *pilāu* and *qawarma,* were now very different from what they had been in Irān or Khurāsān. The amazingly large range of dishes (*alwān*), indulged in by the wealthy or served on festive occasions,[9] would clearly show how luxurious and refined had become the tastes of the well-to-do people, which could only be possible in a rich country like India. Among the articles of dress in common use, the head-gears known as the *chīra* and the *pāg* were certainly of Indian origin and were borrowed from the Rājputs. They would appear to have been in vogue among the dandies of Delhi and other big cities.[10] The tight-fitting cloak for men and the tight-fitting trousers, often worn beneath a loose skirt, for women, on the other hand, were of foreign origin, and were adopted by the Rājputs from their Muslim neighbours. The use of rings, necklaces, ear-rings and other ornaments by men was also due to Indian influence, for such vanities were strictly forbidden to the faithful in the Islamic law. India was famous for its fine cotton and silk fabrics, which now began to be widely used by the gentry among the Muslims who had been accustomed to much humbler and coarser stuffs in their original home-lands.[11] Textile industry flourished in several parts of India—the Deccan, Gujarāt, Bengal, Bihār and Mysore,—under the patronage of the Muslim rulers. It is a significant fact that most of the weavers and master-craftsmen came to be, in the course of time, Muslims, who had either embraced Islām, or were of foreign origin and had brought with them some of their native traditions to India. The names of certain fabrics such as *Sūsī or Daryā'i,* would clearly show that the textile art, developed in Muslim countries, had been grafted on the Indian indigenous art, resulting in great improvement and development.

The same admixture is prominently visible in other branches of useful and fine arts that flourished in the pre-Mughul period. The fine, massive edifices raised by the Khaljīs, the Tughluqs, and the Sharqi kings of Jaunpur, all betray Indian influence and are very dissimilar to those raised in contemporary times in other Muslim lands.[11a] The stone-carvers of India, who were mostly Hindus, were employed in large numbers in shaping the pillars and engraving the floral and calligraphic motifs and designs in these buildings. The use of lintels instead of arches in some of them is also an indication of the architectural synthesis that was brought about in this age. Painting was comparatively little developed in the Sultanate, due possibly to the religious ban on it.

*The cultivation of music has always been a matter of controversy among the Muslims in India. There are two schools of Muslim jurists; one maintains that music has been prohibited, while many liberal thinkers claim that it has been permitted. An Arabo-Irānian music was already in vogue in the Muslim world before the eighth century A.D. Probably this influenced the Hindu music in Sind after the Muslims had conquered it, and Naurūz, Zangola, and Hejaz forms were incorporated by the Indians under the names of Nurochoka, Jangla and Hejaj.

*Khwāja Mu'īn-ud-din Chishtī's band of *qavvāls* sang every evening. Illtutmish put a ban on music, but a member of the Chishti order, who had gone to Delhi, was able to persuade him to withdraw it. Since then musical soirées were organized for the *durbārs* and people began to indulge in them publicly. The *durbār* of his son, Ruknud-dīn Firūz, became a centre of celebrated musicians and dancers of both sexes. Balban was also a great patron of music. He has spoken of Indian music in the highest terms and regarded it as superior to the music of any other country. He is credited with the invention of several new melodies compounded of Irānian and Indian tunes. During Kaiqubād's reign music became the order of the day, and both Jalāl-ud-din and 'Alā-ud-din Khalji were great patrons of music.

*Ghiyās-ud-dīn Tughluq banned music, but the ban was withdrawn by Muhammad Tughluq, and musical entertainment by both males and females is said to have been instituted for the royal *durbār*. He had twelve musicians in his regular service, besides one thousand slave musicians. Ibn Batūtah refers to the popularity of music in the royal court. Firūz Tughluq, though orthodox, was not averse to music, and his acession to the throne was celebrated by entertaining the public for twenty-one days with music. A number of books on music and dance, found at Jvālāmukhī, were translated into Persian at his instance. The Sayyid king Mubārak Shāh was noted for his love of music.[12]

Music, both of secular as well as spiritual character, seems to have reached a high level of perfection, during the period under review. The contributions made by the Muslims to Indian music are generally recognized as of far-reaching consequence, and the devotional *qavvālī* music, practised by skilled artists at the monasteries of the dead or living saints, must have been a powerful factor in strengthening the bonds of unity between the two communities. It is this unity of culture which finds proud expression in the verses of Amir Khusav, who pays glowing tributes to the manifold virtues of India, his birth-place. Similar tributes are scattered in the poems of other writers, like Amīr Hasan Sijizī, Mutahhar of Karra and Jamālī Kanboh.

Among the religious ceremonies and social functions those of the *'aqiqa,*[13] *the* bismillāh,[14] the circumcision, the marriage, and the funeral played the most important part in the life of an individual, and in these also we can easily trace Indian influence. Several ceremonies, connected specially with marriage and death, were common, as they are today, to both the communities,[15] although the Muslims, following the old Arab tradition, continued in India, as elsewhere, to marry cousins and other close relations. The Indian bridal decoration, the *sola singhār*, had already become familiar to the Muslims, and is often mentioned by the name of "*haft-o-nuh* by Khusrav and others. Ibn

Batūtah's acount of the marriage of a Sayyid noble, Saif-ud-dīn, with a sister of Sultān Muhammad Tughluq, provides a revealing picture of the great extent to which the Muslims had adopted the Hindu marriage ceremonies even in those early days. Ibn Batūtah also gives an acount of the funeral ceremonies in connection with the death of his daughter.[16] Among the religious ceremonies the *hajj* or the annual pilgrimage to Mecca was, of course, the most important, but pilgrimages to the shrines of famous saints were also very frequent, especially on the occasion of their *urses* or anniversaries. The close of the Ramazān fast, the Īd-ul-Fitr, was another important occasion for general rejoicing, while the Shab-ī-Barāt, which has several common features with the Hindu festival of Śivarātri, was celebrated by keeping a nightlong vigil and a noisy display of fire-works. Apart from these important festivals more or less of Islamic origin, the Indian Muslims freely participated in the Hindu festivals of a religio-social character, such as the Basant, the Holi and the Dīwāli, which is clearly proved by contemporary historical evidence.

The every-day humdrum life of the common people, devoid usually of amusements or excitements, was frequently brightened up by the royal cavalcades, *jashns* (such as that of the *naurūz*), and receiptions, when the streets were lavishly decorated and beautiful kiosks or pavilions (*qubbas*) erected at regular intervals, in which there were stationed beautiful singing and dancing girls, and where the spectators were treated not only to music but also to pleasant drinks. Glowing acounts of these *qubbas* are found in the writings of Khusrav, Ibn Batūtah and other writers.[17]

The game of *chaugān* (polo), riding, racing, hunting, and archery were very popular as outdoor sports among the nobility and the better classes of society, but the poorer people could seldom indulge in them. Among the indoor games, popular both among the rich and the poor, chess and backgammon (*nard* or *chaupar*) are often mentioned, although they were usually frowned upon by the religious divines as frivolous pursuits beguiling the faithful from more useful and more serious occupations. Drinking of wine, in spite of the strict ban placed on it by Islām, seems to have been very common, especially in the higher classes of society, and convivial wine parties supplied another source of recreation and amusement. To what extent the habit had become prevalent, may be judged from what Baranī says about 'Alā-ud-dīn's determination to root it out.[18] Huge quantities of the precious vintage were hunted out of the hidden cellars and poured out into the streets. Some of it was given to the royal elephants, which made even the pious historian exclaim, not without a touch of envy: "How lucky were the elephants of that age to have thus enjoyed themselves." 'Alā-ud-din's stern measures against the use of wine and other corrupt practices, however, did not produce any lasting result, for in the reign of his son and sucessor, Qutb-ud-din Mubārak Shāh, the people, encouraged by the recklessly dissolute life of their monarch, again reverted to their old ways of life. Jesters, buffoons and mountebanks, who had already become a regular feature of society, had the time of their life under this profligate king, one of whose court jesters, Tamāsha by name, used to walk right into the ranks of the nobles and divines assembled in the *durbār*-hall, in a state of inebriation and revile the greatest of them with impunity. Some of the later monarchs, like Fīrūz Tughluq, again took up the task of reform, but their effort succeeded, if at all, for only brief periods.

It must not, however, be supposed that the majority of the Indian Muslims of the Sultanate period were immoral or irreligious; for even among the nobels we often come across the names of some who were noted for their piety and abstemious lives.[19] Most of the common people, on the other hand, led exemplary moral lives and were deeply religious in their outlook. It is, indeed, a remarkable fact that the middle and lower classes of Muslim society in India have always remained free from the corrupting influence of the court, and staunchly loyal to the Islamic way of life as developed in the peculiar social and economic structure of India. The essentially religious mental attitude, which is a distinguishing feature of the Indian Muslims even today, has certainly been inherited from their forefathers who lived in the middle ages. Indian Islām is very different in some respects from the Arabian Islām of the Prophet's days, but it is a powerful and practical moral and religious discipline which has enabled the Indian Muslims to preserve their unity and identity in this land of diverse cultures and religions.

As we have remarked above, the nobles and other privileged classes among the Muslims held fiefs and estates or large revenue-assignments, which enabled them to lead lives of ease and prosperity. They had enough money to emulate their royal masters in their extravagantly generous expenditure on special occasions, such as feasts, festivals, marriages, etc. They lived in palatial houses with a large number of slaves and domestic servants, male and female. Their houses were usually provided with rich furnishings, richly decorated sofas and divans, exquisitely made glass and china, costly tapestries and valuable carpets from Persia and Bukhara, vases, and gold and silver dishes and bowls. Their stables were stocked with fine horses of indigenous and foreign breeds,[20] and many of them also kept elephants, so that a *fīl-khana* was almost an essential part of a noble's household. They were usually surrounded by a large number of dependants and hangers-on, and were lavish in their gifts to poets and scholars who basked in the sun-shine of their favour. Actually the house of each of these nobles was a miniature replica of the royal court, and it is not strange, therefore, that these nobles' wealth and munificence occasionally excited the jealousy of the kings themselves. Hoarding of wealth was unknown, chiefly because all revenue assignments were personal and not hereditary, and could be cancelled even in the lifetime of the holder.

Next to the nobles, there was a large class of people with modest incomes derived either from small land-holdings or from the royal treasury in return for their services in different capacities. These latter consisted of district officers, revenue collectors, judges, post-masters and others, some of whom were directly connected with the royal household as scribes and secretaries, or as tutors and teachers of the monarch's children. Quite a few of them were also attached to the households of various nobles, and led, on the whole, fairly prosperous and happy lives, possessing their own houses in the cities and the villages. Their mainstay was their landed properties, small or large, and many of them were actively engaged in the cultivation of land. The arts of calligraphy and epistolography (*inshā*), which were assiduously cultivated by most of them, often provided remunerative sources of income.

The lowest strata of Muslim society comprised the peasants and cultivators, usually of Indian origin, workmen, artisans, and domestic servants. Business and trade were mostly in the hands of Hindu merchants among whom the merchants of Gujarāt (usually Baniās) and Multān were famous for their large-scale mercantile activities and fabulous wealth; and their help was constantly sought by the spendthrift nobles and bourgeoisie who found themselves in difficulties. A large number of workmen and artisans—weavers, carpenters, metal-engravers, scribes, etc.—were usually attached to the royal ateliers or *kārkhānas*, while many more of them found employment as retainers of the nobles and the grandees; but most of them worked independently, and following the old Indian practice, had formed themselves into guilds or trade unions. They usually occupied separate and well-marked quarters in the cities which were named after them, as the weavers' marked, the potters' market, and so on. While it is difficult to have any exact idea of the wages earned by these workmen, due to lack of reliable data, it would appear that they were fairly well off and could earn enough to keep themselves and their families in tolerable comfort. This was chiefly because the essential commodities were cheap and plentiful, and they had not yet become used to such luxuries as became common in later times. According to a rough calculation based on information derived from contemporary sources, a modest monthly income of five *tankas* (silver coins) was sufficient for the maintenance of a small family consisting of five members.[21] On the whole, therefore, this class of people also suffered no particular economic hardship. Starvation, unemployment and frustration were usually unknown, except, of course, during famines, which were rather too frequent, due to lack of adequate means of irrigation.

To sum up this brief survey of the religious, intellectual and social condition of the Indian Muslims of the Sultanate period, we could make the following general observations:

1. The religion of Islām, at least its popular form, underwent substantial change, having been profoundly influenced by the Sūfi beliefs which, in their turn, owed a good deal to Hindu Vedāntic and Yogic philosophy. The majority of the Muslims, in spite of the corrupt lives led by some of their kings and nobles, remained, on the whole, religious, and conformed scrupulously to the moral standards set up by Islām.

2. Intellectually, great progress was made in all fields of learning, and this age produced some of the greatest poets and scholars of Muslim India. Many literary products of this period have been irretrievably lost, but those which have survived occupy a place of very considerable importance in Arabic and Persian literature produced in India.[22]

3. Socially, the Muslims of foreign extraction, who came to India from Persia, Afghānistān and Khurāsān, in the early days, unlike the Arabs, held themselves aloof from the Indians for some time, but gradually the barriers between the two communities were removed, and a process of Indianization started, making rapid advance and reaching its climax during the Mughul period. The manifestations of this process were visible in every walk of life, and the Muslims had already adopt many habits, ways and manners of the Hindus.

Hindu Muslim Relations

Reference has been made above[1] to the uncompromising spirit of animosity between the Hindus and the Muslims in India in the thirteenth century A.D. It is necessary to review the changes, if any, that took place in their mutual relation during the period of two centuries and a quarter (1300-1526) covered by this volume.

Influence of One Community upon Another

The Muslims made a large number of converts in India and, by the end of the period, the vast majority of Indian Muslims must have been descendants of Hindu converts.[1a] Even the Muslims who claimed descent from foreigners or foreign immigrants into India lived as close neighbours to the Hindus for generations. It was inevitable, therefore, that there must have been some reciprocal influence between the two communities. Sufficient data are not available for an exact determination of such influence, but it is possible to have a general idea. It has been pointed out in the preceding section that many social practices of Indian Muslims, such as marriage and class distinction, and some of their ideas and beliefs which differ materially from those of their co-religionists elsewhere, were probably due to the influence of the Hindu society. As regards dress, food, language, music, art and architecture, each influenced the other to a certain extent, at least in some regions, mostly in North India.

Even in religious matters there was some mutual influence, as is indicated by Sūfism on the one hand, and the doctrines of medieval Hindu saints on the other. to which detailed reference has been made in Ch. XVI. Muslim saints, particularly of the mystic school, were revered by the Hindus. though, be it noted, the Hindus would not admit them in their houses nor give them food or water in their own utensils.[2] The Hindu mendicants, *yogis*, and astrologers were held in high respect by the Muslims. Some local cults, like those of Satyapīr (True Saint), were popular with village-folks of both the communities. Even in some minor matters, such as the auspicious day for commencing a journey, the Muslims adopted the customs of the Hindus.[3]

In the field of scholarship and literature there was some amount of sympathetic understanding between the two communities. The Muslim scholars studied Hindu philosophy and sciences, such as the systems of *Yoga* and *Vedānta*, medicine, and astrology, while the Hindus learnt from them subjects like geography, arithmetic and chemistry, in which the Arabs had made striking progress. Some Muslim rulers were patrons of Hindu writers, and a few Muslim scholars wrote in Indian vernaculars. A few Hindus also wrote in Persian. The mutual linguistic influence was reflected in the change of Hindi on a line which ultimately led to the development of Urdu.

But all these touched merely the fringe and external elements of life, and even as such, their influence was confined to a small section of the Hindus and Muslims of India, taken as a whole. It is noteworthy, that neither the Hindus nor the Muslims imbibed, even to the least degree, the chief characteristic features of the other's culture which may be regarded as their greatest contribution to human civilization. The ultra-democratic social ideas of the Muslims, though strictly confined to their own religious community, were an object-lesson of equality and fraternity which Europe, and through her the world, learnt at a great cost only in the nineteenth century. The liberal spirit of toleration and reverence for all religions, preached and practised by the Hindus, is still an ideal and despair of the civilized mankind. The Hindus, even with the living example of the Muslim community before their very eyes, did not relax in the least their social rigidity and inequality of men exemplified in the caste-system and untouchability. Nor did the Muslims ever moderate their zeal to destroy ruthlessly the Hindu temples and images of gods, and their attitude in this respect remained unchanged from the day when Muhammad bin Qāsim set foot on the soil of India till the eigheenth century A.D. when they lost all political power. The Hindus combined catholicity in religious outlook with bigotry in social ethics, while the Muslims displayed an equal bigotry in religious ideas with catholicity in social behaviour.

As will be shown later, there was no *rapprochement* in respect of popular or national traditions, and those social and religious ideas, beliefs, practices, and institutions which touch the deeper chord of life and give it a distinctive form, tone, and vigour. In short, the reciprocal influences were too superficial in character to affect materially the fundamental differences between the two communities in respect of almost every thing that is deep-seated in human nature and makes life worth living. So the two great communities, although they lived side by side, moved each in its own orbit, and there was as yet no sign that the "twain shall ever meet".

Status of the Hindus

The political and religious condition under which the Hindus were forced to live in a Muslim State raised a great barrier between the two communities. The political supremacy of the Muslims was absolute; the Hindus not only enjoyed no political status in practice, but could not even aspire to it under Islamic theory. This has been lucidly expressed by Sir Jadunath Sarkar, an eminent historian of international reputation, in an article from which the following passage is quoted:

"The poison lay in the very core of Islamic theocracy. Under it there can be only one faith, one people, and one all overriding authority. The State is a religious trust administered solely by His people (the Faithful) acting in obedience to the Commander of the Faithful, who was in theory, and very often in practice too, the supreme General of the Army of militant Islam (*Janud*). There could be no place for non-believers. Even Jews and Christians could not be full citizens of it, though they somewhat approached the Muslims by reason of their being "People of the Book" or believers in the Bible, which the Prophet of Islam accepted as revealed."

"As for the Hindus and Zoroastrians, they had no place in such a political system. If their existence was tolerated, it was only a use them as hewers of wood and drawers of water, as tax-prayers, "*Khiraj-guzar*", for the benefit of the dominant sect of the Faithful. They were called *Zimmis* or people under a contract of protection by the Muslim State on condition of certain service to be rendered by them and certain political and civil disabilities to be borne by them to prevent them from growing strong. The very term *Zimmi* is an insulting title. It connotes political inferiority and helplessness like the status of a minor proprietors perpetually under a guardian; such protected people could not claim equality with the citizens of the Muslim theocracy.

"Thus by the basic conception of the Muslim State all non-Muslims are its enemies, and it is the interest of the State to curb their rowth in number and power. The ideal aim was to exterminate them totally, as Hindus, Zoroastrians and Christian nationals have been liquidated (sometimes totally, sometimes leaving a negligible remnant behind) in Afghanistan, Persia and the Near East.

"The Quran (IX. 29) calls upon the Muslims 'to fight those who do not profess the true faith, till they pay *jizya* with the hand in humality (*ham sagkhirun*).' This was a poll-tax payable by Hindus (and also Christians) for permission to live in their ancestral homes under a Muslim sovereign.

"In addition to the obligation to pay this poll-tax, the Hindu was subjected to many disabilities by the very constitution of the Muslim theocracy. He must distinguish himself from the Muslims by wearing a humble dress, and sometimes adding a label of a certain colour to his coat. He must not ride on horse-back or carry arms; though wearing the sword was a necessary part of the dress of every gentleman of that age. He must show a generally respectful attitude towards Muslims. The Hindu was also under certain legal disabilities in giving testimony in law-courts, protection under the criminal law, and in marriage. Finally, in the exercise of his religion he must avoid any publicity that may rouse the wrath of the followers of the Prophet.

"Under the Canon Law, as followed in Islamic countries, a man who converts a Muslim to some other faith is liable to death at the hands of any private Muslim, and so also is the apostate from Islam."[4]

Sir Jadunath's exposition of the Islamic theory, and in particular his view of the nature of the *jizya*, has been opposed by some.[5] But his views are fully borne out by the following passage in the *Zakhīrat-ul-Mulūk* by Shaikh Hamadāni:

"There is another mandate relating to those subjects who are unbelievers and protected people (*zimmīs*). For their governance, the observance of those conditions which the Caliph 'Umar laid in his agreement for establishing the status of the fire-worshippers and the People of the Book (Jews and Christians) and which gave them safety is obligatory on rulers and governors. Rulers should impose these conditions on the *zimmis* of their dominions and make their lives and their property dependent on their fulfilment. They twenty conditions are as follows:

1. In a country under the authority of a Muslim rulers, they are to build no new homes for images or idol temples.
2. They are not to rebuild any old buildings which have been destroyed.
3. Muslim travellers are not to be prevented from staying in idol temples.
4. No Muslim who stays in their houses will commit a sin if he is a guest for three days, if he should have occasion for the delay.
5. Infidels may not act as spies or give aid and comfort to them.
6. If any of their people show any inclination towards Islām, they are not to be prevented from doing so.
7. Muslims are to be respected.
8. If the *zimmīs* are gathered together in a meeting and Muslims appear, they are to be allowed at the meeting.
9. They are not to dress like Muslims.
10. They are not to give each other Muslim names.
11. They are not to ride on horses with saddle and bridle.
12. They are not to possess swords and arrows.
13. They are not to wear signet rings and seals on their fingers.
14. They are not to sell and drink intoxicating liquor openly.
15. They must not abandon the clothing which they have had as a sign of their state of ignorance so that they may be distinguished from Muslims.

16. They are not to propagate the customs and usages of polytheists among Muslims.
17. They are not to build their homes in the neighbourhood of those of Muslims.
18. They are not to bring their dead near the graveyards of Muslims.
19. They are not to mourn their dead with loud voices.
20. They are not to buy Muslim slaves.

At the end of the treaty it is written that if *zimmīs* infringe any of these conditions, they shall not enjoy security and it shall be lawful for Muslims to take their lives and possessions as though they were the lives and possessions of unbelievers in a state of war with the faithful"[5a]

It is unnecessary for our present purpose to enter into any further discussion about the correctness of Sir Jadunath's interpretation of the Muslim scripture, but there is no doubt that he correctly represents the view accepted, both in theory and practice, by the Muslim rulers and theologians in India during the period under review.[6] And this is really more relevant to the present issue.

Reference has already been made above[7] to the position of the Hindus in Muslim State according to Islamic theory as explained by the 'wise men', and particularly Qāzī Mughās-ud-dīn of Bayāna, to 'Alā-ud-dīn Khaljī, and the earnestness with which the Sultān carried it into practice.

Muhammad bin Tughluq is generally, and perhaps rightly, regarded as a man of liberal views. The Chinese Emperor asked for his permission to build a temple at Samhal, a place of pilgrimage in the Himālayan hills frequented by the Chinese, which the Muslim army "had seized, destroyed and sacked". But the Sultān, who accepted the rich presents sent by the Chinese Emperor, wrote to him a reply to this effect: "Islām does not allow the furthering of such an aim and the permission to build a temple in a Muslim country can be accorded only to those who pay the *jizya*.[8]

It has been already stated above, that Fīrūz Tughluq. who also looked upon India as a Muslim country, held more bigoted views, for he would not permit the erection of new temples even by those who paid the *jizya*. He, however, realized this tax with utmost rigour even from the Brāhmanas who were up to that time exempted from it.[9]

The true nature of the *jizya* is further revealed by the opposition of the orthodox Muslims to the idea that the Hindus should be allowed to perform their religious ceremonies simply by the payment of the *jizya*. The historian Ziyā-ud-dīn Baranī, a contemporary of the two Tughluq emperors, mentioned above, wrote in righteous indignation:

"........... Should the kings consider the payment of a few tankas by way of *jizya* as sufficient justification for their allowing all possible freedom to the *infidels* to observe and demonstrate all orders and details of infidelity, to read the misleading literature of their faith and to propagate their teachings, how could the true religion get the upper hand over other religions and how could the emblems of Islām be held high..."[10]

It would thus appear that an orthodox section of the Muslims chafed at the Hanafite doctrine which was officially accepted by the Muslim rulers in India. As Qāzī Mughīs-us-dīn pointed out to 'Alā-ud-dīn Khaljī, 'it was Hanifa alone who assented to the imposition of the *jizya* on the Hindus. Doctors of other schools allow no other alternative but 'Death or Islām'. As has been stated above,[11] Sultān Mahmūd followed this policy, and evidently Baranī and men of his ilk yearned for its restoration in the fourteenth century. Baranī gave vent to this feeling in the following passage in his *Fatāwā-ī-Jahāndārī*.: "If Mahmūd .... had gone to India once more, he would have brought under his sword all the Brāhmaṇs of Hind who, in that vast land, are the cause of the continuance of the laws of infidelity and of the strength of idolators, he would have cut off the heads of two hundred or three hundred thousand Hindu chiefs. He would not have returned his "Hindu-slaughtering" sword to its scabbard until the whole of Hind had accepted Islam. For Mahmūd was a Shāfi'ite, and according to Imām Shāfi'i the decree for Hindus is "either death or Islam"—that is to say, they should either be put to death or embrace Islam. It is not lawful to accept *jizya* from Hindus as they have neither a prophet nor a revealed book." The same book shows how Baranī chafed at the idea that the "desire for the overthrow of infidels and the abasing of idolators and polytheists does not fill the hearts of the

Muslim kings", who "permit the banners of infidelity to be openly displayed in their capital and in the cities of Muslims, idols to be openly worshipped ...." "How", asks the indignant historian, "will the true faith prevail if rulers allow the infidels to keep their temples, adorn their idols, and to make merry during their festivals with beating of drums and *dhols*, singing and dancing?"[11a]

If a learned historian and a distinguished Muslim felt no scruple in openly expressing such views in writing, in the fourteenth century A.D., i.e. six hundred years after the Muslims first settled in India, one can well understand why the gulf between the Hindus and the Muslims could never be bridged.

A perusal of the history of 'Afif, another great historian of the period, conveys the same lesson. He puts in the mouth of the *wazīr* of Firūz Tughluq a long speech in which he frankly says that a State should have only two ends in view, namely (1) prosperity of the kingdom and protection of the people, etc.; and (2) destruction of the infidels and expansion of the kingdom. Then he adds with equal candour: "..... through God's grace the destruction of the infidels has achieved remarkable success."[12]

Yahyā, the historians of the fifteenth century, mentions a minor incident of etiquette which perhaps even more strikingly illustrates the fundamental difference between a Muslim and a Hindu ruler. When Ghiyās-ud-dīn Balban proceeded to Bengal to chastise the rebellious Tughril, he sought to enter into an alliance with the Hindu king of Eastern Bengal, Rāi Danuj. An interview between the two was arranged. It was customary for a king to stand up to receive a royal guest. But, Yahyā comments, "the fact that a Muslim king ought not to show proper respect to an infidel made the Sultān pensive". A wily minister suggested a way out of the difficulty. The Sultān sat on the throne with a falcon on his hand, and on the approach of Rāi Danuj stood up and let the falcon go, so that the people would surmise that he left the throne only to set the bird in motion. The Muslim honour was saved by playing a trick upon the unsuspecting Hindu king.[13]

The fact that such an incident was remembered and recorded, nearly two hundred years later, by an eminent Muslim historian, speaks volumes about the way in which a Muslim Sultān was apt to regard even an independent Hindu king, not to speak of lesser potentates or individuals.

It would be tedious to multiply instances of this kind, many of which will be found in the famous historical chronicle of Firishta, while dealing with the history of the period under review.

It is little wonder then that, as the history of the Muslim States in Medieval India clearly shows, the Hindus had hardly any place in the highest branches of administration or in the formulation of its policy. With a few exceptions,[14] here and there, almost all the high offices were bestowed upon the Muslims, whether Indian or foreign. It is interesting to note that many Muslim noblemen or adventurers, coming from Irān or Turān, were immediately appointed to posts of honour, dignity and importance in a Muslim court, which were practically barred to the Hindus. The Bahmanī court was, for long, the scene of rivalry between the foreign and the indigenous Muslim,[14a] but the Hindus had no place there. The Muslim politicians and writers of the period took for granted that the natural distinction was between Muslims and Hindus, and not between Indians and foreigners. The State and society were divided horizontally and not vertically.

As may be easily imagined, the Hindu attitude towards the Muslims was one of sullen bitterness. The Hindus resented the Muslim conquest of India and wistfully looked for the day when the name Āryāvarta, the land of the Āryas, as appellation of their country, would once more be justified by the extermination of the *mlechchhas* (Muslims). The Hindus also looked upon their fellow-religionists in other parts of India as dearer and nearer to them than their Muslim neighbours. The Hindu rulers were also chary in appointing Muslims to high offices or admitting them in their counsels. There were, no doubt, exceptions, which prove the rule, and so far as recorded evidence goes, the Hindus were perhaps a little more liberal in this respect. But, in general, the *kāfirs* and the *mlechchhas* stood as far apart in politics as the poles, as there could not possibly have been any common ground between the two in respect of political feelings and sentiments or historical traditions and ideals. Muhammad Tughluq and Firūz Tughluq spoke the bare truth when they publicly declared that the Sultanate of Delhi was a Muslim State. and all the Muslim rulers of the period under review consciously or unconsciously followed this principle in formulating their policy and principles of administration. This alone can satisfactorily explain why even Muslim rulers, otherwise liberal and fair-minded, did not scruple to follow an extremely bigoted religious policy, even though it wounded the most cherished and sacred sentiments of their Hindu subjects. It is true that the Hindus occupied a large number of junior posts and, towards the close of the period, occasionally a few high offices, in civil administration, and more rarely, in the army. But they had no political status and lived on suffereance in the land of their birth, which was regarded as, and publicly declared to be, a Muslim State and country. The Hindus could, therefore, be hardly expected to be even as much satisfied with their political condition as the Hindus and Muslims at the beginning of the twentieth century when they held the offices even of governors and members of Viceroy's council under the British rule. Whether we look at the intrinsic importance of the posts, or the number of them filled up by the subject people, the Hindus were in much worse condition after three hundred years of Muslim rule than the Indians after one hundred and fifty years of British supremacy. Judged by a similar standard, the patronage and cultivation of Hindu learning by the Muslims, or their contribution to the development of Hindu culture during their rule of three hundred years, pale into insignificance when compared with the achievements of the British rule during half that period in the same direction. If is only by instituting such comparison that we can make an objective study of the condition of the Hindus under Muslim rule, and view it is its true perspective.

Social and Religious Differences

While the political status of the Hindus was not such as to inspire their love or goodwill towards the Muslims, the social and religious differences were so acute and fundamental that they raised a Chinese wall between the two communities; even seven hundred years of close residence (including two of common servitude) have failed to make the least crack in that solid and massive structure, far less demolish it.

In different stages in the history of a people's evolution, they lay special emphasis on certain aspects of life which they hold more dear and sacred than anything else, and on which they place the greatest value. In the age of which we are speaking, religious and social institutions were the most cherished objects of life, of both Muslims and Hindus, and they attached even much more value to them than their descendants put upon political status and economic welfare in the nineteenth and twentieth centuries. And it is precisely in those two highly prized aspects of life that they differed fundamentally from each other.

Religion, which formed the very basis of culture and the keynote of life, both among the Muslims and the Hindus, kept them apart like the two poles. They differed fundamentally in their theological conception, method of worship, and everything connected with daily devotion to God. To the Hindus, images and temples were the most sacred objects, but both of these were anathema to the Muslims. Their philosophical notions and sacred literature, their conception of heaven and hell, of this life and the next, in short the whole outlook on men and things lacked a common basis.

There was a similar contrast between their social rules and regualtions which were indissolubly connected with religion. The democratic ideas of the Muslims, leading to a wonderful equality among the brothers-in-faith, offered a strange contrast to the caste-system and untouchability of the Hindus. The Hindu ideas of physical purity differed from those of the Muslims. In social life there was absolute prohibition of intercoruse by means of inter-marriage or interdining, and their practices and rituals had little in common. Coming down to concrete details we find that these two lived almost in two different worlds. The Muslims relished beef which was extremely abhorrent to the Hindus. The absence of marriage restriction within certain degrees of consanguinity and of rigid widowood, as well as easy methods of divorce and remarriage of females among the Muslims, were repugnant to the Hindus. The laws of succession, disposal of the dead, and modes of eating and greeting were different. The Muslims assumed Arabic names, used Arabic calendar of lunar months, and adopted distinctive dresses. Their congregational prayers were radically different from Hindu mode of worship, and music, which was an essential part of Hindu religious ceremonials, was usually forbidden within the precincts, or even in the neighbourhood, of mosques. The intellectual inspiration of the one was supplied by Arabic and Persian, and of the other by Sanskrit literature. The fact that the Muslims turned towards the west and the Hindus towards the east, while offering prayers or worship to God, though by itself of no great significance, very correctly symbolized the orientation of the two cultures.

Historical Traditions

In addition to social and religious differences, the historical traditions of the preceding centuries drove a wedge between the two communities and kept them apart. The Muslims naturally looked with pride and glory upon their successive military triumphs which laid the Hindus low and made them masters of the country. But no Hindu could possibly recollect them without a sense of shame and humiliation. The wilful destruction of images and temples which the Muslims, perhaps naturally and justly, looked upon as a glory of Islām, outraged the most cherished and deep-rooted sentiments of the Hindus. The massacre and enslavement of the Hindus on a massive scale, generally following upon the victorious campaigns of the Muslims, to which Muslim chroniclers refer with glee, wounded the noblest and most tender feelings and left a lasting scar upon the memory of generations of Hindus.

It would be idle to deny the fact that the spirit with which the military campaigns were undertaken was often as much political as religious, i.e. anti-Hindu. The following extract from the *Tārīkh-ī-Wassāf*, written at the beginning of the period under review, is a good illustration of this view. Referring to 'Alā-ud-dīn Khaljī's camaign in Gujarāt, the author writes:

"The vein of the zeal of religion beat high for the subjection of infidelity and destruction of idols.....With a view to holy war, and not for the lust of conquest, he enlisted .... about 14,000 cavalry and 20,000 infantry ... The Muhammadan forces began to kill and slaughter, on the right and on the left unmercifully, throughout the impure land, for the sake of Islām, and blood flowed in torrents.

"They took captive a great number of handsome and elegant maidens, amounting to 20,000, and children of both sexes, more than per can enumerate........ In short, the Muhammadan army brought the country to utter ruin, and destroyed the lives of the inhabitants, and plundered the cities, and captured their offsprings, so that many temples were deserted and the idols were broken and trodden under foot, the largest of which was one called Somnāt........ The fragments were conveyed to Delhi, and the entrnace of the Jāmi' Masjid was paved with them, that people might remember and talk of this brilliant victory .... 'Praise to be God, the Lord of the Worlds[15]".

It is not strictly relevant to our present purpose to discuss how far the details of the campaign and the motive behind it have been correctly described by Wassāf. If a Muslim writer or chronicler could take this view of things in a serious historical narrative, it is beyond question that the Hindus would exaggerate, and paint in a still darker colour, both the inhuman cruelties and the bigoted religious zeal which prompted them. The effect of such an exulting description, by a member of the community which inflicted the injury, upon those that suffered it, can easily be imagined.

The picture drawn by Wassāf belongs to the very beginning of the period under review. To the end of it reigned Sikandar Lodi, of whom another Muslim writer says:

"He was so zealous a Muslmān that he utterly destroyed diverse places of worship of the infidels, and left not a vestige remaining of them. He entirely ruined the shrines of Mathurā, the mine of heathenism, an turned their principal Hindu places of worship into caravanserais and colleges. Their stone images were given to the butchers to serve them as meat-weights, and all the Hindus in Mathurā were strictly prohibited from shaving their heads and beards, and performing their ablutions. He thus put an end to all the idolatrous rites of the infidels there; and no Hindu, if he wished to have his head or beard shaved, could get a barber to do it. Every city thus conformed as he desired to the customs of Islam."[16]

Such instances can be easily multiplied. Indeed a perusal of the Muslim chronicles leaves no doubt that not only scences like this were witnessed during the period, but were regarded as just and natural by the Muslim divines and learned men of the age. The blood-curdling tales of wholesale rapine and massacre of the Hindus by Muslims, narrated in a single chronicle like that of Firishta, would make one's flesh creep. The Hindus, who must have looked upon such misdeeds as the most heinous crime and the greatest outrage on their religion and society. could hardly be expected to forget or forgive the sacrileges perpetrated in the name of Islām. They would be either more or less than human beings if they could do so. They paid the Muslims back in their own coins, but their opportunities were naturally few and far between.[17] In any case, such recorded historical incidents are few, and contrary instances of religious toleration are by no means rare. The ferocity of Muslim bigotry, renewed at intervals and therefore always of recent memory, fed the ulcer that was eating into vitals of communal amity. No wonder, it created a river of blood between the two communities which centuries of residence together could not bridge.

Facts of History

All these are by no means imaginary pictures or mere theoretical deductions. They are fully supported by such positive evidence as we possess regarding the relation between the Hindus and the Muslims during the period under review.

(a) Ibn Batūtah

We may begin with the picture drawn by Ibn Batūtah, a learned Muslim of Africa, who travelled widely throughout India about the middle of the fourteenth century A.D. during the reign of Muhammad bin Tughluq, one of the most enlightened and liberal-minded Sultāns in India.

Ibn Batūtah confirms the general statement, made above, particularly about forcible conversion, mass-enslavement, and the inferior status of the Hindus as *zimmīs*.[18] Thus he remarks that "other nations embraced Islām only when the Arab used their swords against them".[19] There are several references to Hindu female captives of the highest rank being accorded the most humiliating treatment. Referring to the 'Id ceremony at Delhi in the Sultān's palace he says: "Then enter the musicians, the first batch being the daughters of the infidel rajas—Hindus—captured in war that year. They sing and dance, and the Sultān gives them away to the amirs and *a'izza*. Then come the other daughters of the infidels who sing and dance; and the Sultān gives them away to his brothers, his relations, his brothers-in-law and the maliks' sons" (p. 63). Again, Ibn Batūtah casually observes: "At that time there arrived in Delhi some female infidel captives, ten of whom the vezir sent to me. I gave one of these to the man who brought them to me, but he was not satisfied. My companions took three young girls, and I do not know what happened to the rest" (p. 123). The presents sent by Muhammad bin Tughluq to the Emperor of China included "one hundred male slaves and one hundred slave song-stresses and dancers from among the Indian infidels" (p. 151).

The position of the Hindus as *zimmīs* is occasionally referred to by Ibn Batūtah. "The inhabitants of Habanq", says he, "are infidels under protection (*zimma*) from whom half of the crops which they produce is taken; besides they have to perform certain duties" (p. 241). He refers more than once to actual flights between infidel Hindus and their Muslim neighbours. Most interesting and instructive are the details connected with Alāpur, a small city, most of whose inhabitants were infidels under protection (*zimmī*). The commandant of this place "was one of those heroes, whose bravery was proverbial. Ceaselessly and quite alone he would fall upon the infldels and would kill them or take them prisoner, so much so that his reputation spread widely and he made a name for himself and the infidels feared him". One day he fell upon a Hindu village and was killed in course of the fray. But his slaves seized the village. "They put its male population to the sword and made the womenfolk prisoner and seized everything in it". Later, the Hindus avenged the insult by killing his son (p. 162-63). Immediately after narrating this, Ibn Batūtah mentions an incident which shows the precarious tenure of a Hindu life. When he visited Gwalior he went to see the commandant who "was going to cut an infidel into two halves". At Ibn Batūtah's request the life of the infidel was saved (p. 163).

Ibn Batūtah's graphic account of the barbarous, almost incredible, cruelties perpetrated on the Hindus by the Sultān of Ma'bar has been quoted above.[20] Ibn Batūtah was a near relative of the Sultān and lived in his court. There is, therefore, no reason to discredit the story, incredibly horrible though it might appear to us as it did to Ibn Batūtah. He has also cited other instances of cruelty inflicted upon the Hindus by the same Sultān in the most callous manner. One day while Ibn Batūtah was taking his meals with the Sultān a Hindu (infidel) "was brought in along with his wife and their son who was seven years of age. The Sultān beckoned the executioners ordering them to cut off the Hindu's (infidel's) head"[20a] and then uttered some words meaning "and his wife and son". Ibn Batūtah turned away his eyes while this was being done. Another day the Sultān ordered the hands and feet of a Hindu to be cut off. Ibn Batūtah left the place on pretence of saying prayers, and when he returned he found the unfortuante Hindu weltering in blood (p. 228). Ibn Batūtah's attitude on both the occasions does credit to him and definitely goes against those who excuse the conduct of the Muslim Sultāns on the ground that such cruelties were common in those days.

Ibn Batūtah bears witness to the deliberate and perpetual outrage on Hindu religious sentiments, perpetrated by Muslim rulers and people. In the capital city of Delhi itself, he found near the eastern gateway of the famous Quwwat-ul-Islām mosque "two very big idols of copper connected together by stones. Every one who comes in and goes out of the mosque treads over them" (p. 27).

Some random observations of Ibn Batūtah seem to indicate that the Hindu and Muslims lived as entirely separate communities. Thus he remarks: "In India the infidels occupy one continuous piece of land and inhabit regions which are adjacent to those of the Muslims. The Muslims dominate the infidels" (p. 124). Reference is made to Parwan as "a small city of Musalmans lying in the midst of the territories of the infidels" (p. 163). In the capital city of a Hindu State in Malabar coast, "there are about four thousand Muslims, who inhabit a suburb of their own inside the jurisdiction of the city. There is fighting between them and the inhabitants of the city often" (p. 185). Ibn Batūtah's narrative shows that such communal fights were by no means rare. In another city of the Malabar coast "there were three Muslim quarters" (p. 188). When the Muslim Sultān of Hinawar conquered the Hindu city of Goa, he occupied the Hindu palace and gave the adjacent quarters to his followers, while ten thousand Hindu prisoners were removed to a suburb (p. 196).

The segregation of the Muslim community was rendered necessary, at least to a large extent, by the social rules and habits of the Hindus who regarded the Muslims as unclean and impure (*mlechchhas*). The Hindus maintained no social intercourse with the other community by way of interdining and intermarriage. They were uncompromising in this respect, and regarded the touch of Muslims, or even a scent of their food, as pollution. Ibn Batūtah keenly felt all this when he passed through the Hindu States of Malabar, where Muslims were few and far between. He justly complains that no Hindu would give a vessel to a Muslim for drinking water of a well as he would do to another Hindu. "If one happens to be a Muslim he (Hindu) pours water into his (Muslim's) hands and leaves off when the latter makes him a sign or withdraws. It is the custom among the heathens in the Malabar country that no Muslim should enter their houses or use their vessels for eating purposes. If a Muslim is fed out of their vessels, they either break the vessels, or give them away to the Musalmans" (p. 182). These Hindu ideas of untouchability concerning the Muslims were not confined to Malabar, but extended all over India, and Ibn Batūtah draws a refreshing contrast in this respect between the infidels of Ceylon and those of India. The infidels of Ceylon, we are told, were unlike the infidels of India who would neither admit even Muslim fakirs in their houses nor give them food and water in their own utensils (p. xxxiv). Then he observes in a reminiscent mood: "Occasionally we were compelled to ask some of the infidels of India to cook meat for us. They used to bring it in their own cooking pots and to sit at a little distance from us; they used to bring also leaves of banana tree upon which they placed rice—their principal food—pouring over the rice broth called *koshān* and subsequently they withdrew. Then we used to eat it, and whatever remained would be eaten by the dogs and birds. If any innocent child happened to take anything from that remnant they would beat him and compel him to eat cow's dung which according to their belief purifies" (p. xxxiv).

Reference may be made in this connection to a story, narrated in detail by Ibn Batūtah himself, which throws a lurid light on the relation between the Hindus and Muslims in the very heart of the Muslim empire in North India.

Ibn Batūtah was appointed ambassador to China and proceeded from Delhi in July, 1342, with rich presents, and a guard of thousand horsemen. When they were in the neighbourhood of Aligarh they heard that the city of Jalālī, about eleven miles to the south-east, was besieged by the Hindus, numbering about a thousand horsemen and three thousand infantry. By a surprise attack the Sultān's cavalry guard "killed them (the infidel Hindus) to the last man and seized their horses and arms." The 'infidels', however, continued to raid the suburbs of Jalālī from their base on an inaccessible mountain. In course of one of these, Ibn Batūtah and a few friends were surprised by the raiders and had to flee for their lives. Being hotly pursued, Ibn Batūtah was captured and going to be killed, when one of the captors took pity on him and helped him to escape. After hiding himself in hills, forests, and fields, he came to a road. "But since that road was leading into a village of infidels", Ibn Batūtah took to a different road and hid himself. After seven days, famished by hunger and thirst, he reached "a thickly populated village of infidels". "I begged of them something to eat, but they refused to give anything'. One of them lifted an unsheathed sword to kill him, but let him off after taking his shirt. On the eighth day he chanced to come across a Muslim who took him to a Muslim ruler of a Hindu village (pp. 151-7).

After all this we need hardly feel surprised at the attitude of the Muslims towards the Hindus. The Brāhmans, says Ibn Batūtah, "are revered by the infidels and inspire hatred in the Muslims". (p. 188). The dislike was mutual. "We used to meet infidels on this road at night; but as soon as they saw us they got out of the way until we had passed" (p. 183).

Any one who reads Ibn Batūtah's account would be reminded of what Al-Bīrūnī said regarding the attitude of the Hindus towards the Muslims, and vice versa.[20b] Evidently things had not improved much even after the lapse of three hundred years.

(b) Indian Literature

Unfortunately we possess no chronicle of the period written by a Hindu save and except the second *Rājataraṅgiṇī* of Jonarāja. The terrible tales of persecution of the Hindus by Sultān Sikandar of Kāshmir, as recorded by him, have been narrated above.[20c] But isolated references to the persecution of the Hindus by the Muslims are not altogether wanting. The Muslim sway over South India beyond the Krishnā was of short duration, and confined to Madurā, but the cry of anguish from this region in the far south has been preserved in a local chronicle of Madurā. The misery caused by the Muslims in this sacred city is also narrated in detail by Gaṅgādevī, the consort of prince Kampana of Vijayanagara. A few extracts are quoted below:

"The temples in the land have fallen into neglect, as worship in them has been stopped. Within their walls the frightful howls of the jackals have taken the place of the sweet reverberations of *mṛidaṅga* .... The sweet odour of the sacrificial smoke and the chant of the Vedas have deserted the villages which are now filled with the foul smell of roasted flesh and the fierce noise of the ruffianly Turushkas. The suburban gardens of Madurā present a most painful sight; many of their beautiful coconut palms have been cut down and on every side are seen rows of stakes from which swing strings of human skulls strung together. The Tāmraparṇī is flowing red with the blood of the slaughtered cows. The Veda is forgotten, and justice has gone into hiding; there is not left any trace of virtue or nobility in the land and despair is writ large on the faces of the unfortuante Drāviḍas".[21] In spite of possible exaggeration, the general truth underlying this doleful and dismal picture is borne out by Ibn Batūtah's description of the monstrous cruelty perpetrated by the Muslim Sultān of Ma'bar or Madurā.[21a.]

Vidyāpati, the famous poet of Mithilā in the 15th century A.D. has given a gruesome account of the oppressions of the Hindus by the Turks.[21b] After describing the vital differences between the two in social and religious customs he mentions how the Turks force the Hindus to work without pay, place the leg of the dead cow on the heads of Brāhmaṇas, lick the sandalwood mark on their foreheads, tear off their sacred thread, break temples and build mosques in their place, abuse the Hindus and assault them.

The medieval religious writers of Bengal, particualrly the Vaishnavas, have left a vast literature which contains casual references to the miserable plight of the Hindus in Bengal. These Vaishṇavas were the most inoffensive and peaceful members of the Hindu community and their views cannot be regarded, by any stretch of imagination, to be tinged by political or racial bias of any kind. This literature reflects the state of things prevailing in Bengal three hundred years after the Muslims had conquered it. It is important to bear this in mind, for it had been held by some that "after the first shock of conquest was over, the Hindus and Muslims prepared to find a *via media* whereby to live as neighbours".[22] A positive and definite ideas of the neighbourly relation between the two during the fifteenth and sixteenth centuries A.D. may be formed from the contemporary Bengali literature.

The *Chaitanya-maṅgala* of Jayānanda describes as follows the plight of the Brāhmaṇas of Navadvīpa, the birth-place of Chaitanya, shortly before his birth (A.D. 1485); "The king seizes the Brāhmaṇas, pollute their caste, and even take their lives. If a conchshell is heard to blow in any house, its owner is made to forfeit his wealth, caste and even life. The king plunders the houses of those who wear sacred threads on the shoulder and put sacred marks on the forehead, and then bind them. He breaks the temples and uproots *Tulasī* plants, and the residents of Navadvipa are in perpetual fear of their lives. The bathing in the Gaṇgā is prohibited and hundreds of sacred *Aśvattha* and jack trees have been cut down. The numerous Yavanas (Muslims) who reside in the Piralyā village ruined the Brāhmaṇas. The feud between the Yavanas and the Brāhmaṇas is everlasting, and the terrible village of Piralyā is close to Navadvīpa. Misled by the false report of (the people of) Piralyā that a Brāhmaṇa was destined to be the king of Navadvīpa...the king (of Gauḍa) ordered the destruction of Nadiyā (Navadvīpa). Sārvabhauma Bhattāchārya left Gauḍa with his family and kinsmen and fled to Orissa where he was honoured by its ruler Pratāparudra." Some time later, the king of Gauḍa changed his attitude and had the broken houses and temples repaired, but the Brāhmaṇas whose caste was polluted remained for ever outside the fold of Hinduism."[22]

Such pogroms of Hindus were not accidental or merely passing episodes. As Jayānanda so tersely puts it, the feud between the Yavanas and the Brāhmaṇas was everlasting. So we find that, far from improving, the communal relation became even worse during the benign rule of 'Alā-ud-dīn Husain Shāh (A.D. 1493-1519) who is generally regarded as the most liberal-minded Muslim ruler of Bengal.

Vijaya Gupta, one of the eulogists of Hussain Shāh, gives a gruesome detailed description of the outrage on Hindus by the Muslim *qāzis,* Hasan and Husain. These two made a pastime of baiting the Hindus in all possible ways. Anyone found with the sacred *Tulazi* leaf on his head (an obligtory Vaishṇava custom) was taken to the *qāzī* with hands and feet bound, and heavy blows were administered to him. The *piyādā* (peon) tore away the sacred thread from a Brāhmaṇa and spat saliva in his mouth. On one occasion a Muslim *mullā* happened to pass by a hut in a wood where some shephered boys were worshipping the goddess *Manasā* with the symbol of sacred earthen pots to the acompaniment of music. In righteous indignation the *mullā* made an attempt to break the pots, but was severely trounced. The *mullā* brought it to the notice of the two *qāzī* brothers who exclaimed: "What! the scoundrel (*harāmzādah*) Hindus make so bold as to perform Hindu rituals in my village! The culprit boys should be seized and made outcaste by being forced to eat Muslim bread." So the two brothers gathered a large number of armed Muslims and proceeded towards the shephered's hut. The mother of the *qāzīs*, a Hindu girl forcibly married by the former *qāzī*, vainly tried to dissuade her sons;

they demolished the shephered's hut, broke the sacred pots into pieces, and threw away the offerings to the goddess. The affrighted shephered boys had concealed themselves in the wood, but some of them were hunted out and seized.[23]

Iśāna Nāgara, another contemporary writer, descriebs the condition of the Hindus under Husain Shāh as follows:

"The wicked *mlechchhas* pollute the religion of the Hindus every day. They break the images of the gods into pieces and throw away the articles of worship. They throw into fire *Śrīmad-Bhāgavat* and other holy scriptures, forcibly take away the conch-shell and bell of the Brāhmaṇas (two necessary articles of worship), and lick the sandal paints on their bodies. They urinate like dogs on the sacred *Tulasi* plant, and deliberately pass faeces in the Hindu temples. They throw water from their mouths on the Hindus engaged in worship, and harass the Hindu saints as if they were so many lunatics let large."[24]

The two great biographies of the great Vaishṇava saint Chaitanya, namely, the *Chaitanya-charitāmṛita* and the *Chaitanya-bhāgavata,* contain many stories of the religious bigotry of the Muslims and the consequent persecution of the Hindus. Both the books refer to a famous episode in the life of Lord Chaitanya. He had introduced the system of public worship in the form of *kīrtan* (a sort of congregational song loudly sung together by a large number of men in public streets to the accompaniment of special musical instruments). This enraged the Muslim *qāzī*, and one day when Chaitanya's devotees were singing the name of God in the streets of Nadīyā (Navadvīpa in Bengal), he came out, struck blows upon everybody on whom he could lay hands, broke the musical instruments, and threatened with dire punishment all the Hindus who would dare join a *kīrtan* party in this way in his city at Nadīyā. To prevent the recurrence of public *kīrtan,* the *qāzī* patrolled the streets of Nadīyā with a party. The people of Nadīyā got afraid, but Chaitanya decided to defy the *qāzī's* orders, and brought out a large *kīrtan* party which was joined by thousands. The *qāzī* was at first wild with anger and held out the threat that he would destroy the caste of all the Hindus of Nadīyā; but terror seized him when his eyes fell upon the vast concourse of people in a menancing attitude. He fled, and his house was wrecked by the angry crowd. The *Chaitanya-bhāgavata* does not describe the sequel. But the other work,

Chaitanya-charītāmṛita, describes how Chaitanya sent for the *qāzī* who was now in a more chastened mood, and the two had a cordial talk.[25]

As is usual with religious books, the author of the *Chaitanya-charitāmṛita* attributes the change in the *qāzī's* attitude to a miralce. A more rational explanation of the *qāzī's* forbearance is probably to be found in the attitude of the Sultān. Shortly after the above incident, the author describes the visit of Chaitanya to Rāmakeli, a village near the capital city of Gauḍa. When Sultān Husain Shāh heared of the great ovation paid to the saint by millions of people along the whole route, he was surprised, and observed that one whom such a vast crowd follows without any expectation of material benefit must be a saint. He ordered the Muslim *qāzīs* not to injure him in any way and allow him to go wherever he liked.[26]

It would be wrong to infer from this, that Sultān Husain Shāh had a tender heart for the Hindus. At least the contemporary Hindus thought otherwise. Even after Husain Shāh issued the above order, the intimate followers of Chaitanya argued: "This Husain Shāh had destroyed numerous temples in Orissa; the liberal views he expressed were but a passing phase, and might be changed at any moment by evil counsels of Muslim officials".[26a] So they sent an urgent message to Chaitanya to leave the vicinity of the capital. One of the Hindu courtiers of the Sultān, when asked about Chaitanya, deliberately misrepresented him as an ordinary *sannyāsī,* in order to avert the Sultān's wrath against a great Hindu saint.[2]

Sanātana, a trusted Hindu official of the Sultān, became an ardent devotee of Chaitanya. So he (Sanātana) spent his time in religious exercises in his house, and ceased to attend the court on plea of illness. One day the Sultān paid a surprise visit and found Sanātana hale and hearty, engaged in religious discourse with twenty or thirty Vaishṇavas. The Sultān got very angry and kept Sanātana in confinement. Sultān Husain Shāh was then making preparations for a military expedition against Orissa, and asked Sanātana to accompany him. But the latter refused, saying: "You are going to torment our gods (i.e. destroy the images and temples); I cannot go with you."[28] This firm reply to the iconoclastic Sultān offers a striking contrast to the fulsome eulogies paid to him by some contemporary Bengali poets. One of them, Vijaya Gupta, mentioned above, describes Husain Shāh as an ideal king whose subjects enjoy all the blessings of life, and compares him to the epic hero Arjuna. Another goes even further and describes the Muslim Sultān, notorious for breaking Hindu temples, as the incarnation of Kṛishṇa in the Kali Age. All these merely indicate the degree of abject surrender and the depth of moral degradation of the Hindus of Bengal caused by three hundred years of political servitude and religious oppression.[28a] Evidently a new spirit was infused into them by Chaitanya, at least for the time being.

Throughout the *Chaitanya-bhāgavata* there are casual references to Hindus being constantly oppressed by the fear that the public performance of *kīrtan,* and even singing religious songs loudly in one's own house, would provoke the Sultān and bring untold miseries upon the people of Nadīyā. A section of them was therefore angry with the Vaishṇavas, and once a rumour was spread that the Sultān had sent two boats full of soldiers to Nadīyā to arrest those who sang *kīrtan.* Many people expressed their amzement that Chaitanya and his followers were engaged in loudly singing *kīrtan* at Rāmakeli near the capital city, Gauḍa, without any fear of the terrible Muslim king living so near.[29] These incidental references constitute more valuable data than even the full-fledged stories of the sacrilegious conduct of the *qāzis* for making a proper estimate of the wretched condition of the Hindus. They had to live in perpetual dread of the religious bigotry and intolerance of the Muslims during the rule of even the most enlightened Muslim Sultān of Bengal. No wonder that many Hindus embraced Islam to get rid of this ignominious fate. Duarte Barbosa who visited India during the reign of Husain Shāh observes with reference to Bengal: "The Heathens of these parts daily become Moors to gain the favour of their rulers".[30]

But the Vaishṇava literature also shows the brighter side of the relation between the Hindus and Muslims. When the *qāzī* of Nadīyā met Chaitanya after the tumultuous riot mentioned above, he reminded the latter that his (Chaitanya's) maternal grandfather was his (*qāzī's*) uncle according to the customary usage of the village, and therefore Chaitanya was his nephew. It is thus apparent that although there was no interdining and intermarriage between the Hindus and the Muslims, some sort of cordial neighbourly relation was fostered between the two communities living together in the same village or city. This is quite natural. But the pity of it is, that even such neighbourly feelings could neither mellow the bigoted fury of the Muslims against Hindu religion, as is proved by the conduct of the *qāzī* himself; nor relax in any way the social bigotry of the Hindus which got the better not only of humanitarian feelings, but also of their age-long virtues of respect for guest and mercy towards helpless seekers of shelter, as examplified by the refusal of food and water to a hungry and thirsty foreigner, Ibn Batūtah. Incidental references have been made in the above stories to the forcible marriage of a Hindu girl by a Muslim, and dubious methods adopted to make the Hindus lose their caste. Other corroborative concrete instances of these are met within contemporary literature. These were also so many sore points with the Hindus which widened the breach between the two communities.

Three different lines of evidence—Muslim chronicles, the acount of Ibn Batūtah, and contemporary Indian literature—all agree in testifying to the fact that the basic and fundamental differences between the two communities continued, as before, during the period under review. No doubt, mutual understanding was developed and there was a greater amount of cordiality in the normal social relation between the two. Each was influenced by the other, in varying degrees, not only in different spheres of life, but also in ideas, beliefs, and even superstitutions. But all these merely affected the external and superficial in man and society, and left untouched the core of the heart and the mind. It was only necessary to scratch the skin to bring out the Hindu and the Muslim in every Indian, indivdually or collectively.

—*M.W. Merza*

References

A Hindu Society

1. On Chaitanya's attitude towards caste, vide S.K. De, *Early History of the Vaishnava Faith and Movement in Bengal,* pp. 80-81n. On caste in Sikhism down to the time of Guru Govind Singh, vide Teja Singh and Ganda Singh, *A History of the Sikhs,* Vol. I, pp. 66-67.
2. The above dates, which are approximate, are taken from P.V. Kane, *History of Dharmaśāstra,* Vol. IV, pp. ix-xi.
3. For references to these views, vide Kane, *op. cit.* Vol. II, Part I, p. 56.
4. For references; vide Saletore, *Social and Political Life in the Vijayanagara Empire,* Vol. II, pp. 33 ff. 122 ff. Mahalingam. *Administration and Social Life under Vijayanagara,* pp. 143-44, 240 ff., 245 ff.

5. References in Mahalingam, op. cit. 137 ff.

5a. *IBH*, 63, 151. *TA* III. 597. The Editor is responsible for this para.

5b. *Vivādaratnākara*, 139 ff.; *Parāśara-Mādhava*, II, 238 ff.; *Vyavahāravivekoddyota*, 214 ff.; *Vyavahārasāra*, 152 ff.; *Vivādachandra*, 46 ff.; *Vivādachintāmaṇī*, 63 ff; *Vyavahārakāṇḍa*, 291 ff.

6. *E.C.* VIII, p. 40 (gift of female slaves mentioned in incsription of 1382), *Annual Report of Epigraphy*, 1905, p. 46 (reference to bond-servant). For references to slavery in the preceding periods vide the earlier volumes, s. v.

7. For references, vide Saletore, op. cit. Vol. II, p. 166 ff., p. 362; Mahalingam, op. cit., p. 262 ff.

7a. Quoted in the preface to the edition of the *Vyavahārasāra*. See Bibliography.

8. For the history of the controversy about the validity of marriage with the maternal uncle's daughter in the *Smṛitis*, vide Kane, *History of Dharmaśāstra*. Vol. II, Part I, pp. 458 ff.

8a. *Parāśara-Mādhava*, I, 485 ff.; *Madanapārijāta*, 155 ff.; *Gṛihastharātnākārā*, 55 ff.

8b. *Gṛihastharatnākara*, 86.

8c. *Madanapārijāta*, 89.

9. Vide Yule and Cordier, *Cathay and the Way Thither*, Vol. II, p. 139 (Friar Odoric), Yule, Mirabilia (Jordanus), *IBH, 21-22.*

9a. Full reference in *Vivādaratnākara*, 409 ff.; less detailed references in *Madanapārijāta*, 191-192; *Parāśara-Mādhava*, II, 322-23; *Vyavahāravivekoddyota*, 315-17; *Vyavahārasāra*, 203-4; *Vyavahārakāṇḍa*, 342; *Vivādachintāmaṇi*, 189-90.

9b. *Vyavahārasāra*, 249-50.

9c. *Vivādachandra*, 92-93.

9d. *Vivādachintāmani*, 236.

9e. *Vyavahārasāra*, 237.

9f. *Vivādachandra*, 82-83.

9g. *Parāśara-Mādhava*, II. 369; *Vyavahāravivekoddyota*, 376.

9h. *Vivādaratnakara*, 511-15; *Madanapārijāta*, 670; *Vyavahāravivekoddyota*, 377-79; *Vivādachandra*, 81; *Vyavahārakāṇḍa*, 380-1; *Vivādachintāmaṇi*, 218-21.

10. *Vivādaratnākara,* 516-18; *Madanapārijāta.* 665-69; *Vivādachandra,* 382-84; *Vyavahāravivekoddyota,* 380; *Vivādachintāmaṇi,* 221-24; Śūlapāṇi on Yājña-*valkya*, I, 144-45.

10a. *IBH,* p. 171 (diet among the Marāthā people): Saletore, op. cit. Vol. II, p. 305 ff. Mahalingam, op. cit., p. 281 ff. (diet of people in Vijayanagara Empire).

11. For references see Saletore, op. cit., 159 ff., 297 ff., Mahalingam, op. cit. 263 ff., 284 ff.

12. In the above passage the author observes that the Brāhmaṇa though addicted to all sense-enjoyments, is not disqualified because of the efficacy of his Vedic studies and his five daily sacrifices in removing sins, while his earthly divinity is not lost by eating forbidden food and the like because of the similar efficacy of single *mantras.* Quoting in the next place a *prima facie* view which favours membership of a *parishat* for a Śūdra of good character and conduct in preference to a Brāhmaṇa of bad character living in the same village, the author rejects the same on the ground that, as between the claims of birth and character, the superiority of the former is to be considered principally, while the latter is to be considered as far as possible.

13: Vide Yule and Cordier, *Cathay,* Vol. II, p. 145 (Odoric); Yule, Mirabilia (Jordanus), *IBH,* p. 23.

14. Yule and Cordier, *Cathay.* Vol. II, p. 137; Yule, Mirabilia (Jordanus).

Muslim Religion and Society

1. Vol. V, 467 ff.

2. See, for example, how Qutb-ud-din Mubārak Khalji and later on Ghiyās-ud-din Tughlūq fell out with Hazrat Nizām-ud-din Auliyā. The former, indeed, threatened the saint with dire consequences if he failed to present himself at his court on an appointed date, but was himself murdered before that date.

3. Thus we have the months Mirānji, Madār and Khwāja Mu'in-ud-din corresponding to the Arabic months of Rabi'al-Sānī, Jumād-al-Awal and Jumād-al-Sānī, and named after Shaikh 'Abdul Qādir Gilānī of Baghdad, Shāh Madār and Khwāja Mu'īn-ud-dīn of Ajmer respectively.

4. See *Chashma-i-Kauthar* (p. 361 ff.). He was a native of Jaunpur where he was born in A.D. 1443. He gained numerous adherents, particularly in Gujarāt and Hyderābād.

5. See above, p. 146.

6. This title originally indicated a non-Sayyid Arab, a descendant, usually, of one of the first three Caliphs of Islām, but later on became indiscriminately used for any Muslim who was not of Sayyid, Mughul

or Afghān origin. Thus all the new converts to Islām came to be designated as *Shaikhs*.

7. Khusrav mentions the *katāra* in one of his verses. *Sari an du chashm gardam ki chu Hindudān-i-rahzan I Hamarā zletigh-i-abrū bejigar zadeh katāra II.* "May I be a ransom for those two eyes which like the marauding Hindus, with their sword-like eye-brows, strike at even one's liver with a *katāra.*"

8. The Arabs probably had beçome familiar with *tambul* in very early times, but it was unknown in Central Asia. According to al-Mas'udī, it had become popular in al-Hijaz and Yemen in the fourth century (Murūj, II, p. 84).

9. See Khusrav, *Qirān-us-Sa'dain* (Aligarh edn.), pp. 183-185. Ibn Batūtah gives a graphic account of the dishes and dinner etiquettes (IBH, 15, 120, 180).

10. Khusrav says;

    Ay Dihlī o ay butān-i-sādeh I Pag basteh o risha kadj nihādeh II.

    "Oh Dihlī and oh her beardless beauties! Turbans tied (round their heads) and the turban-tails placed awry."

11. Khusrav speaks particularly of two varieties, the Deogiri and the Maradevnagri. See the *Nuh Sipihr*, the *Ashīqa*, etc. Cf. also the-*Khazāin-ul-Futūh*. (Edited by Mirza, p. 22).

11a. Cf. Chapter XIX.

12. The Editor is respopnsible for the preceding three paragraphs, which are based on an article by S.N.H. Rizvi in *Is. C.*, XV, 331.

13. Shaving of the new born child's natal hair, corresponding to the Hindu *chūḍākaraṇa*.

14. The first lesson given to a child, consisting usually of the recitation by the teacher of a Qur'anic verse which the child was asked to repeat.

15. Such as *chauthi, chāla etc.* It may be interesting to note in this connection that the Indian practice of erecting a *mandha* (*maṇap*) for the bride has a curious resemblance to the Arab custom which finds expression in the phrase *banā 'alaiha*" (built or erected a tent over her) in the sense of "married her".

16. *IBH*, 78 ff., 211, 120.

17. See Khusrav: *Nuh Sipihr* (ed. Mirza, pp. 376 ff.) and Ibn Batūtah (Egyptian edn.), Vol. II, p. 38; *IBH, 63*.

18. See p. 23 above.

19. The large number of mosques, inns, tanks and wells built by them bear eloquent testimony to their religious zeal.

20. Called *kohī* and *bahri* by khusrav and others; *Kohī*, because they were procured from the hill districts of Konkan, etc., and *bahrī*, as they were imported from over-sea countries, chiefly Arabia.

21. See Ashraf: Life and Conditions of people of Hindusthan, *JRASBL*, I. pp. 233-237.

22. Cf. Chapter XV, Sections D and E, particularly the three paragraphs marked with asterisk on pp. 538-9, which originally formed part of this section, and were transferred to the section on literature. (Ed.).

Hindu-Muslim-Relations

1. Vol. V. 497-502.

1a. Recently, Kazi Abdul Wadud has challenged the theory, to which 'wide currency was given by the scholarly writings of Risley, Beverly and Hunter,' namely, "that the Musalmans of Bengal sprang from the lower strata of the Hindus of the province, and that the aword of Islam was primarily respónsible for the conversation." He has mostly relied on the arguments advanced by Khundkar Muhammad Fazle Rabbi in his book. The Origin of the *Mussalmans* of the Bengal, among which he cites the following as the "most weighty"; "How to account for the comparative paucity of Mussalmans in Northern India, the seat of Muslim power for centuries, whee the notorious sword of Islam could not have been shy". It is forgotten that this objection may be advanced against any explanation that is offered to acount for the large number of Mussalmans of Bengal, including those of Mr. Rabbi and Kazi Wadud, namely, (1) that a fairly large number of Mussalmans were not indigenous to Bengal, but went there as soldiers, Government officials and traders; (2) Bengal was a stronghold of Pathans. If the first argument had any validity, we would expect more Muslims in Upper India than in Bengal. As to the second, Bihar, and to a certain extent, Orissa, were also strongholds of the Pathans, and yet these two regions contain a much smaller percentage of Mussalmans than Bengal. ("The Mussalmans of Bengal" by Kazi Abdul Wadud in Studies in the Bengal Renaissance, edited by Atulchandra Gupta, pp. 460 ff.).

2. *IBH*, p. xxxiv.

3. *IBH*, 151-2.

4. *Hindusthan Standard*, Puja Issue, 1950.

5. Cf. Vol. III, p. 456, f.n., 1; also Ch. XIV of this volume, p. 450.

5a. *Sources of Indian Tradition* (Columbia University Press, New York, 1958), pp. 489-90.

6. Confirmation and illustration of the adoption of Sir Jadunath's theory into practice meets us at almost every step in the Muslim historical chronicles and the political history of the Sultanate sketched above (cf.

specially, pp. 25, 59, 104 ff., 147, 158). Cf. also the *Fatāwā-i-Jahāndāri* of *Ziyā-ud-din* Barani (IBH, 260 ff.). For the *jizya*, cf. Vol. III, 455-6.

7. P. 25.

8. *IBH,* 150.

9. Above, pp. 104.5.

10. *IBH,* 261.

11. Above, Vol. V, p. 499.

11a. *Sources of Indian Tradition,* p. 489.

12. *TKB,* II. 110.

13. *T.M.,* 40. It is difficult to believe the story, but the fact that a distinguished historican of the period thought fit to give currency to it shows clearly the attitude of the Muslims towards the Hindus in the age in which he flourished.

14. The case of Medinī Rāi, in Mālwa (pp. 183-4), is a striking example. But even in this case his later career supports the theory enunciated here. There are a few cases on record where Muslims occupied a high post in Hindu State and vice versa. But the very small number of such cases supports the view mentioned in the text. The careers of Gaṇeśa and his son, sketched above (pp. 208 ff), are other striking illustrations of the wide gulf that separated the Hindus and Muslims in politics. It is noteworthy that in spite of perpetual rebellions and usurpations, no Hindu ever succeeded in gaining the throne or maintaining it in a State ruled over by the Muslims.

14a. See pp. 268 ff.

15. *HIED,* III, 42-44.

16. *HIED,* IV, 447.

17. Rāṇā Kumbha claims to have imprisoned the *Yavanīs* (i.e. Muslim women) and also broken a mosque. When Medini Rāi was powerful in Mālwa, "Musulmān and Sayyid women were taken by the Rājputs and were turned into slave girls" (*TA, III, 597).* The massacre and rapine of the Muslims by the Hindu kings of Vijayanagara are referred to by Firishta.

18. For the significance of the term *zimmī*, see above.

19. These figures within brackets refer to pages in *IBH.*

20. Pp. 233-4.

20a. In this quotation the word 'Hindu' has been substituted for 'enemy', as being the correct translation of the original word 'kāfir' (see above, p. 245, f.n., 19).

20b. Cf. Vol. V, pp. 500-501.

20c. See above, pp. 378 ff.

21. *Further Sources of Vijayanagara History,* I. 40.

21a. Above, pp. 233-4.

21b. Cf. *Kirtilatā.*

22. Tara Chand, *Influence of Islam on Indian Culture,* p. 137.

22a. Cf. D.C. Sen, *Baṅgabhāshā o Sāhiya,* 6th Edition, pp. 319-20.

23. *Manasā Mangala* also called *Padmā-Purāṇa* (in Bengali), pp. 54 ff.

24. *Advaita-prakāśa* (in Bengal) Ch. IX, p. 39.

25. For this episode cf. *Chaitanya-bhāgavata,* Madhyakhaṇda, Ch. 23 (pp. 271 ff); *Chaitanya-charitāmṛita,* Ādi-līlā, Ch. XVII (pp. 122 ff).

26. *Chaitanya-charitāmṛita,* Madhya-līlā, Ch. I, p. 138.

26a. *Chaitanya-Bhāgavata, Antyakhaṇda,* Ch. IV, p. 358.

27. *Ibid. Chaitanya-bhāgavata, Antya-Khaṇda,* Ch. IV, p. 358.

28. *Chaitnya-charitāmṛita,* Madhya-līlā, Ch. XIX, p. 326.

28a. For a different view on this point cf. p. 219.

29. *Chaitanya-bhāgavata,* pp. 14, 140, 356.

30. M.L. Dames, *The Book of Duarte Barbosa,* 11, 148.

4

Islamic Education

The beginning of the eighth century A.D. marked the modammedan invasions in India. Mahamūda Ghaznavi invaded the country and plundering her, established innumerable schools and libraries with the looted wealth in his own country. Afterwards when the Muslim rulers established permanent empire in India, they introduced a new educational system here. At that time, ancient Brahmanical and Buddhist education was prevalent in the country. From time to time many efforts were made to destroy Indian education and culture at the hands of number of muslim rulers such as Bakhatiar, Allahuddin, Firoz and Aurangazeb etc. Bakhatiar, destroying the Buddhist universities attempted to propagate and spread Islamic education.

Thus we see that partly through the State efforts and partly those of wealthy people, Indian education gradually assumed a new form in this era. We also note that contemporary Hindu education could not help being influenced by this new system of education. Its vogue spread to the extent that many Hindu scholars having acquired proficiency in Persian and Arabic sought responsible posts in the courts of Muslim rulers. The Islamic education too, on its part, was considerably influenced in the fields of Philosophy, Medical science and Vocational education. Islamic education was divided mainly into three categories: (i) Maktab (Primary education); (ii) Higher Maktab; and (iii) Madrasha (Higher education). Being classified thus into above-mentioned divisions, the Islamic educational system spread a network of institutions throughout the country a detailed account of its gradual progress will be given in the following pages.

The aims of Islamic education were multifarious. In order to fulfil these aims, the new system of education was to serve as the chief instrument directed to that purpose. It is, however, to be noted that the objects of the spread of education have been different with different rulers. Akbar and Aurangzeb had quite different aims concering education from those of other rulers. While Akbar aimed at organising the nation on a new pattern by harmonising political, religious and social aspects of the society, the sole objective of Aurangzeb, on the contrary, was to spread Islamic education and culture by destroying Hindu culture and education. We can put the aims of Islamic education briefly as follows:-

(i) The very first aim of Islamic education was to spread the light of knowledge among the followers of Mohammedanism. According to the Prophet, knowledge is nectar and salvation is impossible without it. This explains the supreme importance attached to the acquisition of knowledge by the Prophet, Mohammad. He preached to the people that distinction between essential duty and wrong action, religion and irreligion could be accomplished only through knowledge and as such according to Mohammad the "acquisition of knowledge is incumbant upon all the faithful, men as well as women."

(ii) The second aim of education was to spread and propagate religion. The spread of Islam was regarded as religious duty and the belief that only a propagator of religion could be Ghazi, or martyr was prevalent among them. Therefore, Islam was spread in India through education on a large scale. In Maktabs study of the Quran used to be started from the beginning and children were acquainted with the fundamental principles of Islam. In Madrasahs also tenets of Islamic religion were taught in the form of philosophy, literature and history. The Muslim rulers in India being prompted by religious sentiments patronished education and sought to preserve it, because according to Muhammad "No present or gift of a parent, out of all the gifts and presents to a child is superior to a good liberal education." Hence construction of school buildings began to be regarded as sacred a duty as to erect a mosque, so much so that a Maktab would necessarily be built and attached to a mosque. The

Mohammedan hermits, the rulers of religious bent of mind and the citizens all of them regarded teachers and students as sacred and pious so much so that some persons expressed their wish to be cremated in the very premises of the Madrasahs. According to the prophet the ink of the scholars is more holy than the blood of the martyr. Muslims regarded general education as integral part of Islamic education. Being instigated by vehement fanaticism, they destroyed ancient Buddhist and Hindu temples, schools and other educational centres and erected on their ruins mosques and Madrasahs.

(iii) Their next object was to evolve a special system of morals based on Islamic doctrines and to expound ancient Islamic laws, social traditions and special political principles.

(iv) They also wanted to achieve materialistic prosperity. The inherent weakenss of Islamic education was that it allured people with the fine bait of high posts, honourable rank, medals and grants of *'jagirs'* in order to encourage them and keep the interest of students from declining. Hence the Muslim rulers occasionally encouraged students by making them commanders of the army (*Sipah Sālār*) or *Kāzī* (Judge) in civil administration or *'Vazir'* (Minister) in the executive department of the empire. "Learning was held in high esteem and the learned were loved and respected all over the country. The state also encouraged them in every possible way. Judges, lawyers and ministers of religion were taken from these classes."[2] Many Hindus, with a view to reaping these benefits felt allured to receive Islamic education, and having attained proficiency in Persian, were appointed on high posts in the state. Thus to prepare the students for practical life, was one of the principal objects of this education.

(v) Lastly, its object was somewhat tinged with political motives and interests. The Mohammedans had entered a land; the civilization, culture and political knowledge of which was far superior to theirs. Hence it became indispensable for them to create some such political

circumstances as might strengthen their rule in the country. We find Akbar's educational and political policy to be a concept step in this direction.

State Patronage and Growth of Education

In the beginning of the 8th century, the Mohammedans invaded India. At the time, the Buddhist system of education was in vogue throughout the country along with the existence of some Brahmanical educational centres at some places. As has already been indicated, there was sufficient growth and spread of education at that time. There were important and famous educational centres such as Nalanda in Bihar and Valabhi in the west, which were disseminating higher education in the country. Besides these, there were other famous universities—one at Kashi in northern India and another at Bikramasila. A reference to them has been made already in the previous chapter. Dhar was another famous centre of education in Malva. It should be noted that the first Mohammedan invaders did not make any efforts with regard to expansion of education in India. Mahamūd Ghazanavi, the famous invader, though he was a lover of education and fine arts and promoted the cause of education in his own native country with the booty obtained from India, did not put any efforts for advancement of Indian education. His main object of invading India, in fact, was plundering and carrying away the booty to his own country. In 1192, Mohammad Ghauri invaded India and laid the foundation of Muslim empire in the country. He dismantled the temples at Ajmer and built mosques and schools in their place. One of his eminent commanders named Bakhtiar invaded Southern India and destroyed Buddhist universities, thus causing much harm to ancient Indian education and culture. He established a number of Madrasahs. Afterwards, certain rulers belonging to slave dynasty such as Iltutmish, Razia and Balban too encouraged education in the country. Some of these Muslim rulers were great patrons of arts and literature and kept religionists, artists, historians and poets in their courts. Balban was one of them. Famous poet Amir Khushran and Amir Hassan Dehlwi who had earned a wide repute even abroad for their Persian works were the contemporaries of Balban. During the 13th century, religious works, literature, history and fiction were produced on a large scale. The Sultans of Delhi also made proper provision for the education of Mohammedan masses. Nearly every Muslim colony had two Maktabs. These emperors also established Madrasahs and sanctioned liberal grants for them. Sultan Iltitutmish founded one Madrasah at Delhi and another at Multan. Nasiriyya Collage called after the name of Nasir-ud-Din was a famous institution constructed by the slave king. It should, however, be remembered that provision for cultural improvement was specially for people belonging to higher stratum of society and the standard of masses in culture and education was on constant decline.

Zalal-ul-Din was an erudite emperor in Khilji dynasty. But during the term of reign of Ala-ud-Din Khilji, education received a tottering blow because in the early period of his reign he withdrew state financial aid from educational institutions and diverted the amounts so released towards and reorganisation of his army after confiscating the estates attached to educational institutions. But according to the views of Barni, the, most marvellous phenomenon during the reign of Ala-ud-Din was that eminent persons of other nations, scientists and skilful artists flocked in the metropolis. The capital of Delhi, owing to the presence of such unparalleled scholars, had become the 'envy of Baghdad, rival of Cairo and equal of Constantinople." Later on Ala-ud-Din came to be recognised as "the strengthner of the pulpits of learning and religion, and the strengthner of the rules, of colleges and places of worship." According to Ferishta in the reign of Ala-ud-Din there were as many as forty-five Doctors of arts and sciences, who worked as Professors in the universities. Abdul Haq Haqqi informs us that "during the time of sultan Ala-ud-Din, Delhi was the great rendezvous for all the most learned and erudite personages."[3]

The Tughluq dynasty contributed much to the growth of education. Ghiyas-ud-Din and Mohammad Tughluq were themslaves scholars and lovers of education. The court of Mohammad sheltered many a poet, philosopher, physician and logician. He would enter into metaphysical discussions with them. Maulana Muiuddin Umarani was a famous literateur of that period. Both of these rulers awarded scholarships to deserving students and constructed Maktabs. During the term of reign of Firoz Shah, Delhi had grown into a famous educational centre. He encouraged the scholars by extending financial help to them. His bounty can be evidenced by the fact that as many as 180, 000 slaves received education at Delhi.[4] It is said that of these slaves, 12,000 turned to be serious scholars, tradesmen and artisans.[5] He constructed near about 30 Madrasahs where teachers and pupils resided together. A permanent teacher was appointed in every Madrasah which was attached to some mosque and liberal financial help was given to these institution. Ziauddin Barni and Shamse-Shiraj composed their works under the patronage of Firozshah. A keen student of History himself, he wrote his autobiography named *'Fatuhat-i-Firozshahi.'* He had got hold of a very big library well-stocked with many valuable Sanskrit works as a result of Kangra-conquest. Firozshah got innumerable books of the library translated into Persian. Thus owing to his personal love and taste for education, Muslim education, politics, religion and literature made considerable progress during that period.

After the death of Firozshah, many of the provincial rulers under him became independent. They too made creditable efforts to promote education in their own small states. In southern India, the rulers of Bahamani dynasty established many Maktabs and Madrasahs. Mahmūd Gāvan caused a big Madrasah to be erected which included a well-furnished library containing thousands of books. Maktabs were opened in rural areas too for the expansion of Islamic education. In Bahamani kingdom, the standard of education also rose considerably. Besides these, Bijapur, Golconda, Malwa, Khandesh, Jaunpur, Multan, Gujerat and Bengal also became famous centres of education. Jaunpur was famous for its arts, literature and learning of higher nature in that age. Some of the chiefs and wealthy nobles also opened Maktabs for the spread of primary and religious education. Some learned teachers taught pupils at their own houses.

Education in northern India had proceeded on downward slope at the time of the invasion of India by Babar. Babar, though himself a scholar and poet, could do nothing during the short term of his reign for the spread of education. However, the History written by Syed Maqabar Ali, the Vazir (counsellor) of Babar, informs us that construction of Maktabs and Madrasaha was also one of the main duties of 'Shuhrat-i-Aam' (Public works Department) Emperor Humayūn also founded a very big and famous Madrasah at Delhi and Sheikh Hussain was appointed as the Principal of that Institution. He estalished a library at Delhi and converted the Aaramgah or Luxury palace of Shershah into a library. A Madrasah was also started in the tomb of Humayūn. This Madrasah, which was situated on the roof of the tomb, was a prominent institution once upon a time and learned and influential teachers were appointed for teaching-work. Humayūn himself had a liking for studies— his favourite subjects being geography and astrology.

Shershah Sūri opened a Madrasah at Narnaul and made provisions for mass-education. These Indian rulers at that time meant by the term 'education' mainly Islamic education which included study of the Quran, reading, writing and elementary arithmetic.

After the death of Humayūn, Akbar suceeded to the throne. The period of Akbar's reign marks the beginning of a new era in the history of medieval education. Though he was quite illiterate yet he possessed very sharp and brilliant talents. His period is characterised by an unprecedented progress of education, fine arts, literature, philosophy and history. His court sheltered many erudite scholars and Akbar used to enter into discussions with them. He patronized religious scholars of different creeds and thus contributed much to the growth of learning. He framed rules and curricula for mass education with the help of his learned counsellor Abul Fazal. He introduced improvement in the traditional system of education through state mandates. Moreover, for the improvement of muslim masses, he got the curriculum changed for the purpose. He instituted a very vast and rich library at the metropolis well-stocked with eminent volumes on different religious creeds, literatures, and philosophical treatises. He established Madrasahs at Agra, Fatehpur Sikri and other places. He got many Sanskrit volumes translated into Persian which he himself would listen to the recitation of some other person. The Hindus had begun to study Arabic and Persian in order to avail of the benefit of state service. They showed keener interest in the study of Persian owing to Akbar's policy of religious tolerance. Akbar established schools for the education of Hindu children also.

Jahangir, the son of Akbar, though he himself was not a lover of education, was, nevertheless, learned and encouraged scholars. He had a love of books. He was also a great patron of the art of painting. He had issued a mandate that in case any wealthy citizen or traveller died without any heir, his estate should be taken by the State and money obtained from its proceeds should be spent on the construction and repairing of Madrasahs and improvement of education. After his enthronement Jahangir got these Madrasahs repaired which had been the abode of animals and wild birds for thirty years; he now peopled them with teachers and pupils.

Shahjahan though he patronised fine arts such as music, painting, sculpture, etc. did not make any appreciable attempts in the direction of the improvement and expansion of education. He only preserved the policy of his forefathers. He constructed a big Madrasah at Delhi and got another one named *"Darul-Baqi"* repaired. Shahjahan was an eminent scholar of Turkish and he would spend some hours of night in reading books. His son, Dara Shikoh was an erudite scholar and well-versed in Hindu Philosophy. He had a thorough knowledge of Arabic, Persian and Sanskrit. He had translated the Upanishadas, Bhagavada Gita, Yog Vasishtha and Ramayan. He worte a commentary on *Sūfi* philosophic system. It is said that if Dara Shikoh were to take the reins of empire in his hands, history of Indian education and fate of India would have been quite different.

It is, all the same, true that Islamic education had not attained universality. There was nothing like modern Education Department for the purpose of organised and systematic expansion of education and its administration. Spread of education was regarded as the religious duty and the money spent by the State on education was considered to have been spent on charity. During the period of Shahjahan, there came a French traveller named Bernier to visit India. He has given a very disappointing account of the contemporary education. He writes: "A profound and universal ignorance is the natural consequence of such a state of society as I have endeavoured to describe. Is it possible to establish in Hindustan academies and colleges properly endowed? Where shall we seek for founders? Or, should they be found, where are the scholars? Where the individuals whose property is sufficient to support their children at college? Or, if such individuals exist, who would venture to display so clear a proof of wealth. Lastly, if any person should be tempted to commit this great imprudence, yet where are the benefices, the employments, the offices of trust and dignity that require ability and science and are calculated to excite the emulation and the hopes of the young student?"[6]

In fact, when we cast our glance upon the educational efforts of the then rulers and private patrons, the statement made by Bernier appears to be a gross exaggeration and a fallacy. He has however, omitted to refer to those Indian educational centres where secular and spiritual education of a higher order was being imparted on a large scale without state help depending merely on private enterprise and thus great educational centres had come into being in solitary places. It is true that the term "college" did not mean any such big educational institution where innumerable students might be receiving education. Undoubtedly, Bernier had presented the picture of Indian education with the standard of European educational institutions in his mind. As a matter of fact, the schools and Madrasahs of India should not have been so famous at that time that they might compel the attention of visitors towards them. Generally a place was attached to mosque where the religious preachers gave education to the assembled pupils. Otherwise we get referenes mostly to the repairing of old Madrasahs.

Aurangzeb was a sworn enemy of Hindu education. He had demolished many Hindu temples and educational institutions and erected mosques, Maktabs and Madarasahs on their ruins. Unlike Akbar, he considered Islamic education as the only true education and accordingly made efforts for its promotion. Referring to Mirat-i-Alam, Elliot has quoted: "All the Mosques in the empire are repaired at the public expense. *Imams,* criers to the daily prayers and readers of the Khuthwa have been appointed to each of them so that a large sum of money has been and is still laid out in these disbursements. In all the cities and towns of this extensive country pensions and allowances lands have been given to learned men and professors and stipends have been fixed for scholars according to their abilities and qualifications."

Aurangzeb, in spite of his narrow and fanatic views, was a learned scholar of Turkish, Arabic and Persain. Knowledge of the Quran and Hadis was on the tip of his tongue. The downfall of education which had commenced during the period of Shahjahan had, for some time during the reign of Aurangzeb, come to a standstill. Aurangzeb introduced improvement in quality as well as quantity of education, as it manifested by his talks with his own teacher. A reference to this talk will be made later on. He made education more suitable to the practical aspect of life by amending the curriculum. He established state Maktabs and Madrasahs and spread Islamic religious doctrines and education. He enriched the state library with innumerable Islamic books. He had brought cart-loads of books from the library of Bijapur.

As has been pointed out, Aurangzeb confined his efforts only to the education of the Mohammedans. He issued *Farman* or Royal orders to the provincial rulers to the effect that Hindu temples and educational institutions be demolished and in their places, mosques and Maktabs be erected. He also passed orders that special provision should be made for the provinces of Gujerat and Oudh which were educationally backward. In 1678, he made special provision for the education of the *Boharas* of Gujerat and appointed state teachers. Further, having made their education compulsory, he ordered that he should be informed of their progress indicated by the monthly examinations.

State of Education after Aurangzeb

The symptoms of the downfall of Moghul Empire had become evident even during the reign of Aurangzeb. Rebellion by the provincial Subedars and the rise of the Marathas shook the Moghul empire to the very foundation. Under such circumstances, therefore, when war, anarchy, plundering and seditions were rampant, it was futile and quite useless to expect the rulers to devote their attention to the progress of education and literature. It is, nonetheless, true that in different provinces the wealthy people had established some Madrasahs. The Madrasah of Ghaziuddin at Delhi is worth mentioning 'More or less secular village schools for both Mohammedans and Hindus continued to exist, but the schools and colleges attached to temples and mosques which were then receiving any help from states had to be closed down dispersing the teachers and the students. In an unsettled country there could be no progress in education. A few of the successors of Aurangzeb tried in a feeble way to keep the torch of education lighted but could hardly make their influence felt in the eighteenth century.'[7] The conquests of Marathas and English rulers led to the downfall of the seats of muslim education in India.

It is an acknowledged fact that the education imparted in these Maktabs and Madrasahs was not for the masses but was meant specially for those who wanted to be benefited by it. Thus education developed during the reign of Mohammedan rulers. Both Hindus and Muslims were influenced by the system of education of one another and eventually a uniform educational system was evolved.

The Maktabs and Madrasahs which were attached to mosques would generally go out of existence with the death of their founders and teachers and pupils would leave those buildings. The entire period of 700 years of Mohammedan rule was dotted with intermittent warfare; hence the rulers could not devote undistracted attention to the improvement and expansion of education. Besides state efforts, private venture too helped a lot the growth of education during the period. As a matter of fact, noble and wealthy class of the society contributed to the development of education through liberal donations and benefactions. The schools established by private efforts proved to stand on a more firm footing than the state Madrasahs, because the latter would callapse soon for want of proper patronage. When in 18th century the cauldron of anarchy, maladministration and sedition was seething in India through the activities of the Maratha, Muslim, Sikh, English and French communities, universal and wide-spread ignorance had become a common phenomenon and a matter of course. In the absence of employment and state ranks there was nothing to inspire the drooping spirits of young students with hope and courage. Trade, industry and agriculture of the country were in a ruined state. This naturally resulted in unprecendent downfall of education in this period and the entire country was shrouded in a dark veil of ignorance. The English and Christians established some schools for Hindus and Mohammedans, as well as Maktabs, Madrasahs and Tols in Bengal; but all these efforts were insignificant and quite inadequate. In modern times too, there are certain Maktabs running in the mosques where education in the Quran is imparted by *Imāms* and *Maulavīs* and these institutions are under the direct supervision of the State Education Department.

References

1. Hazrat Shaikh Isa Dehlawi's name may be mentioned in this connection who expressed his last wish that he should be buried in the place where the students of the Madrasah used to keep their shoes.
2. Jaffar: *Education in Muslim India;* p. 4.
3. Jaffar: *Education in Muslim India;* p. 46.
4. F.E. Keay: *Indian Education in Ancient and later times;* p. 144.
5. N.N. Law: *Promotion of Learning in India;* pp. 54-55.
6. Bernier: *Travels.*
7. J.M. Sen: *History of Elementary Education in India;* p. 34.

5

Education and Culture

The Political History of India from Timūr to Bābur does not make happy reading. During the first half of the period, despite its struggle for survival, the Sultanate went on shrinking. Some stability was attained in the second half, some lost territory was reclaimed, but then all was lost to Bābur in the end. In the political sphere, therefore, the fifteenth cenury was a period of decay and disintegration.

But in the social and cultural sphere this period of a century and a quarter was of sustained progress and great achievements. It saw the development of new patterns in architecture. Many works of merit were produced in classical as well as regional languages. Many reformers and poet gave a new tone to society by their teachings and writings. The fifteenth century was thus a century of cultural advancement, of new trends in social behaviour and, above all, an age of socio-religious reforms. We will now turn to review the social and cultural achievements of the period under study.

Architecture

In its heyday the Lodi empire extended from the Indus in the west to the bend of the Ganga in Bihar in the east. In the north it went up to the sub-montane belt of the Himalayās and in the south its boundary ran along a zigzag west-to-east line including Nagor, Mandrael, Narwar, Chanderi, Chunār and Khalgaon. Even when the empire was not so extensive, or conditions so favourable, the Saiyyad and Lodī Sultans, following the traditions of old, gave attention to art and letters, and constructional work went on throughout the one and a quarter century of their rule.

The Khaljīs and the Tughlaqs were mighty builders. They had build enthusiastically, repaired and conserved old buildings, and developed a robust style of their own. But the continuity of architectual exuberance of the Tughlaq times received a setback at the hands of Timūr. Timūr invasion swept everything before it. Besides the treasure of the State and the wealth of the capital, he carried away with him many good craftsmen, architects and stone-workers to Samarqand to build for him there, while many others, following the confusion of his attack, migrated to various provincial capitals. Without money and without artisans it was not possible for the rulers of Delhi to accomplish much. During the first decade after Tīmūr's departure, perhaps only one building was constructed, an Idgāh by Mallū Iqbāl Khan, in an inscription on which he heartily cursed the "Kāfir" conqueror. The first two Saiyyads restored some political stability. Khizr Khan and Mubārak Shāh even founded two cities, but they (Khizrābād and Mubārakābād) have practically disappeared because of their poor construction owing to limited financial resources.

The buildings constructed during the Saiyyad and the Lodī regime fall into two groups, (a) tombs and (b) mosques. The tomb-construction began to take a definite shape. It was based on two different conventions, one octagonal in plan and the other square. The prototypes of the first pattern are the three royal tombs of Mubārak Shāh Saiyyad (died 1434), Muhammad Saiyyad (d. 1445) and Sikandar Lodī (d. 1517). They deserve a detailed study for they reveal the stages in the evolution of the octagonal process which had begun in the tomb of Khan-i-Jahān Telangānī, the Prime Minister of Firoz Shāh, constructed in 1368-69[1], and found its culmination in the magnificent mausoleum of Sher Shāh Sūri. This type remained popular for well-nigh two centuries, and even provided the inspiration for some of Akbar's monuments.

The tomb of Mubārak Shāh Saiyyad[2] is 30 feet each octagonal side, 74 feet wide, and the height of the dome, excluding the finial, is 50 feet. Here, the central dome is raised higher than in the original prototype, the Telangānī tomb. The height of the verandah, too, is increased; pinnacles (*guldastās*) are provided at the angles of the polygonal drum; kiosks (*Chhatrīs*) repalce subsidiary domes, and an arched lantern crowns the summit in place of the usual finial.[3] But there is one defect also. In the upper part the structure rises above the spectator's eyes and from the average line of sight these parts and foreshortened. The result is a slightly stunted elevation.

This defect is removed in the tomb of Saiyyad Muhammad, erected some ten years later by his son and successor 'Alāuddīin Ālam Shāh.[4] This tomb which lies in Khairpur to the north-east of the tomb of Safdar Jung, has the same dimensions as those of Mubārak Shāh, but the height of the central dome as well as the kiosks is elegantly elevated. Besides, there is also symmetry and cohesion in its several parts. Many of its features—use of local grey-stone and pierced stone-screens—were inherited from preceding centuries, but some new ones, chiefly decorative in character, were added to them. These include the use of blue enamelled tiling, refined treatment of surface ornament incised on plaster and embellished with colours, and the lotus finials on the domes, etc. The inner walls are decorated with quotations from the Quran in incised plaster. Besides Muhammed Saiyyad's there are seven more graves, obviously of other relatives.

The tombs of Saiyyad Mubārak and Saiyyad Muhammad are now more or less isolated structures, any supplementary features that may have surrounded them having disappeared. On the other hand the tomb of Sikandar Lodī,[5] constructed by his son and successor Ibrāhīm in 1518, is better preserved and is more finished in form. It is similar in design and dimensions to that of Muhammad Shāh, but in this mausoleum the use of enamelled tiles has been much extended; tiles of several colours—green, yellow, azure and dark blue—are disposed in a variety of patterns. There is a marked tendency towards more lavish ornamentation. A significant structural deviation is also noticeable. In the tombs of the two preceding monarchs the dome is solely of uniform thickness of stonework, but in the present instance the dome is composed of an inner and outer shell of masonry, with a distinct space between the two. Such a device was quite well known in Iraq, Persia, and other parts of western Asia, but in India, Sikandar's tomb provides the first "successful" example in the application of the "double dome".[6] It imparted a loftier and more imposing exterior, and provided the interior with larger space. Since later on, the later domes of India were constructed on this same principle, the emergence of the device in the Lodī period is of special significance.[7] Another noteworthy feature of Sikandar Lodī's mausoleum was its walled enclosure "which occupies a place midway between the fortified enclaves of the Tughlaq tombs and the decorative garden of the Mughals".[8]

The octagonal method of tomb-construction seems to have been confined to the royal family: The square-plan type of tomb was, perhaps, reserved for nobles and others of high rank, although some of them are even larger and more imposing than the royal tombs. The square type curiously enough found favour during the Saiyyad and Lodī time only, and all its examples fall within the fifteenth century. In Delhi and its neighbourhood there are at least seven such mausoleums. They are now known by their local names only, and it is difficult to say whose memory they commemorate. They are Barē Khan Ka Gumbad (or Dome), Chhotē Khan Ka Gumbad, Bara Gumbad, Shīsh Gumbad, Tomb of Shihābuddīn Tāj Khan, Dādī Ka Gumbad and Polī Ka Gumbad.[9] They are square solid buildings with domes carried on squinch arches and an octagonal pillared kiosk (light open *Chhatrī*) on each corner of the roof.

Bara Gumbad, so called because of its lofty dome 80 feet to the top, lies some 300 yards north-east of the tomb of Muhammad Shāh Saiyyad. An inscription over the southern Mihrāb, incised in plaster, points to its construction in 1494 (900 H). It is a beautiful structure as its domes rest on corbelled pendentives most elaborately carved and finished. At the north and south ends of the apartment are oriel or projecting windows, whose prototype may be found in the back wall of the Quwwat-ul-Islam mosque at the Qutb. The Bara Gumbad has a mosque attached to it which is profusely decorated throughout with conventional foliage and verses from the Quran in incised palster relieved by coloured tilework.

Cunningham compares the eastern gateway of the Bara Gumbad with the famous 'Alāi Darwāzā constructed by Alāuddin Khaljī, and his opinion is shared by Fergusson.[10] In constrast to the rich internal treatment of the 'Alāī Darwāzā[11] the walls of the Bara Gumbad are left uncarved. But in its grandeur it is perhaps unequalled in the ruins of Delhi save by its prototype.[12] although it is far removed "from that ideal structure"[13] Shīsh Gumbad, or the Glazed Dome, is situated some 50 yards to the north of the Bara Gumbad. The tomb of an unidentified dignitary, its ceiling is decorated with floral carvings in incised plaster and quotations from the Quran. The exterior is ornamented with the blue glazed tiles in two shades which must have lent it a very striking appearance and which give the tomb its name.[14]

It would be nedless to make a detailed study of all the "Gumbads" mentioned above and many more like the Hijrē Ka Gumbad (Dome of Hermaphrodite) and Nīlī Gumtī, so called because of its blue tiles. The treatment in all cases is almost the same. A single chamber comprises the interior which is square in plan and the dome is supported by a squinch arch at each corner. There are sunken archways, those on the west contain the *mihrāb*. This gives a feeling of monotony and these structures seen one after the other look rather stereotyped.

In the sphere of mosque construction the Saiyyads could not boast of any large ones of the public or congregational order;[15] but with the accession of Sikandar Lodī, a new leaf is turned in this field. A devout Musalman, he is said to have built mosques throughout his kingdom.[16] But most of them were of a private nature, mostly attached to the tombs. However, there are some notable structures like the mosque attached to the Bara Gumbad and Moth Ki Masjid, which in their specialised form of design provide a motif for Jamala Masjid (constructed in 1536) and Qila Kuhnā Masjid of Sher Shāh (built in C 1550) in the last of which they ultimately reach perfection.

The mosque attached to the Bara Gumbad is a kind of domestic chapel, and represents the Lodī technique in embryo.[17] This technique is definitely improved in the Moth Ki Masjid, built ten years later (1505) by Miān Bhuā, the Prime Minister of Sikandar Lodī.[18] Moth Ki Masjid stands on a raised platform. The gateway is faced with red sandstone ornamented with marble. The eastern angles of the enclosure are marked by domed *chhatrīs* supported on eight red stone pillars and contain traces of blue tile decoration.

This mosque[19] is much larger than the one attached to the Bara Gumbad, and measured nearly one hundred and twenty-five feet across. Consequently it provided much more scope for the skill of the craftsmen and "it epitomises in itself all that is best in the architecture of the Lodīs".[20] In the central portion the system of squinch arches found in earlier buildings continues, but in the side aisles a form of stalactite pendentive is introduced in the angles.[21] Free intermixture of white marble, red sandstone and enamelled tiles lends a colourful effect to the decoration, which contrasts effectively with the bold quality of the masonry. The spandrels above the arches are full of carvings in plaster with exquisite arabesque designs of typically Islamic character. Percy Brown suggests: "There was evidently a very talented group of craftsmen, engaged in this art during the fifteenth century, reminiscent of that much greater school of artists who, at about the same time were perpetuating such wonders in a similar technique on the walls of the Alhambra in Spain.[22]

Sikandar Lodī was by far the greatest builder of the fifteenth century. Inscriptions on various buildings in northern India indicate his love for architectural activity. He is credited with constructing a canal in A.D. 1492-93[23] a Baolī in Rajputana[24] and mosques in almost all important cities including Lahore, Karnal, Hansi and Makanpur (District Kanpur), besides many in Delhi and Agra.[25] There are also so many nameless mosques and tombs belonging to the Lodī period which, from their design and material of construction, can safely be attributed to Sikandar's time.[26] Like Firōz Tughlaq, Sikandar Lodī was not only a great builder but also a great repairer. In his time in A.D. 1492 (897 H) was built the mausoleum of Amīr Khusru. An inscribed frieze at the entrance doorway of the Qutb Mīnār credits him with repairing this world famous edifice in A.D. 1503 (909 H),[27] although the nature of the repairs is not known. A few more buildings of his son and sucessor Ibrāhīm Lodī are also extant, like the tomb of Khwājā Khizr (completed in 1522) and Rajōn Ki Baolī, with a mosque attached to it. But Ibrāhīm's political difficulties left him little time for much constructional activity.

Besides the Imperial style of architecture, two other local styles, those of Jaunpur and Gwalior, deserve special attention.

Otherwise an obscure place, Jaunpur was brought into prominence in 1360 by Firōz Shāh Tughlaq, who built it into a city. It assumed independence a little before Tāmūr's invasion and thereafter continued its own course undisturbed. Even when it was engaged in wars against Delhi and other neighbouring kingdoms, its rulers continued to lend patronage to art and learning. The buildings that the Sharqīs of Jaunpur have left speak of their aesthetic architectural taste. Unfortuantely many of Jaunpur's finest monuments were destroyed by Sikandar Lodī after defeating Husain Shāh in 1495. The few that have survived include several large mosques, three of which still remain tolerably entire, and a considerable number of tombs and palaces. The Atālā mosque, the Khālis Mukhlis, the Lāl Darwāzā Masjid, the Jhanjhri mosque and the Jama' Masjid are some of the best specimens of Indo-Muslim architecture in India.

The construction of the Atālā mosque was started in about 1373 during the reign of Fīrōz Shāh Tughlaq and was completed in about 1408 in the reign of Ibrahīm Sharqī (1401-1440). It was erected on the site and from the material of an earlier Hindu temple said to have been built by Raja Vijāya Chandra Dēva of Varanasi.[28] Built on the orthodox plan, it consists of a square countryard, measuring 177 feet on each side, with the prayer chamber on the west and colonnaded cloisters on the other sides. The domes over the prayer chamber and its back wall, the tapering minarets, the *kangūra* cornices and the arches and trellis windows are of the Tughlaq style. On the other hand the imposing propylon (75 feet high), propylon screens and surface decoration give it, and the Jaunpur style, its distinctive character. The Atālā mosque is so like a Hindu arrangement "that one might almost at first sight be tempted . . . . to fancy it was originally a Hindu monastery",[29] but it also exhibits the saracenic arcuate style in as great a degre of perfection as is exhibited at any period, prior or subsequent. The one defect pointed out in this edifice is that the propylon was made so lofty that the domes are hidden from view, but the architects seem to have so designed the building that while the massive propylon looks grand and imposing from the front, the domes seen from the sides and the rear are equally beautiful.

Another mosque belonging to the reign of Ibrāhīm Sharqī was built by two governors of Jaunpur, Maliks Khālīs and Mukhlis, who have given their names to it. The Jhanjhri Masjid was also built by Ibrāhīm in honour of Hazrat Sa'it Sadr Jahān Ajmalī.[30] The former is a plain structure, but the latter, though badly mutilated, was very similar in design to the Atālā mosque as is indicated by its propylon screens. The Lāl Darwāzā Masjid, so called because of its vermillion-painted gate, was built by Mahmūd Shāh (1440-52) and the Jama Masjid by Husain Shāh (1452-78). Both these are more or less based on the design of the Atālā Masjid, although the latter edifice is more imposing than the former. The architect of the Lāl Darwāzā mosque is said to have been a Hindu, named Kamaū, the son of Visadru, and it is likely that the architect of the Atālā Masjid was also a Hindu.[31] Thus the architecture of Jaunpur had all the beauty and grace of the Hindu art employed to the best advantage in the construction of their mosques.[32] The massive propylon gives the facade almost the look of a south Indian temple, and constitutes the most distinctive element of the style. The peculiarities of this style—the best blending of the Hindu and the Muslim—extended into other important cities of Jaunpur kingdom like Kalpi, Varanasi, Ghāzipur and Āzamgarh.

The architecture of Gwalior, annexed to the Sultanate in 1518, can be best described in one word—grandiose. Perched on a high hill, the fort and palace of Raja Mān Singh (1486-1518) and the palace added by his sucessor Vikramāditya, are the most remarkable examples of the Hindu architecture of northern India during the period under review, Bābur was struck by their beauty and wrote: "They are singularly beautiful palaces (of Mān Singh and his successor Vikramāditya), wholly of hewn stone. The palace of Mān Singh is more lofty and spendid than that of any other Rajas... The five large domes are covered with plates of copper gilt. The outside of the walls they have inlaid with green painted tiles."[33] The copper is gone, but the tiles still look exquisite. A visitor to Gwalior is even today struck by its grandeur, and Fergusson rightly remarks that these palaces furnished points of imitation to Mughal emperors as well as Hindu princes.[34]

The Imperial or Delhi, Jaunpur and Gwalior styles are the chief styles of the Sultanate. The buildings in the Punjab have undergone such large-scale renovations in sucessive ages that the forms in which they now exist cannot be called pre-Mughal. In Sindh nothing of note was constructed during this period. But the rise of Bengal, Malwa, Gujarat, Bahmanī and Vijāyanagar as independent kingdoms gave fresh impetus to architectural activity. The capitals and other cities of these independent States were decorated by their monarchs according to the best of their ability and resources. Thus the break up of the Sultanate at the close of the fourteenth century did not prove to be an unmitigated curse, for throughout the fifteenth century different schools of architecture flourished in these various States; and although their study does not fall within the framework of this work, a brief survey of their accomplishments would be good for a comparative study, and for having a glimpse into the overall picture of the architectural achievements of the country as a whole.

In Bengal, the early Muslim buildings bear traces of the Hindu temple architecture since they are mostly superstructures on the original Hindu, but the climate of Bengal is so singularly inimical to the preservation of architectural remains, that the extant ones belong only to the period of over two centuries (A.D. 1338-1576). Besides, Bengal is practically without stone. Therefore, the Muslim rulers constructed their edifices with heavy short pillars of stone supporting poined arches and vaults of brick, and the style so developed may rightly be called the "brick style" of Bengal. The Purbiya dynasty of Bengal (A.D. 1352-1487) did not do anything much to entitle them to a place in political history, but since they possessed one of the richest regions of India, they spent their wealth lavishly in adorning their capital with beautiful buildings. Jalāluddin Muhammad Shāh (1414-1443) was a great builder. His Eklakhi mosque is bold architectural enterprise and though smaller than the Ādina mosque (built by Sikandar, Shāh, 1358-89), it is a great improvement upon it. A very interesting antiquity of Bengal is the Minār standing just outside the fort of Gaur. For two-thirds of the height it is a polygon of twelve sides; above that it is cicular till it attains the height of 84 feet. There is said to have been an inscription ascribing its erection to Saifuddīn Fīrōz Shāh II (A.D. 1488-90). There are also several gateways, the finest one being the Dākhil or Salāmī gateway, the northern, entrance to Gaur fort, said to have been built by Ruknuddīn Bārbak Shāh (1460-74). It is made of brick, but in strength and grace it is second to none in its class found anywhere.

To the west of the shrunken Sultanate of Delhi had risen two powerful kingdoms, Malwa and Gujarat. The Ghorīs of Malwa declared independence about the same time as the Sharqīs of Jaunpur. The Ghorī dynasty of Malwa made Māndū their capital. It occupies one of the noblest sites occupied by any capital in India.[35] It is an extensive plateau four or five miles east and west and three miles north and south, abounding in water and fertile in the highest degree. This Māndū, the Ghorī and Khaljī dynasties adorned with all kinds of beautiful buildings.

The finest building in Māndū is the Jama Masjid, commenced by Hoshang Shāh and completed by Mahmūd Khaljī I in 1454. "Though not very large, it is so simple and grand.... that it ranks high among the monuments of its class."[36] The tomb of its founder stands behind the mosque. Its stern style is relieved by three perforated marble screens of exquisite beauty. More beautiful than all these—mosques and tombs—are the palaces of Māndū. The massive and picturesque "Jahāz Mahal is situated between two great tanks, almost literally in the water, like a ship. The other palaces of note are the palace of Bāz Bahādur (built apparently by Nāsiruddīn Khaljī in 1509),[37] the pavilion of Rupmatī and the Hindōlā Mahal built much later.

The Māndū architecture in a word is massive, elegant and saracenic. Red sandstone and marble, both white and coloured and locally available, have been freely used, the first for constructive and the other for decorative purposes. The builders clung steadily to the pointed-arch style and unlike Jaunpur and Gujarat, the Hindu principles do not seem to have influenced the style of Māndū.[38]

About the architecture of Gujarat, Fergusson remarks: "Of the various forms which the saracenic architecture assumed in India, that of Ahmadabad may probably be considered as the most elegant, as it certainly is the most characteristic of all. No other form is so essentially Indian."[39] For long Gujarat had been a bulwark of Jainism and it contained a considerable number of big and beautiful Jain and Hindu temples. Even after its conquest by 'Alāuddīn Khaljī in A.D. 1299, the Chalukyan style of architecture continued to persist. When Muzaffar Shāh, a converted Rajput of the Tank clan,[40] and the governor of Gujarat, declared his independence there was, as it were, conversion of Rajput government into Muslim, of Rajput architecture into Muslim. In A.D. 1411 his grandson Ahmad Shāh, moved his capital to Karnavati, which was then renamed Ahmadabad,[41] and he and his sucessors decorated Ahmadabad and other towns for the next two centuries.

Ahmad Shāh decorated his capital with all kinds of elegant buildings—fort, mosques, gates and tombs. From the fort to the gateway known as the Tin Darwāzā and thence to the Jama' Masjid it was an achievement in town-planning. The Jama' Masjid of Ahmadabad was completed in A.D. 1423 and is "generally considered the high water-mark of mosque design in western India, if not in the entire country".[42] Its spacious courtyard of 49,500 square feet and some 300 tall, slender, closely set pillars simulate "a thick grove of silver pine trunks".[43] It was but fitting that his son and sucessor Muhammad Shāh (1442-51) interred Ahmad Shāh in front of the eastern entrance to the Jama' Masjid and sustained his style in his tomb.

In Muhammad Shāh's reign the tomb of Shaikh Ahmad Khattri was built in 1446 at Sarkhej (6 miles S.W. of Ahmadabad). Many other mausoleums and mosques were built there by him and by his two successors Qutbuddin (1451-58) and Mahmūd I Beghara (A.D. 1459-1511). During the time of the latter came Gujarat's greatest days. He founded Mahmūdābād (17 miles S.E. of Ahmadabad) and decorated it, at the same time enhancing the beauty of Ahmadabad and other cities of Gujarat like Batwa and Champanir. The tomb of Shaikh Mubārak Saiyyad, erected about 1484 near Mahmūdābād, represents the arcuate style of Gujarat in its finished form. This tomb clearly betrays the style of Lodī tombs at Delhi and it is not improbable that some Delhi craftsmen were attracted to Gujarat. In 1492 the mosque of Muhāfiz Khan, "a gem of architectural refinement" was built. But the most famous mosque is that of Sīdī Saiyyad built sometime between 1510 and 1515. Although almost an insignificant building, it has acquired world-wide fame because of the perforated stone screens in its sanctuary. Great skill is shown in the even manner in which the pattern is spread over the whole surface.[44] What the Gujaratīs had been able to accomplish on hard stone in the fifteenth century, the Mughals could do on marble only in the seventeenth and perhaps not so well.

Of sanctuaries and mosques there is no dearth in Ahmadabad, Champanir and other prominent towns of Gujarat. Structures of the secular variety are also by no means inferior to the religious buildings. Among these is the palatial scheme at Sarkhej, consisting of a large artificial lake with Mahmūd Beghara's palaces occupying two of its sides. The *wavs* or step-wells of Gujarat are known for their artistic beauty. Two of these are the Bai Harir's *wav* in Ahmadabad constructed in 1499 and that at Adalaj built about the same time. Indeed in beauty and in construction the architecture of Gujarat was far superior to the contemporaneous architecture of the Sultanate of Delhi and for the matter of that to that of any other State in the country.

Like any other Muhammadan dynasty, the Bahmanīs too were great builders. Their architecture betrays Sarcenic influence. The mosques at Gulbarga and Bidar are beautiful specimens of Deccan art, but the most remarkable architecture is that of Bijāpur. The Gol Gumbad (tomb of Muhammad Ādil Shāh) has traces of Ottoman influence and so have some of the other tombs and mausoleums. The kings of Bījāpur were mighty builders. Their city-walls; colleges and libraries, though ravaged by time, still speak of their artistic tastes and accomplishments.[45]

Equally impressive is the architecture of Vijāyanagar and Rajputana. The kings of Vijāyanagar built palaces, temples, public offices, aqueducts and irrigation works with great enthusiasm. And what they built, they decorated. Nuniz speaks of their "wonderful" system of irrigation, and Portuguese chroniclers and Abdur Razzāq speak highly of the beauty of Vijāyangar painting and sculpture. Most of the buildings of this great kingdom are now in ruins, and yet they exhibit a grandeur which forces itself upon one's eyes. The famous Hazāra temple built during the reign of Krishna Deva Raya is "one of the most perfect specimens of Hindu temple architecture in existence".[46] Vitthalswāmī temple too "shows the extreme limit in florid magnificence to which the (South Indian) style advanced."[47]

In Rajasthan, the palace of Rana Kumbha (A.D. 1418-68) in Mewar is "grandiose", and shows the same "beauty of detail which characterises his buildings in general".[48] Its ruins show kiosks covered with domes resting on lintels and columns, amidst Hindu balconies.[49]

Reverting to the imperial style of the Delhi Sultanate, it may be remarked that the Saiyyads and the Lodīs built little, but whatever they built they decorated well. Many of the constructional and decorative details of the fifteenth century were inherited from the preceding centuries, yet there are some innovations introduced. The use of blue enamelled tilings for decoration, surface ornamentation of incised plaster embellished with colours, lotus finials on domes, stunted turrets, *guldastās*, diminutive kiosks or *chhatrīs*, fuller domes and pinnacles are contributions of the Lodīs to Indo-Muslim architecture.[50] The double dome was adopted by the Mughals, so also the octagonal mausoleum. Sikandar Lodī's tomb enclosure anticipates the ornamental garden tombs of the Mughals. The use of enamelled tiles continued to be popular in future years. All this was no mean contribution of the fifteenth century to Indo-Islamic architecture. In the words of Sir John Marshall; "Out of the universal chaos which followed on the invasion of Tīmūr, there emerged a vigorous and catholic spirit of design—a spirit replete with creative energy and imagination—which under the Saiyyad and Lodī dynasties gave encouragement once more to the latent genius of Hindustan and at the same time derived new inspiration from the never failing source of Islamic art in Persia."[51]

Music and Painting

About the art of painting during this period little is known. The Sultans of pre-Mughal India were great builders, but they do not seem to have had much liking for paintings. The Hadīs forbids painting of all human forms, and thus places a ban on the development of this art.[52] Moreover, paintings either on paper or in plaster are not as durable as sculptures in stone, and when most of even the stone edifices of these times have been reduced to a dilapidated state, it is fruitless to search for any contemporary paintings. Even so we cannot say that the art of painting had ceased to exist. Ibn Batūta appreciated the "strikingly beautiful paintings and mosaic" of the palace of Hazār Sitūn.[53] We also know that Fīrōz Tughlaq forbade paintings on buildings, which shows that they were a common feature. But not much can be said about this art in this period.

Like architecture and painting, dance and music have also been the soul of India through the ages. The sculptures, on the surviving temples have kept alive the glorious memory of dancing in ancient times. Commoners and kings held these fine arts in the highest esteem.[54]

With the advent of Islam, the art of music and dancing entered upon a new phase. Music is prohibited in Islam, but human nature ever asserted itself against the austere laws of the faith. Muslim rulers and nobles always patronised music throughout the medieval times. Contact with Iran, rise of Sūfīsm and their stay in Hindustan made Muslim rulers lovers of music and dance. Indian classicial music and dance. Indian classical music survived throughout the Sultanate period, although classical Indian dancing almost died out in northern India because it had drifted from the aesthetic sphere into that of the courtesans and the dancing girls.

The Khaljīs were great patrons of music.[55] Amīr Khusru, himself a renowned musician, gives interesting details about contemporary musicians and musical instruments in his *A'ijāz-I-Khusravī*.[56] Though a puritan, Fīrōz Tughlaq got a number of books on music and dance, he had obtained from the Jwālā Mukhī temple, translated into Persian.[57] Even the terrible Tīmūr, who had learnt about the beauty of Hindustani music, listened to Indian artistes when he was in this country and profusely rewarded them.[58]

But the upheaval caused by Tīmūr's invasion dispersed the musicians of Delhi to the far-off courts of Gwalior, Jaunpur and Gujarat which remained centres of musical art throughout the fifteenth century. Husain Sharqī of Jaunpur was a great lover of music and he is said to have invented the Khayāl. Another great centre of music in northern

India was Gwalior. Raja Mān Singh and his queen are said to have been proficient composers and singers. It is said that the Raja called a conference of musicians to make a proper classification of Rāgas.[59] Undoubtedly he was the founder of the Gwalior school of classical music.[60] He is said to have revived the Dhrupad style which had been neglected and therefore forgotten since the days of Amīr khusru.[61] He was the author of a treatise on music entitled *Mān-Kutuhal*.[62] He also got the *Rāgadarpana,* a treatise on Indian classical music translated into Persian. In his court flourished masters like Baijū, Pandvī, Lohang. The master musician was Nāyak Bhikshū. It is, therefore, not surprising that Tānsen originally belonged to Gwalior. In the far-off Vijāyanagar empire the art of music developed rapidly. Both Krishna Dēva Raya and the Regent, Rāma Raya, were proficient musicians, and during this period some new treatises on music were produced, about which we shall study a little later.

At Delhi music gradually regained its position with the stability of the Sultanate. The Saiyyad kings do not seem to have neglected this art and Mubarak Shāh was known for his love of music.[63] The orthodox Sikandar Lodī also was a great lover of music. Although to keep up a show of religious austerity he would not allow anyone to sing or play in his presence, all the celebrated artists used to come and perform before the King's favourite noblemen like Mīrān Saiyyad Rūhullā and Saiyyad Ibn Rasūl, whose tents, by the Sultan's orders, were pitched near those of the king's.[64] Thus the clever and virtuous monarch filled his ears with melody without damaging his reputation for piety. In the palace, instruments were regularly played on. Shahnāī was played every night, commencing at 9 o'clock.[65] A number of beautiful singers and players played on instruments like Chang, Qanūn, Tambūr and Vīnā.[66] According to 'Abdulla, the Sultan's favourite tunes were Mālkaus, Kalyān, Kanada and Husainī;[67] according to Ahmad Yādgār they were Kedār, Adāna, Husainī and Rāmkalī, while according to Rizqulla Mushtaqī, his favourites were Gaur, Kalyān, Kanada and Maqām-i-Husainī.[68] This list shows that Sikandar loved to listen to almost every important Rāga. Sikandar Lodi's services in promoting the art of music were laudable. Under his patronage was written and to him was dedicated the *Lahjāt-i-Sikandar Shāhī,* a treatise on music by 'Umar Yahiyā.[69] Yahiyā was a scholar of Arabic, Persian and Sanskrit and his work is based on many Sanskrit treatises like *Sangīt Ratnākar,*[70] *Nrtya Sangrah, Sangīt Kalpataru* and the works of

Matang.[71] Probably the *Lahjāt* is the first book in Persian on Indian music.

Promotion of Learning

Throughout the medieval period of Indian history the Sultans were keenly interested in the promotion of learning. Iltutmish, Balban and 'Alāuddīn Khaljī established a number of Madrasās in Delhi and elsewhere. During Fīrōz Tughlaq's reign numerous colleges and monasteries were established throughout the country. Besides, his various Kārkhānās provided vocational training to thousands of youngmen.

After Tīmūr's invasion not much is known about the educational system until Sikandar Lodī came to power. Himself a poet and litterateur, Sikandar encouraged learning in every way. He established Madrasās in all parts of his kingdom and appointed distinguished scholars to the charge of the colleges at Agra and other places. He wanted to raise the percentage of the educated, especially among the Afghans, and therefore insisted on compulsory education of his military officers.[72] According to the author of the *Akhbārul Akhyār,* the Sultan invited learned men from Arabia, Iran and Central Asia to India and many of them adopted Hindustan as their home. Shaikh Husain Tāhir, who lived during the reigns of Bahlūl and Sikandar, was known as a walking encyclopaedia.[73] Two distinguished brothers, Shaikh 'Abdulla and Shaikh 'Azizullā Tulambī, were invited from Multan and appointed Principals of the colleges at Agra and Sambhal respectively. 'Abdulla[74] produced forty good disciples of whom Miān Ladhan, Jamāl Khan Dehlvi, Miān Shaikh of Gwalior and Miān Saiyyad of Badaon are well known.[75] Sikandar Lodī himself often attended Abdulla's lectures. He used to enter the classes with silent steps, listened with humility, and when he left he offered the customary salutation.[76] Shaikh 'Azāzullā's two distinguished disciples were Miān Hātni Sambalī and Shaikh Ilah Diya Jaunpuri. The Sultan founded schools at Mathura and Narwar also, which were open to all without discrimination of caste or creed.[77] Learning thus "spread in the country".[78]

Two important points may be noted in connection with the educational system in the medieval times. The first is that there was hardly any secular approach to education. The location of Muslim and Hindu schools in masjids and temples respectively, was enough to give a religious bias to education. Hindu scholars concentrated on the study of religious books like the Vedas and Shāstras besides logic, grammar and literature. The subjects of study in Muslim schools likewise were of a religious nature. Great emphasis was laid on theological education (*manqūlāt*). Besides grammar, literature and logic, the other most important subjects were Hadīs (Tradition), Fiqh (Jurisprudence), and Tafśir (Exegesis). In the words of Dr. Yūsuf Husain, "the institutions of higher learning in the Muslim countries, called Madrasās, had develoepd into centres of learning with a distinct religious bias. They were essentially schools of theology, with auxiliary linguistic studies. These Madrasās were the strongholds of orthodoxy and were subsidised by the State.[79]

The second point of importance is that the standard of education was high. Education was neither compulsory nor universal. Only those who had a keen desire to acquire knowledge joined the schools. There were no printing presses, no text books, no "made-easy" notes. The students devoted their whole time and concentrated attention to study; and lack of printed books necessitated strenuous taxing of the memory. Grammar was the basis of study of languages and there was no other short-cut for acquiring mastery over it. Religious and philosophical studies interspersed with high-brow discussions required thorough grounding in the subject. Thus while only a few persons took to scholastic pursuits, those who joined schools and colleges took to their studies in right earnest.

Persian Literature

Although there were separate schools for Sanskrit and Persian studies, there were some Muslim scholars who learnt Sanskrit and Hindu scholars who learnt Persian. Muslims had learnt much from Hindu medicine, philosophy and astronomy, and translated many works on these subjects from Sanskrit into Persian. This was possible only when the translators possessed mastery of both the languages. Similarly Hindus too had started taking to the study of Persian. A contemporary Brahman scholar of Persian was Pundit Dongar Mal. He was a poet, a scholar and a professor of Persian.[80] He wrote both in Hindi and Persian, and his style combined the grace and mystic note of the Sūfi classics.[81] Similarly a Muslim theologian, Shaikh Rizqulla (1491-1581), wrote lyrics on the love of Krishna in Hindi under the titles of *Wujūb-Jap-Niranjan*, "the work being unfortunately lost to us".[82]

Indeed from the days of Firōz Tughlaq onwards many works were translated into Persian from Sanskrit; Sanskrit possessed a rich Literature. Fīrōz Shāh Tughlaq got a work on Hindu Philosophy translated into Pesian and named it *Dalāyal-i-Fzhroz Shāhī.* In the fifteenth century the work of translating Sanskrit works into Persian went on apace. King Zainul 'Ābidīn of Kashmir (1420-70) possessed good knowledge of Persian, Hindi and Tibetan. Under his patronage the *Mahābhārata* and *Rājtaranganī* were translated into Persian. Jonarāja (d. 1459) carried on Kalhan's *Rājtaranganī* in the same style, his pupil Srīvara covered, the period from 1459 to 1486, while Priya Bhatta and his pupil Shuka carried on the tale to some years after the annexation of Kashmir by Akbar.[83]

Miān Bhuā, the Prime Minister of Sikandar Lodī, got together many Indian and foreign scholars to write books on every science.[84] He appointed physicians of India and Khurāsān to prepare a treatise on Medicine. They consulted works of "Charak, Sushrut, Jānu Karan, Bhoj ...., Chintāman, Chakrāvat, Kīrat and many others,[85] and completed in A.D. 1512 a work called the *Tibb-i-Sikandari* also known as the *Madanush-Shifāi Sikandarī.* The chief author of the work is mentioned as Miān Bhuā, son of Khawās Khan and Minister of Sikandar.[86] In view of the fact that the works of so many scholars of medicine were consulted in the preparation of the treatise, the contention of 'Abdullah that it was a translation of a Sanskrit work entitled *Ayur Mahāvaidak,*[87] does not seem to be correct, more so because the title *Ayur Mahāvaidak* is itself open to doubt. Obviously the *Madunush-Shifāi Sikandarī* was the result of years of patient research based on the works of many ancient masters of Indian Medicine "which were popular in those days". Both Rizqulla and 'Abdulla aver the "there is no work of greater authority on medicine in India" than the *Madunush-Shifāi-Sikandarī.*[88] Similarly many works of Persian were adapted into Indian languages. *Katha Kautuk* was written by Srīvara on the theme of Yūsuf and Zuleikhā by the Persian poet Jāmī.[89]

Besides works of translation many original works of merit were product during this period. Muhammad bin Shaikh Zainuddīn compiled a lexicon entitled *Farhang-i-Sikandari alias Tuhfa-us-Sa'dāt.* A very uncommon work of its kind. it was completed in A.D. 1510 and dedicated to Sultan Sikandar.[90] Another famous writer of the time was Zahīr Dehlvī. Sultan Sikandar conferred the title of Zahīr on him. Other writers of note were Maulānā Hasan Naqshī, Maulānā 'Ali Ahmad Nishānī and Nūrul Haqq.[91] But the greatest intellectual of the age was perhaps Shikh Jamāl Kambū. He was a theologian, poet and writer and a great traveller. Badaonī says that his Diwāns alone consisted of eight to nine thousand couplets. Shaikh Jamāl's real name was Shaikh Fazlulla *alias* Jamāl Khan.[92] He was the author of a number of works of which *Siyār-ul-'Ārifin, Masnavī Mehr O Māh* and the *Diwān* are well known.[93] The *Siyār-ul-'Ārifin* is a biography of saints commencing from Khwājā Mu'inuddin Ajmeri and finishing with the author's own spiritual guide, Shaikh Shamsuddīn. Jamāl's poetry vibrates with exalted passion.[94] Sikandar Lodī, himself a good poet, used to submit his verses to Shaikh Jamāl for his opinion.[95] Eleven lines of his composition in praise of the saint are still preserved in the *Makhzan-i-Afghānī*.[96]

The list of the authors and works given above is obviously not complete or exhaustive. But it is indicative of the type of literature produced in the Persian language in the fifteenth century. The works of translation as well as the original ones cover a long range of subjects—medicine, philosophy, theology, lexicography, biography and poetry. Examples of lyrical poetry quoted here exhibit extreme delicacy of feeling and expression; passioante love and deep disappointment; the depth of mysticism and sūfism. Similar works of mystic poetry were produced in other languages also (but of that a little later).

However, the Persian literature of the day was deficient in one major sphere—historical literature. Ever since the foundation of Turkish rule in Hindustan, many works of historical merit were produced, so that from the *Tājul Ma'āsir* of Hasan, Nizāmī to the systematic treatise of Shams Sirāj 'Afif a continuous history of two centuries is available to us. In fact there are various contemporaneous accounts for the reigns of the Khaljīs and the Tughlaqs. But in the fifteenth century there is only one contemporary work, Yahyā bin Sarhindī's *Tārīkh-i-Mubārak Shāhī,* dealing with the first thirty-four years of the Saiyyad rule. Although a single contemporary work covering a long period of about thirty-four years is hardly enough for giving a correct picture of the times, yet at least it is there. For the next three generations, in fact till the coming of Bābur, very little seems to have been written, and the period under review is sadly lacking in historical literature.

Arabic Works

Most of the Arabic works of the period were confined to commentaries on the Quran and Hadis. Saiyyad Muhammad, better known as *Gīsū-darāz* (1321-1422), was a very popular Sūfī saint of his times and wrote the *Ar-Risalātu fi Masā'ili Ruyati ul-Bāri Ta' alā*. The Shafi'ite savant, 'Alī bin Ahmad Mahā'imī (d. 1431), of Arab extraction, wrote a commentary on the Quran and another on Fiqh entitled *Fiqh-I-Makhdūmī*. He also wrote several works on various Sūfī themes. Sa'aduddin Khairābādī (d. 1477) also wrote on Fiqh and Tasawwuf. *Qāzī* Shihābuddīn, entitled Malikul 'Ulema (d. 1445)[97] lived at Jaunpur in Ibrāhīm Sharqī's reign and wrote many books on Islam. Another scholar of Jaunpur of the same period was Shaikh Ilah Diya Jaunpurī, the author of many excellent works like *Hedaya-i-Fiqh*, a commentary on Kāfiya, and notes on the *Tasfsir-i-Madārik*.[98] Similarly Badruddin Muhammad, who was born in Egypt in 1424, but migrated to Gujarat in 1517, also wrote a number of treatises on the Islamic religion. In the words of M. Ishaque, "..... the authors who made any contribution to Arabic literature in India were Arabs or Persians or persons of Arab and Persian lineage ..... Generally speaking, the works produced in India are on religious subjects, *taswwuf* and grammar. They mostly comprise commentaries on the Quran, Hadis, Fiqh and grammar."[99]

Sanskrit Literature

There was great literatry activity in Sanskrit throughout the country. Of the Sanskrit writers on religion and philosophy in the fifteenth century the most famous are Rudradhara, Misāru Misra and Vāchaspati Misra of Bihar. Indeed, from the thirteenth century to the fifteenth, Smriti literature "flourished in Mithila so luxuriantly that the writers came to be regarded as forming a separate school".[100] Rudradhara wrote several works on Dharmashāstras including *Shuddhiviveka* and *Srāddhaviveka*. The former deals with purification in all its aspects; while the latter with the Srāddhas. Rudradhara belonged to the early years of the fifteenth century. To the middle of the century belonged Misāru Misra, the celebrated author of *Vivādchandra*, dealing with laws and procedure, and *Padārtha-chandrikā*, dealing with the Nyāya Visēshaka system. But the doyen of the Mithila writers was Vāchaspati Misra, who was adviser in Dharmashāstra of Mahārājā-dhirāja Harināarāyana and his son

Rūpnārāyana. He was a prolific writer having to his credit more than a dozen works. His *Vivādchintāmani* holds a prominent position in Hindu law. He belongs to the latter part of the fifteenth and earlier part of the sixteenth century.[101] About the same time (i.e. early sixteenth century, c. 1510) Dalpat Rai, a Brahman officer in the army of Ahmad Shāh I of Gujarat, wrote an encyclopaedic work on *Dharmashāstra.*[102] To this same period belongs Raghunadan Misra of Bengal, a renowned commentator on the Smiriti. Under the patronage of Madan Singh, who ruled (1425-50) over Gorakhpur and Champāran, was written the *Madanpradip* dealing with the various Sanskāras; Visheshwar Bhatta wrote the *Madanpārijata,* dealing with Sanskāras, under king Madanpāla, who ruled at "Kashtha on the Yamuna". Vallabhachārya in his *Anubhāshya* on the Brahmasūtras propounded the Suddhavaita system or pure monism.

In Vijayānagar, literary activity in Sanskrit was more manifest. It was because the south was not long under direct Muslim influence. Sāyana, the famous commentator on the Vedas, served as Minister under Hari Hara II, and his brother Mādhava under Bukka. Krishna Dēva Raya was a great patron of Sanskrit and Telugu literature. "The numerous inscriptions show that a knowledge of Sanskrit was widely diffused and court-poets and writers were pastmasters in drafting official documents."[103] The Jains also produced a great deal of religious and secular literature. A great Jain writer of the middle of the fifteenth century was Sakalakīritti.

Drama and poetry form the soul of Sanskrit literature, and a large number of *Kavyās* and dramas were written during the period of our study. To the early part of the fifteenth century belongs the *Pārvati-Parinya* of Vāman Bhatta Bāna. Gangādhara wrote the *Gangādās-Pratāp-Vilāsa* which deals with the struggle of the Champanir prince, Gangadāsa Pratapdēva, against Muhammad II of Gujarat (A.D. 1443-52). In Bengal, Rūpa Goswāmī, Minister of Sultan Hussain Shāh, composed the *Vidagdha Mādhava* and the *Lalitā Mādhava* about A.D. 1532.[104] The Dramas of Rūpa Goswāmi reveal poetical powers of a high order.

Ramchandra, son of Lakshman Bhatta, composed in 1524, *Rasik-ranjana* at Ayodhya which combines the erotic and ascetic sentiments. Vidyāranya of Vijāyanagar wrote the *Shankaravijāya,* supposed to contain a biography of the great Shankarachārya. Two other court poets of Vijāyanagar were Diwākar and Madhava. To this period also belongs the Gujarat historical *Kavya Gurugunā Ratnākar,* written by Somnath in 1485.

Many works were also produced on the science of grammar, lexicography and poetics. Ramchandra (A.D. 1400) wrote his *Prakriyā-kaumudi* in which he has rearranged the material of Pānini. At Ahmadabad, in 1458, was written *Nyāyāratha-manjūsha,* a commentary of Hēmchandra's grammar. Punjarāja, a minister of Ghayāsuddīn of Malwa (1469-1500) wrote the *Sisuprabodh* on Alankāra. In Bengal some of the best commentaries on Pānini were written by Nandan Misra, Pundarīk Vidyāsāgar and Srīman Misra. Lexicographers like Brahspati Rāyamukta, the famous commentator on the Amarkosh flourished during the fourteenth century and Appāraya in the fifteenth. Gangānanda, a court poet of Mahārājā Karna of Bikaner (1506-27) wrote the *Kāvyadakini* which deals with poetical blemishes (*doshas*). He also wrote *Karnābhūshana,* a treatise on poetical *rasas.* Works on music were a special feature of this period, and these were written both in the north and the south. *Matanga Bhārata* was written by Lakshmana Bhāskar in the fourteenth century. Vidyāranaya of Vijāyanagar wrote *Sangitsāra* on music. Similarly there were works written on medicine, astronomy, astrology and polity.

According to A.B. Keith production of Sanskrit literature had sufffered in quality under Turkish rule. The later additions to *Rājtaranganī* by Jonrāja, Srīvara and Prīya Bhatta were not so meritorious as the work of Kalhana himself.[105] Keith is also of the opinion that in the process of Turkish conquest Sanskrit drama "took refuge in those parts of India where Muslim power was the slowest to extend".[106] True, the creative period had long been a matter of the past; the "immense" quantity of production in every branch in general lacks originality. And yet the fifteenth century was not a period of stagnation. On the other hand the works of Vāchaspati Misra, Mādhavacharya and Vallabhachārya as well as those on music and grammar do credit to the period of our study.[107]

Development of Regional Languages

Besides the work produced in classical languages, the fifteenth century in particular saw the development of Hindi and many other regional languages. Many causes contributed towards this development.

Because of the new political set-up, stressees of the times, and lack of patronage from the kings, Sanskrit lost its old position. A common medium of expression was the natural outcome of the contact between the foreigners and Indians. Thus developed Hindustani, a great poet of which was Amīr Khusru. His Hindustani or Hindvī later bifurcated into two channels of Hindi and Urdu. This was the position in Madhya Desa. In the various kingdoms into which the country had been divided consequent upon the invasion of Timūr, regional languages like Maithili, Bengali, Marathi and Gujarati developed rapidly under the patronage of their kigns, and these were enriched by the writings of philosophers and poets. Because of all these factors the fifteenth century beame an age of development of regional languages and their literatures.

The beginnings of all literatures are to be found in poetry, for man feels first and reasons afterwards. The first poet of Hindustani was Amīr Khusru, Tūtī-i-Hind or Parognet of India.[108] Khusru was the first to employ Persian metres in Hindi, a language he loved and praised[109] and in which he wrote many couplets. By the fifteenth century Hindi had got a definite shape as is evident from the works of Kabīr, Raidās and many other saints of the fifteenth century, whose contribution to the development of languages will be studied later on. Suffice it here to say that these saints travelled extensively. They preached in Hindi and most probably conversed with the people in the same language wherever they went. Thus Hindi or Hindustani seems to have been understood all over northern India and had attained the position of a national language. However, it had its variations in various regions of the country. Rajasthani developed in Rajasthan, western Hindi (both Brajbhāsa and Kharī bolī) in western U.P., Avadhī in eastern U.P. and Bihari in Bihar. Kharī boā did not become popular till the eithteenth century,. but during the fifteenth century many books in Avadhī were written. Qutban, a disciple of Shaikh Burhān of the Chishtia order and a protege of the Sultan of Jaunpur composed, in 1501, his *Mrigāvatī*. It is a Rajput romance with little allegorical elements; but Manjhan's *Madhu-mālatī* (composed in the early years of the 16th century) has great imagery and deep allegory.

The development of Urdu was very gradual and imperceptible. Hindi and Urdu are of the same parentage and in their nature they are not different from each other. Urdu, under the patronage of Muslim kings, sought inspiration from Persian while Hindi continued to draw from its original fount Sanskrit.[110] Khwājā Bandā Nawāz Gīsū-Darāz (1321-1422), who lived in the Deccan, was the first writer of deccan Hindi. His inspiriing prose work, the *Mirātul 'Āshiqīn,* is replete with Arabic words, and is looked upon as the earliest work in the Urdu form of Hindi. Persian words are found interspersed in the writings of Kabīr and Jaisī also, and the foundations of Urdu were laid during our period of study.

As in the Madhya Desa, so also in Bengal, Sanskrit ceased to be a living language after its conquest by the Turks. In the absence of the printing press and with very few hand-written works existing, it became the exclusive care of the pandits. It lost touch with life and reality and "ploughed a lonely furrow in the barren fields of hyper-subtle scholasticism".[111] Muslim Sultans and nobles were interested in encouraging art and literature, and got Sanskrit books translated into Bengali. The first Bengali translation of the *Mahābhārata* was undertaken at the command of Sultan Nāsir Shāh in the fourteenth century. But the father of Bengali poetry was Krittivāsa Ojhā who translated the *Ramayana* in the fifteenth century (c. 1418)[112] Maladhar Vasu translated the *Bhāgwat Purāna* in 1473-1480 at the command of Sultan Rukanuddīn Bārbak Shāh, from whom he received the title of Gunarāj Khan.[113] Sultan Husain Shāh of Gaur (1493-1519) patronised Vipradās Piplai and Vijaya Gupta, the author of *Mansā Mangal.*[114] At the command of Pārangal Khan, a general of Husain Shāh, Kavindra Paramēsvara translated a larger portion of the *Mahābhārata.* From the early fifteenth century the tradition of reciting in Bengali the *Ramayana* and *Mahābhārata* stories and the stories relating to Krishna gained currency.[115]

Muslim sovereigns of Bengal rendered great service to Bengali language and literature by granting recognition to Bengali in their courts. Following their example, the Hindu Rajas of Bengal also began to patronise the language of the people. But still greater service to the cause of the language was done by the Vaishnava philosophers and Bhakti poets of Bihar and Bengal. In the twelfth century Jayadeva had written "his masterpiece"[116], the *Gīta Govind,* This lyrical epic was full of the passionate but divine love of Rādha and Krishna. Chandī Das (A.D. 1417-78) and Vidyāpati (A.D. 1433-81) wrote equally beautiful lyrical poetry in Bengali and Maithili. Besides devotional songs, Vidyāpati wrote historical poems also. His historical poem *Kirtilatā* describes an episode in the life of his patron Hindu Raja. Incidentally it gives a very vivid picture of the life of Jaunpur city of his day, Chaitanya also himself contributed much to Bengali lyrical poetry.[117] In the opinion of D.C. Sen, the author of the monumental work entitled the *History of the Bengali Language and Literature*, Bengali was raised to the status of a literary language by the Vaishnava hymn writers just as Pali was by the Buddhists.[118]

In Maharashtra also the Bhakti poets from Namdēva onwards enriched the regional Marathi language. The Abhangs of the Maratha bhakts have a soul-stirring appeal and are sung even to this day in the villages and towns of Maharashtra. So also is the case with the religious songs of Narsi Mehta (1415-81) and his followers in Gujarat. In the Punjab, Guru Nānak gave a new religion and also a new script—Gurmukhī (meaning from the Guru's lips)—to the people. His compositions like *Āsa-di-war, Japjī, Dākhni Onkār, and Sidh Gosht,*, though devoid of any pretensions to literary perfection, are works of excellent merit. Equally important is the emergence of the Apabhramsa literature of the Jains of this period. Up to the the eleventh century the Jains stuck to Sanskrit, but afterwards their philosophical and poetical works came to be written in the language of the people. In the *Apabhramsa,* rhyme, which is regarded as a speciality of modern Indian languages, is profusely used; and it gave shape to the Kanarese and Tamil languages in the south.

General Remarks

In conclusion it may be noted that in the cultural sphere the fifteenth century was a period of great activity. It contributed much to art and literature. Imperial as well as provincial architecture provided motifs to Mughal architecture. Dance and music flourished as never before. They received the patronge of kings and the people; besides many works on music were produced during this period. Similar was the case with regard to the other fields of art, science and literature in which many works of merit were produced both in Persian and Sanskrit. Hindi took a definite shape; the Sant Kavyās and Vaishnava hymns are a special feature of this period. Almost all regional languages developed and flourished. In the political field, the first half of the fifteenth century was a period of decay; the second half of upheavals; but in the cultural field it was an age of sustained progress. There was a continuous progress of synthesis in spie of all conflicts—politial, social and intellectual. In fact these conflicts provided an urge for synthesis and counteracted the reactionary tendencies which have been sometimes emphasised by the careless exaggerations of historians.

—*K.S. Lal.*

References

1. Percy Brown, *Indian Architecture* (Islamic Period), Additional Plates, P.C. III, fig. I.
2. Arch. Sur, Ind. Rep., IV, 65.
3. Sir John Marshall, C.H.I. III, 594.
4. Arch. Sur, Rep., XX, 158; Carr Stephen, *Archaeology and Monumental Remains of Delhi, 161-2; Chronicles, 336;* Āsār, Chapter III, 42; J.A.S.B., XXXIX, 82; List, III, 32-33.
5. In Arch, Sur. Rep., IV, 184-85, A.L. Carlleyle located Sikandar's tomb at Agra near Sikandara. But Sir Saiyyad Ahmad Khan identifies it with the fine building in a walled enclosure at Khairpur, old Delhi. Āsār, I. 89.

   Niāmatullah's positive statement about Sikandar Lodi being buried in a garden by the side of his father's tomb sets at rest the doubts about the location of the tomb. *Makhzan,* 65(a).
6. Percy Brown, 27-28; Marshall, *op. cit,* 596.
7. Arch Sur. Ind. Report, IV, 69; Carr Stephen, 170-71; Āsār., Chapter, III, 46; Hearn, *Seven Cities of Delhi,* 130; Rodgers, 89-90; J.A.S.B. XXIX, 1870, 84; Cole, *Reports of the Curator of Ancient Monuments in India.* 3 Reports, Second Report, 1882-83, Government Press, Calcutta, C. XI; List, III, 38-41.
8. Marshall, 595 n.
9. Percy Brown, 28.
10. Arch. Sur. Ind. Rep., IV, 67 ff; XX, 155-57; Fergusson, II, 210.
11. K.S. Lal, *History of the Khaljis,* 377-79.
12. Carr Stephen, 196-97; Asar, III, 52; J.A.S.B., XXIX, 1870, 70-88.
13. Percy Brown, 29.
14. Arch. Sur. Rep., XX, 158; List., III, 36-37.
15. There is one of Mubārak Shāh at Badaon, of no great architectural significance. Arch Sur. Rep. XVI, 26; J.A.S.B., 1872, 111-12, Epi. Indo-Moslemica, III, 1909-10.

16. T.A., I, 336; *Makhzan*, 76(a).

17. Percy Brown, 29.

18. There is a story behind the construction of this mosque. Once the Emperor gave a grain of *moth* to his Prime Minister Miān Bhuā. The latter, thinking the grain to be suspicious, it having touched the royal palm, sowed in into the ground and obtained a few more grains. The process was repeated and crop obtained. The crop was sowed as seed and a huge harvest was collected. In course of time, from the income of that one *moth*, the mosque was built up. This is how it came to be known as Moth Ki Masjid. *Khulāsat-ut-Tawārīkh*, 278.

19. Arch. Sur. Rep., IV, 67, 90. *Archaeology*, 1902-3, 77; Carr Stephen, 166-67; Āsār., Chapter, III, 44; Rodgers, 89.

20. Sir John Marshall in C.H.I., III, 596.

21. Percy Brown, 29-30.

22. Percy Brown, 30. Cf. Also Sir John Marshall, *op. cit.*, 596-97.

23. P.A.S.B., 1872, 48.

24. Arch. Sur. Rep., XX, 131.

25. Arch. Sur. Rep., XVII, 105.

    Ibid., XXIII, 115; P.A.S.B., 1873. 141. Epi Indica, II, 1894, 137. Rodgers, *Revised List of Objects of Archaeological Interest in the Punjab*, 50, 151.

26. List, II, Delhi Province, Monuments Nos. 101, 104, 107 and many ohers.

27. Epi. Ind., 1919-20, 4; Carr. Stephen, 59-60. Āsār, III, 18. Asiatic Researches, XIV, 487. J.A. Page, *A Guide to the Qutb*, Delhi, 21.

28. Fuhrer and Smith, *Sharqi Architecture of Jaunpur*, Arch. Sur. of India, 1889, plates, 29-40.

29. Fergusson, II, 227.

30. Marshall, *op. cit.*, 627.

31. *Ibid.*, 628.

32. Cunningham, Arch: Sur. Rep., I, 287; Fergusong, II, 227-8.

33. B.N. (B), II, 608-9. Bābur visited it on 27 September, 1528.

34. Fergusson, II, 176.

35. Fergusson, II, 247.

36. *Ibid.*, 248.

37. Fergusson, II, 250.

38. J.B.B.R.A.S., 1903, 339-40 gives a detailed study of the buildings of Dhar and Mandu.

39. Fergusson, II, 229.

40. For Tank or Tak clan see Elliot, *Races of the N.W. Province*, Beames's Edition, I, 109, 114; Cunningham, Arch. Sur. Rep., II, 8; Tod, *Rajasthan*, Madras edition, I, 103 ff.

41. Havell, *Aryan Rule in India*, 341.

42. Percy Brown, 51.

43. *Ibid.*, 52 and plate XXXV, Fig. I.

44. Burgess, *Muhammedan Architecture of Ahmadabad*, 41, ff. and plates 46-51; Arch. Sur. of Western India, VII, 1901. Fergusson, II, 236-7 and plate 394; P. Brown, 58, and plate XLI. Fig. I.

45. Ferishta, II, 302.

46. Longhurst, *Hampi Ruins*, Memoir of the Archaeological Survey of India, 124-32.

47. Fergusson, I, 401.

48. Fergusson, II, 172.

49. Rousselet, *L'Inde des Rajahs*, 232-33, cited in Fergusson, II, 172 and Tara Chand, 246.

50. Fergusson, II, 176. Also B.N. (B), II, 608-14.

51. C.H.I., III, 593.

52. Islamic Culture, XXIV, 1950, 218-225.

53. I.B., 58-59.

54. The Hindu system of notation is perhaps the oldest; it was carried to Europe in the eleventh century A.D. G.S. Ojha, *Madhya Kalin Bharatiya Sanskriti*, 193-4.

55. T.F.S. (B). 128-29, 188, 199-200; Ferishta, I, 84; Aiyangar, *South India and Her Muhammedan Invaders*, 113-16.

56. *A'ijās-i-Khusravi*, Bk. II, 180.

57. Badaonī, I, 249.

58. Abdul Ghanī, *op. cit., I, 31.*

59. His great-grandfather Dungar Singh, who maintained friendly relations with rulers of other counries, sent a valuable work on music to Sultan Zainul Ābidīn of Kashmir. Mohibbul Hasan, *op. cit.*, 73.

60. V.N. Bhatkhande, *A Short Historical Survey of the Music of Upper India*, 18.

61. Islamic Culture, XXIX, 1955, 20.

62. Blochmann, Āīn, I, 681; Harihar Nivas Dwivedi, *Mān Singh aur Mān-Kutuhal* (Hindi) 41, 43.

63. T.M.S. 211.

64. T.D., 40.

65. *Ibid.*, 41. گشتن یک پهر از شب; E.D., IV, 449.

66. T.S.A., 48.

67. T.D., 41. In Persian music there are, according to the *Ghayāsul Lughāt,* twelve Maqāms (or modes) of which Husainī is the tenth.

68. T.S.A., 48

69. Islamic Culture, XXVIII, 1954, 411.

70. By Sārang Deva, a contemporary of 'Alāuddin Khalji (1296-1316).

71. Islamic Culture, 1954, 414. A MS of the *Lahjāt-i-Sikandar Shāhi* is in the Lucknow University Library. Another is in the Madras University Library.

72. T.A., I, 336.

73. He died in 1503 and lies buried at Delhi. T.D., 60-63; List, III, 158; *Akhbārul Akhyār,* 195-6.

74. He died in 1541 and was buried at Shaikh Sarāi, Delhi, List, III, 142; *Akhbārul Akhyār,* 330-31.

75. Islamic Culture, XXX, 1956, 110.

74. Badaonī, Ranking, I. 427.

77. Yūsuf Husain, *Glimpses of Medieval Indian Culture, 74.*

78. T.A., I, 336; T.D., 44.

79. Yūsuf Hussain, *op. cit.,* 69.

80. Badaonī, Ranking, I, 426; Islamic Culture, XIII, 1939, 408-14.

81. A *matla'* (opening couplet) of his is full of feeling:
Had not thy glance been the dagger, my heart had not bled to-day;
Had not thy look been the serpent I never had lost my way.
(Cited in Badaonī, Ranking, I, 426).

82. N.B. Roy, *op. cit.,* xxii; *Akhbārul Akhyār,* 174.

83. Keith, *History of Sanskrit Literature,* 174.

84. W.M., 32 (a)

85. The dots indicate portions which have been eaten away by worms in the MS. of the *Madanush-Shifāi Sikandari,* 3(a).

86. B.M. Catalogue, II, 471.

87. T.D., 44.

88. W.M., 32(a), T.D. 44. The work has been published by the Newal Kishore Press, Lucknow.

89. A Berriedale Keith, *A History of Sanskrit Literature*, 361.

90. British Museum Catalogue, II, 493.

91. E. and D. VI, 487.

92. *Akhbārul Akhyār*, 227-29. His tomb is in Mehraulī. Āsār., 47; Carr Stephen, 173; Arch. Sur. Rep., IV, 67, 90.

93. T.S.A., 47 and n.1.

94. Cf. "I wear a garment women of the dust of thy street
And that too rent to the skirt with my tears."
Also
"My heart's desire is fixed on thy abode
Oh thou that art long absent from my sight;
By day and night the thought of thee alone
My constant partner is......"
(Cited in Badaonī, Ranking, I, 429-30)

95. Badaoī, Ranking, I, 429; Dorn, I, 89.

96. Some of the lines express the Sultan's deep regard for the saint-poet
"Oh Jamālī, the store-house of eternal wealth,
The wayfarer of the path of faith.
You went round the world,
....
You had been a jewel but now turned into a full treasury
....
I may lose the sight of my eyes by the glare of the sun,
But the moon of your face will not be remote from me."
(Cited in *Makhzan,* 71 (a-b)

97. Ferishta, II, 595; *Encyclopaedia of Islam*, I, 932.

98. Badaonī, Ranking, I, 428-29.

99. *The Delhi Sultanate*, 533.

100. Cited in Ishwari Prasad, *Medieval India,* 550.

101. The dates of these Mithila writers have been discussed by Mehendale and Pusalkar in *The Delhi Sultanate,* 478-79.

102. Proceedigns of the Indian History Congress, 1951, Jaipur. 142.

103. Ishwari Prasad, *Medieval India*, 552.

104. Keith, *Sanskrit Drama*, 250-51.

105. Keith, *History of Sanskrit Literature*. 174.
106. Keith, *Sanskrit Drama*, 242.
107. Mehendale and Pusalkar in *The Delhi Sultanate*, 490.
108. Ram Babu Saksena, *A History of Urdu Literature*, 10.
109. *Ashiqa*, E. and D. III. Appendix 556.
110. Saksena, *Urdu Literature*, 2.
111. J.C. Ghosh, *Bengali Literature*, 19.
112. Ghosh, *op. cit.*, 34-36.
113. *Ibid.*, 37.
114. *Ibid.*, 45-46.
115. S.K. Chatterjee in *The Delhi Sultanate*, 513.
116. D.C. Sen, *A History of Bengali Literature*, 194. Also Keith, Classical Sanskrit Literature, Heritage of India series, 121.
117. Ghosh, *op. cit.*, 39 n.
118. Sen, *op. cit.*, Introduction.

6

Organisation of Education

Primary Education (Maktabs): The aim of Islamic primary education was to teach the pupil knowledge of the alphabet and religious prayers. This was done in the Maktabs. The term 'Maktab' is derived from Arabic 'Kutub' (he wrote) and means a place where writing is taught. These Maktabs were attached to mosques. Usually when a mosque was built, the building of Maktab was also constructed along with the mosque. The Maktab was the chief place where primary education was imparted to children. Though some of the well-to-do people would engage a teacher for the education of their children at their own houses, yet majority of the children of a locality assembled in the Maktab and received regular education there. Besides Maktabs there were the Khanqahs or monasteries and *Dargāhs* or shrines where education was imparted to the children of Islam. Generally a Maulavi or a religious preceptor was appointed at these places by the builders of Khānqahs or *Dargahs*. The offerings made at these shrines by the devotees contributed towards the maintenance of the Maulavis apart from the regular help they received from the patrons of these shrines.

Admission: There was a special method of admission to the Maktabs. Just as in the Brahmanical system of education, the ceremony 'Vidyarambha' or Upanayana was observed, similarly education among Mohammedans used to commence with the formal observance of a ceremony known as *'Bismillah'*. "When a child is four years, four months, and four days old, the friends of the family assemble and the child is dressed in his best clothes, brought into the company and seated on a cushion in the presence of all. The alphabet, the form of letters used for computation, the introduction to the Quran, some verses of chapter LV. and the whole of chapter LXXXVII are placed before him, and he is taught to pronounce them in succession. If the child is self-willed, and refuses to read, he is made to pronounce the *Bismillah*, which answers every purpose, and from that his education is deemed to have commenced."

Curriculum: A reference is available about the education of the princes that "Whilst the princes remain in the harem, under the eye of their father, a eunuch is charged with their education. They are taught to read and sometimes to write in Arabic and in Persian. Their bodies are formed to military excercises, and they are instructed in the principles of equity. They are taught to decide rationally upon the subjects of dispute which occur, or on suppositions suits at law. Finally they are instructed in the Mohammedan religion, and in the interests of nation, which they may be called one day to govern"[1].

The children of general masses also received education in Maktabs besides the princes. Some Hindu children too, learnt Persian in the Maktabs. In the beginning, the child was taught the script through the help of eye and ear. The knowledge of the script was followed by the study of the thirtieth chapter of the Quran which contained verses of daily prayer and *"Fatiha"* (verses recited at the time of burial ceremony). Much attention was paid to the correctness of pronunciation. Hence the children were taught the Pandenamah' of Sadi. The child was not required and expected to understand it. It was followed by teaching in the art of writing and the Persian grammar was caused to be crammed by the pupils. Afterwards the *Guliitan* and *Bostan* of Sadi were taught and explained to them which helped their knowledge of morals. Good writing was an essentiality and therefore, four to five hours a day were devoted to its exercise. Then the pupil was taught certain poetic works as *Yusuf* and *Zuleikha*, *Laila* and *Majnu*, and *Sikandernamah* etc. Besides these, elementary Arithmetic, mode of conversation, correspondence, drawing of petitions etc. were also included in the primary education.

As has been pointed out above, the script of the alphabet was Persian, yet Urdu too formed one of the chief subjects of study. Besides Quran, education in *Khalikbari*, *Karimah* and *Mamkimah* was also given. Thus the students got some practical knowledge having finished their primary education.

Higher Education (Madrasah): In the medieval period, higher Islamic education was imparted in the Madrasahs. The Madrasahas were those places where eminent scholars used to deliver lectures. A number of erudite teachers conducted their teaching work in different subjects through lectures. These teachers were usually appointed by the State and certain altruistic wealthy persons. The student, having finished his Maktab career, was eligible to the admission to Madrasahs. On this occasion no formal ceremony was obsered.

The administration of the Madrasahs was conducted by private managing body or respectable benefactors. The State used to sanction financial aid to these institutions but in view of the non-existence of any the State Education Department, their management was not in the hands of State. Generally land grants were given to the Maktabs and Madrasahs or some specific sum of money in the form of state grant was assigned to them. At certain places, Government provided for the lodging and boarding of the students in hostels. But these provisions were made by individual rulers being prompted by religious sentiments or sense of self-honour. Moreover, higher education was also encouraged by appointing students to high and honourable posts under the state.

Curriculum: Higher education in the Madrasah can be put under two categories: (i) Secular and (ii) Religious. The course covered a period of some ten to twelve years in all. Secular education included in its curriculum subjects as Arabic grammar, prose, literature, logic, philosophy, law, astrology, arithmetic, history, geography, medicine, agriculture and composition, etc. The medium of instruction was mainly Arabic, though Aurangzeb emphasised the use of mother tongue in place of Arabic as medium of education, because he felt that a child was incapable of acquiring proficiency in Persian or Arabic even after the education in them for twelve years. With regard to prayers, he thought that they could be done in mother tongue and thus learning could easily be simplified. The Religious education included a comprehensive and profound study of the Quran, commentary on Quran, traditions of the Prophet, Mohammad, Islamic law, and sometimes the tenets of *Sufi* creed. In the beginning, the Mohammedans had specially stressed secular education. They felt the dire necessity of multiplying their number in India, and to this end, they converted many Hindus into Muslims and initiated them into Islam. These converts needed religious education. Hence in course of time religious education dominated the scene. The curriculum of education was changed anew during the reign of Akbar. The Emperor adopted the policy of religious tolerance. He, therefore, anticipated some danger to the safety of his empire in providing only Islamic education to the Hindus. In addition to that, the prevalent system of education appeared to be quite unsuitable to practical life. He established Madrasahs for the Hindu children where they were taught Hindu religion, philosophy and literature along with Persian.

The Hindus had already begun the study of Persian with a view of availing themselves of the benefit of State service. The name of Raja Todarmal deserves special mention in this connection. But Emperor Akbar was not satisfied with the contemporary system of education. He, therefore, introduced improvement in the system and by broadening the sphere of curricula, made it much more suitable and beneficial to the practical needs of life. Abul Fazal has given the following account about contemporary educational system in *"Ain-i-Akbari"*: "Every boy ought to read books on morals, arithmetic, the notation, peculiar to arithmetic, agriculture, mensuration, geometry, astronomy, physiognomy, household matters, the rules of govt., medicine, logic, the *tabli, riyazī* and *ilahi* sciences, and history; all of which may be gradually acquired. In studying Sanskrit students ought to learn the Vayākarn, Niyai, Vedanta, and Patanjal. No one should be allowed to neglect these things which the present time requires".

Describing an incident about Aurangzeb, Bernier has written that after the enthronement of the Emperor Aurangzeb, his former teacher went to him with some aspirations. The Emperor refused to interview him; still the teacher persisted. Being weary with his presence, one day Aurangzeb called him to him and said: "Pray what is your pleasure with me, Mullah-gy (Mullah ji) Monseiur the Doctor? Do you pretend that I ought to exalt you to the first honours of the State? Let us then examine your title to any mark of distinction. . . . .. . You taught me that the whole of Franguistan (Europe) was no more than some inconsiderable island, of which the most powerful Monarch was formely the King of Portugal, then of Holland, and afterward the King of England.............Admirable geographer! deeply read historian! was it not incumbent upon my preceptor to make me acquainted with the distinguishing features of every nation of the earth; its resources and strength; its mode of warfare, its manners, religious, form of government, and wherein its interests principally consist; and, by a regular course of historical reading, to render me familiar with the origin of State, their progress and decline; the events, accidents, or errors, owing to which such great changes and mighty revolutions, have been affected? Far from having imparted to me a profound and comprehensive knowledge of the history of mankind, scarcely did I learn from you the names of my ancestors, the renowned founders of this empire. You kept me in total ignorance of their lives, of the events which preceded, and the extraordinary talents that enabled them to achieve, their extensive conquest. A familiarity with the languages of surrounding nations may be indispensable in a King, but you would teach me to read and write Arabic..........Forgetting how many important subjects ought to be embraced in the education of a Prince, you acted as if it were chiefly necessary that he should possess great skill in grammar...........and thus did you waste the precious hours of my youth in the dry, unprofitable, and never-ending task of learning words!..........If you had taught me that philosophy which adapts the mind to reason..........If you had inculcated lessons which elevate the soul and fortify it against the assaults of fortune...........If you had made me acquainted with the nature of man.........I should be more indebted to you than Alexander was to Aristotle.............Answer me, sycophant, ought you not to have instructed me on one point at least, so essential to be known by a King; namely, on the reciprocal duties between the sovereign and his subjects? Ought you not also to have foreseen that I might, at some future period, be compelled to contend with my brothers, sword in hand, for the crown, and for my very existence? Such, as you must well know, has been the fate of the children of almost every King of Hindoustan. Did you ever instruct me in the art of war, how to besiege a town, or draw up an army in battle array? Happy for me that I consulted wiser heads than thine on these subjects! Go! Withdraw to thy village. Henceforth let no person know either who thou art, or what is become of thee."[2]

Probably this description may be somewhat exaggerated. Nonetheless, it throws sufficient light on the curriculum and aims of education of that period. Though Aurangzeb was not as broadminded and of catholic views as Akbar in matters of education and religion, yet he was a capable and strong ruler despite his narrowmindedness. He examined the defects of educational system and realized the necessity of their being remedied. The above-quoted conversation of Aurangzeb indicates that he was fully conscious of the enormous waste of time involved in the learning of words and grammar. He had an aversion to hypocrisy and vanity in spite of being in favour of religious education. He had strong faith in such a system of education as might prepare the child for the practical aspects of life. He did not like the idea that the precious time of the children should be wasted in learning ancient and classical literature only. In reality, he was in favour of rendering higher education of more practical utility by including in the curriculum, the study of history, geography, philosophy, art of warfare, politics and diplomacy. Akbar, on his part, had also aimed at making education more useful and substantial. It appears that after Akbar the educational curriculum and system had deteriorated again. That is why we find Aurangzeb so very eagar to improve it. It should, however, be remembered that Aurangzeb's attention was more towards the education of Princes than to that of masses and consequently subjects of practical utility could not be included in the curriculum of general education. In modern times too, the educationists are trying their level best to achieve this end.

Thus we see that the subjects taught in the Madrasahs were various and of different kinds. These Madrasahs can well be compared to the colleges of modern times. Owing to the predominance of higher Arabic and Persian literature, grammar, prosody and poetry, special emphasis was laid in medieval Indian institutions too upon bookish and theoretical learning like contemporary European institutions. This learning was based upon a knowledge of pure literature, poetry, logic, philosophy and dry and rigid grammatical principles. Education was imparted simply for the sake of education and not for the sake of life. It was only a means of display of pedantry. The time of teachers and pupils was spent in jugglery of words over any philosophical issue or in appreciating different aspects of literature.

History has certainly remained the main feature of this age. There was comparatively nothing by way of true history in ancient India, but during medieval period, we generally find historians in the court of nearly every Mohammedan ruler. Some of the Emperors themselves have given an account of historical events in their own autobiographies.

The subject of Law was also taught in these Madrasahs. Not unlike the Buddhist and Brahmanical systems of education, the basis of Islamic education too was religion; and law during this period was based on religious works as the Quran and long-standing traditions and conventions. Medical science was based on Greek (Yūnānī) system. In this field, the Islamic education was of a lower standard and less developed than in ancient Indian system of education. Music, though it was not a popular subject, was nevertheless, taught generally. In metropolitan cities some institutions taught music alone. In royal courts, the musicians were highly honoured. Tānsen was unique jewel of the court of Akbar in the sphere of music. The Mohammedans generally followed the prevalent Indian system in the field of handicrafts and architecture, and receive special training in them. Still the stamp of other Muslim countries like Turky and Persia was unmistakable over these arts. The Turks were very fond of beautiful mansions. They, therefore, had sent for Muslim architects from Central Asia. Education in architecture and sculpture was imparted in India in traditional form only.

Method of Teaching:The method of teaching in the Maktabs was very simple. At the time when the child could speak articulately, '*Qalamā*' was caused to be crammed by it. Afterwards, the child learnt some verses from the Quran by rote. When it attained the age of nearly seven years, religious education was started with the study of the holy Quran. The child was taught reading and writing and simple arithmetic. The surviving Maktabs are still following the same method of teaching.

The vogue of cramming and memorising was prevalent in this period also. The method of education in Maktabs was mainly oral. The Emperor Akbar realized that much of the precious time was merely wasted in learning useless words. Hence he introduced improvement in the method of teaching. It is writen in *Ain-i-Akbari*— "In every country, but especially in Hindustan, boys are kept for years at school where they learn the consonants and vowels. A great portion of the life of the students is wasted by making them read many books. His Majesty orders that every school boy should first learn to write the letters of the alphabet, and also learn to trace forms."

"He ought to learn the shape and name of each letter which may be done in two days, when the boy should proceed to write the joined letters. They may be practised for a week, after which the boy should learn some prose and poetry by heart, and then commit to memory some verses to the praise of God, or moral sentences, each written separately. Care is to be taken that he learns to understand everything hiself, but the teacher may assist him a little. He then ought for some time to be daily practised in writing a hemistich; the verse; the former lesson. If this method of teaching be adopted, a boy will learn in a month, or even in a day what it took others years to understand, so much so that people will get quite astonished"[4]

Thus we find that Akbar introduced a scientific method of teaching. This method could not remain in force for long and died out gradually; as we hear Aurangzeb also complaining of the wasting of time in learning the alphabet of Arabic and Persian and a "long and continuous task of learning words".

As has been indicated above, higher education was conducted in Madrasahs. There too the method of teacing was, in the main, oral. The teachers adopted lecture method as is implied in the term "Madrasah" which is derived from Arabic *'dars'* i.e. a lecture, lesson. Along with this method, students were encouraged in developing the habit of consulting books. Practical and experimental education in *tibii, riyazi* and *ilahi,* was provided. *Tibii* included physical sciences; and *riyazi* included sciences which treat about quantity and comprise mathematics, astronomy, music and mechanics; while *ilahi* consisted of divine sciences comprising everything connected with theology and the means of acquiring knowledge of God.

Individual attention was paid to an all round development of students. Each student was given his own subject and lesson of study so that he might develop knowledge freely and individually. His progress was blocked by being placed with weaker students. Though only capale and eminent teachers undertook the duty of teaching, yet like Buddhist system of education, the 'Monitor-System' was prevailing, i.e., in the absence of a teacher, or in order to relieve the teacher for sometime of the burden of teaching work, able students of higher classes would, with the permission of the teacher, undertake the duty of teaching students of lower classes. Teaching of reading and writing was done separately i.e., other work could be taken up only after finishing the previous one. This resulted in an unnecessary waste of time owing to the slow progress of students implied in the process itself. Akbar, in order to remove this defect followed the ancient Indian tradition and prescribed the simultaneous process in reading and writing for the students.

Analytical and Inductive method was also adopted in the Madrasahs where higher education was provided in such subjects as religion, logic, philosophy and politics. Formal disputations upon important issues were the usual features of royal courts. The courts of Firoz Tugluq and Akbar were famous for such discussions.

Another method which was also in vogue during medieval period was self-study. Students would study in solitude with the occasional guidance of teachers. This method involved learning by rote.

Punishment: It is, however, a truism to say that during medieval period, under Islamic system of education, an attempt was made to understand the psychological working of the child's mind. Guilty students were given very severe corporal punishment. In the absence of any scheduled rules of punishment laid down by the state, teachers were free to exercise their individual discretion in matters of punishment. Discipline, moral conduct and humility were regarded as the essential attributes of students. Any student found guilty of a breach of them was publicily caned, whipped or beaten with fists. Possibly a peculiar mode of punishment i.e. causing the guilty child to stoop in a grotesque posture, like a cock had been the invention of this period. According to this mode of punishment the students were made "to hold their ears by taking their hands from under their thighs while sitting on the tiptoe."[5] For certain special faults, the child was hung from a peg with his hands and feet all tied up with a rope.

Rewards: It must be borne in mind that while guilty students were punished severely for breach of discipline or neglect of studies, on the other hand, rewards were given to able and intelligent students of unimpeachable character and thus they were encouraged. There was the convention of awarding *Sanads* or certificates and *tamghas* or medals to the students at the end of their academic career at some specific stage. Students would be awarded scholarships from royal courts and students of the Madrasahs were appointed on high and honourable posts in judicial courts, secretariat and army under the state at the end of their scholastic career. "The appointment was made by a board of examiners, who were the distinguished members of their class, best suited to ascertain the learning and suitability of a candidate, who, if declared successful, was formally invested by them with his new character by tying an *amamah* (turban) round his head." Some respectable wealthy nobles and citizens also encouraged students by awarding stipends to them.

References

1. Quoted by F.E. Keay: *Indian Education in Ancient and Later Times;* p. 130(1942).

2. Bernier: *Travels;* page 155.

3. H.I.E. 7.

4. Quoted by Nadvi in *Muslim Thought and its Source* p. 117.

5. Jaffar: *Education in Muslim Indir.* p. 26.

7

Education and Social Condition

The society and culture during the Mughal Age was not entirely new or radically different from the culture of the preceding or succeeding ages. The Indian culture in all ages has been fundamentally the same, and the differences we notice at different times are, generally speaking, those of detail and not of the essence. So, an attempt has been made to describe, under a few major heads, the various facets of the society and culture during the period under review.[1]

Dress

The dress of the poor people of various communities was very much alike. Workmen, tillers of the soil and other labourers contented themselves with a cotton *langota* tied round the waist and reaching down to their knees. Bābur refers to it in his memoirs.[2] During winter common people, except paupers, put on small quilted coats which lasted for years. In northern India even the poor put on turbans to protect their head from heat or cold. In the cold weather quilted caps were common in some parts of northern India, especially in Kāshmīr and the Punjab. The upper classes spent lavishly on their dress, and wealthy Muhammadans wore both *shālwārs* and breeches or tight trousers. Over their shirts they put on narrow waist-coats. The *qābā* or a long coat coming down to the knees was worn as an upper garment. The rich also carried over their shoulders shawls of very fine woollen fabric of various colours. It was the fashion to tie one's waist with a scarf of beautiful and costly multi-coloured stuffs. Men carried arms and adorned themselves with a *kātār* or a dagger. The Mughul rulers were very particular about new fashions and invented many new dresses. Akbar employed skilled tailors to improve the style of costumes in his wardrobe. The *Āīn-i-Akbarī* describes eleven types of coats.[3] Father Rudolf found Akbar clad in a *dhoti* of the finest and most delicate silk. Monserrate writes about the dress of Akbar: "His-Majesty wore clothes of silk beautifully embroidered in gold. His Majesty's cloak comes down to his hose and boots cover his ankles completely and (he) wears pearls and gold jewellery."[4] Turbans wore the common head-wear of all communities,[4a] those of the Muslims were usually white and round-shaped, while those of the Hindu were coloured, straight, high and pointed. Stockings were not used by any section of the people. The general style of the shoes was Turkish viz., pointed in front and open above with low heels to be easily undone when necessary. The men of taste had their shoes made of velvet of several colours or of brocade covered with silk leather, and sometimes set rubies and diamonds on the instep of their shoes. Ladies had not many varieties of dresses. The common apparel of the womenfolk was a piece of cloth called '*sạri*' wrapped round the middle part of the body and thrown over the head and an *āngiyā* or a small jacket worn round the chest. Breeches or *shālwārs* and shirts were common among Muhammadan ladies. *Ghāgrā* too was popular among them. The rich women put on *qābās* of the Kāshmir wool. Some of them also used Kāshmīr shawls of fine finest quality. Ladies, both Hindu and Muhammadan, covered their heads with a *dopāṭṭā* of fine cotton, or silk wrought with silver or gold threads, according to their means. Muhammadan ladies, whenever they moved out, put on white shrouds or *burqās*. There were of course, exceptions and local variations from the general types.

Toilets

Hair dyes, recipes for the cure of baldness and the removal of hair from the body were known from ancient times and practised in medieval age. Soaps, powders and creams had their substitutes in *ghasul,* myrobalans, *opatanah,* and pounded sandal wood. Soap was known and used in India from ancient times. Precious scents of diverse kinds were in use. The *Āīn-i-Akbarī* gives a long list of scents and their prices.[5] Nūr Jahān's mother prepared a new *itar* from roses and named it *itar-i-jahāngirī*, Abu-'l-Fazl, in the *Aīn-i-Akbarī*, describes 16 items for a woman's toilet which include bathing, anointing, braiding the hair, decking the crown of her head with jewels, sectarian marks of caste after decking with pearls, jewels and gold, tinting with lamp-black like collyrium, staining the hands, chewing betel leaf and decorating herself with various ornaments, as nose-rings, necklaces, and wearing a belt hung with small bells, garlands of flowers, etc. Hindu ladies usually tied their hair behind their heads. Sometimes they twisted up their hair upon the top of the head like a pyramid, sticking gold bodkin in the centre. The use of the false hair has also been referred to.[6] Hindu ladies considered it auspicious to put a vermillion mark and to anoint the parting of their hair. Collyrium was used for the eyes. It was usual for high class ladies to use *missia* for blackening between the teeth and antimony for darkening their eye lashes.[7] Indian women frequently used *mehidi* (henna leaves) to give red colour to their hands and feet. It served as a nail polish to redden their finger nails. They reddened their lips by chewing betel-leaf which served them as a lip-stick.

Ornaments[7a]

Women were anxious to adorn, one might say even load, themselves with a variety of bulky ornaments Ladies bedecked every limb of their bodies from head to foot with different types of ornaments. Abu-'l-Fazl enumerates 37 in his list in the *Āīn-i-Akbarī* *Chauk, Mang, Kotbiladar* (perhaps the modern *Chandraman*), *Sekra,* and *Binduli* adorned the head and the forehead. *Karnphul, Pipal Patti, Mor Bhanwar* and *Bali* were the different types of ear-rings. Nose-ornaments seemed to have been introduced by Muhammadans. *Nath* and *Besar* were their different types. *Laung* or a flower-bud—a small stud of single diamond or ruby fixed at the corner of the left nostril—enhanced the beauty of the face. Around the neck were worn necklaces of gold, pearls, and other precious stones which contained five to seven strings of gold beads. The upper part of the arms was ornamented with *bazubands,* and *tad. Gajrah* or *Kangan,* a bracelet, adorned their wrists. They decorated their wrists up to the elbow with bracelets called *Churis. Chhudr Ghanṭikā* and *Kaṭi Mekhalā* were the two varieties of gold belts. Rings were worn on toes and fingers. *Jehar* served as an ankle ornament. *Ghunghry* were worn between the *Payal* (ornaments of legs) and *Jehar* (ankle ornament). *Bhank* and *Bichwah* were the ornaments used for the instep while *Anwat* decorated big toe.

As for men, Muslims were usually against ornaments; some of them, however, put on amulets. Hindus, on the other hand, adorned themselves with ear and finger rings. Rajputs put on bracelets as well. All the Mughul Emperors except Aurangzīb adorned themselves with rich jewellery on important occasions.

Diet[8]

Khichari[9] was the most popular dish of the common people who could ill afford to spend on dainty dishes. Rice formed the chief food of the people of the East and South. The Gujarātis preferred rice and curd. Jahāngīr refers to the food of the Kāshmīris which usually consisted of boiled rice and boiled salted vegetabels,[10] chiefly a leafy plant called *karam*. The people of the North, however, generally took *chappatis* of wheat, *jowar* or *bajra*. The middle classes managed to have three meals a day. The poor, too, managed to have light refreshments in the form of some parched pulse or other grains between the three regular meals. The upper classes invariably used wheat flour, boiled rice and cooked vegetables of various sorts. Hindus in general being vegetarians, confined themselves to pulses, curd, butter, oil and milk and its several preparations. They prepared rice, aromatic birinjes and puddings of rice mixed with almonds and raisins. On his abstinence days, Jahāngīr would take *lazizah,* i.e., *Khichari,* prepared in the Gujarāti style.[11] Abu-'l-Fazl gives a detailed list of various vegetables ad meat and sweet dishes in the *Āīn-i-Akbarī*.[12]

Muhammadans prepared rice and aromatic birinjes as *qabuli, duzdbiryan, qimah palao,* and pudding of rice mixed with almonds and raisins and strewn with butter and pepper. Sweet dishes consisted of *halwa,* sweetmeats, and comfits prepared from refined sugar and *faluda*.[13] An idea of the variety of dishes served at a noble's dinner can be had from the description of Asaf Khān's banquet to Sir Thomas Roe[14] and that of the Governor of Ahmadābād to Mandelslo.[15] Mukundarāma's gorgeous description of feasts and vegetable dishes leaves us in little doubt as to their popularity among the upper class Hindus.[16]

Kitchens and Utensils

The utensils used in Hindu kitchens were all made of brass or bronze, while those of the Muhammadans were earthen ware or made of copper. The Mughul kings used gold or silver utensils and were fond of precious China and glassware. Aurangzib, however, used earthen or copper vessels. Hindus paid great attention to cleanliness and a special place called *chauka* invariably rubbed over with cow-dung was reserved for cooking meals, which none was allowed to enter with shoes on. Bathing was a pre-requisite before meals. Hindus would at the outset put apart a small portion of their food as an humble homage to the gods. Akbar used to put apart the share of the dervishes before he commenced his meal.[17]

The ordinary people used the leaves of the trees, stitched together with rushes, as plates. In the case of the Rājās and other rich men, food was brought from the kitchen in bowls or vessels of silver or gold. Table manners required not to use one's left hand or lick the fingers. Wives did not make it a custom to join their husbands at tables, but took meals separately. The kitchen and table manners of the Muhammadans were quite simple, though not always as clean as those of the Hindus. They were free to cook wherever and whenever they liked and eat everything except the flesh of swine. A *dastarkhwan* was spread on the floor and dishes arranged thereon. The whole family sat together and partook of the dishes jointly. No napkins were used and the procedure of washing was not always adhered to.

The manner of cooking in the royal kitchen and the process of sending in of plates and the measures adopted to check poisoning have been elaborately described in the *Āīn-i-Akbarī*.[18]

Intoxicants

Wine, opium, *bhang* and tobacco, were the most common intoxicants indulged in Mughul times. Betel, tea and coffee were also sometimes included in this class. The masses were generally opposed to intemperance which was looked upon as a vice and even a sin. The strict prohibition enforced by almost all the Mughul kings was no less a factor in discouraging the use of wine among the people. Severe punishments were inflicted for excessive drinking and disorderly conduct. The nobles, however, indulged in heavy drinking and many of them fell victims to alcohol. All the Mughul emperors excepting Aurangzīb took wine several times a day. Bābur and Jahāngīr were renowned drunkards. Humāyūn was more fond of opium. Aurangzīb totally abstained from wine while Akbar and Shāh Jahān would not pass the limits of decency.

Nira, Mahua, Kherra, Bhadwar, Jagre, and *toddy* were some of the well-known varieties of country wine. Some superior kinds of wines were also imported from foreign countries like Portugal and Persia. Opium was in use among a large-number of people especially Muhammadans and Rajputs. The latter would double the dose on the eve of a battle. Its stimulating effect animated them with extraordinary courage and bravery to fight more valiantly and heroically. Some of the Mughal emperors particularly Humāyūn and Jahāngīr were very fond of this intoxicant. Tobaco gained rapid popularity among common people soon after its introduction in India in 1605 by the Portuguese. Smoking became so habitual with one and all in the short interval of a decade or so that Jahāngīr had to order its prohibition by special enactment in 1617 on account of its harmful effect.[19] The decree, however, remained a dead letter and several travellers refer to its wide popularity. Manucci mentions Rs. 5,000 as tobacco duty for a day in Delhi alone.[20]

Betel was in most common use among all classes of people throughout India. It was necessarily chewed after meals but most of the people went on taking it throughout the day. Its choicest varieties were *Bilhari, Kakar, Jaiswar, Kapuri, Kapur Kant,* and *Bangalah. Makhi* leaves of Bihār and *Keroah* of Orissa were also much sought after.

Tea and coffee were not taken as beverages in those days but as intoxicants. These drinks were taken by quite a large number of people especially those of Coromandel Coast. There seems to have been coffee shops, if not coffee houses, in some of our cities like Delhi and Ahmadābād.[21]

Houses and Furniture[22]

Mughul palaces, or more appropriately palace-fortresses, were usually situated on the bank of a river or a stream. Some of these were built on rocky eminences "just turning into or overhanging lakes or artificial pieces of water." These palaces consisted of two parts—inner and outer. The inner part contained the quarters of the queens, the princesses, the private council hall, the retiring rooms, the luxurious *hammams,* etc. while the other part comprised *Dīwān-i-Ām, Dīwān-i-Khās*, the arsenal, the store house, etc. in their proper places. There were also pavilions for witnessing animal fights and for musical entertainments. Stables for horses, elephants, cows, etc. were also provided. Akbar's palaces at Āgra, Allahābād and Lahore may serve as good examples of Mughul conception of royal palaces.[23] Most of the Hindu palaces built during the 16th and 17th centuries, particularly in the capitals of the States in Rājputana, viz., Bikāner, Jodhpur,

Jaisalmer, Orchha, Datia, Udaipur and the city of Amber (Jaipur), are unsystematic in their compositions and are built more for convenience and comfort than for architectural considerations. In their planning and construction, as is natural, Mughul style predominates. As for example, the Jahāngīr Mandir at Orchha was so designed that every part fulfilled its function and expressed purpose; its rooms were devised for seclusion, its terraces for the cool air, its corridors for convenience; each compartment, court hall and passage, had its specific use and was introduced into the scheme in accord with the requirements of its inmates. The houses of the nobles were luxuriously built, preferably in the middle of a garden, and had spacious lawns, tanks, choultries, etc. The house had to be so constructed as to provide for the two wings known as the *mardana* and the *zenana*. A drawing room where the nobles received visitors, and held court, a *khwabagah,* or the bed-room, kitchen, lavatories, besides a courtyard were the necessary requisities. Climatic conditions also necessitated a terrace where the family could sleep during summer nights. The roofs of the buildings were kept flat for the purpose. A *'barsati'* or a room at the terrace was also provided. The European travellers praise the houses of the rich which, to quote Pelsaert,[24] "were noble and elegant, spacious and pleasant." The houses of the merchants at Surat were built of brick and lime and had several storeys; the houses in Kāshmīr were built of wood due to frequent earthquakes. Bernier saw at Āgra the mansions of nobles "interspersed with luxuriant and green foliage in the midst of which the lofty stone houses of the *banias* or Hindu merchants have their appearance of old castles buried in forests". There were lofty and spacious houses of the upper classes at Delhi, Lahore and Masulipatam. In Malabar these houses were built of teakwood and did not possess more than two storeys. The houses of the traders, merchants and the petty *umras* were modest in their appearance as compared to those of the nobles. They lacked elaborate carvings, embellishments, and beautiful gardens. Some of them were built of brick, burnt tiles and lime; others of clay and straw. In the villages the well-to-do *zamindārs* had several huts grouped together. These houses[24a] were airy and commodious. Some of them were two-storeyed and had beautiful terrace roofs. The main features of these buildings in the cities were the provision of eave or *chajja* above the cornice of each storey with its great width, its cast and shadow, which helped to keep the entire building cool during summer.

The houses of the poor were thatched huts without any cellars or windows. The addition of a second hut and a granary was considered as making a house a comfortable abode. These huts had only a single opening for air, light and entrance. The floors of the houses were of pounded earth spread over with cow-dung. In their huts they had only a mat to sleep upon and a pit or hole in the ground to keep their rice in. They had only a pot or two for cooking purposes.

The houses of the rich, especially the nobles, were, however, luxuriously furnished. Their *dīwān khānās* or drawing rooms were decorated with costly carpets from Kāshmīr, Lahore or even imported from Persia and Turkey. *Jajams* and *shatrinjis* and *baluchis* were sometimes spread over the mattresses. Big cylindrical cushions were a part of the furniture and no drawing room could be considered complete without them. Gujarāti and Banarasi curtains were particularly liked. The latter were embroidered with silk. Sind had a reputation for leather hangings. Bernier gives a very interesting account about the *dīwān khānās* of a noble.[25]

The Indian mode of sitting did not necessitate chairs which were rightly regarded as superfluous and uncomfortable. Fryer and Pelsaert's observations regarding the complete absence of chairs are, however, exaggerated. 'Abdur Razzāq, the Persian Ambasador to Vijayanagara in 1443 A.D., and Sir Thomas Roe refer to their use. The seats, sometimes cushioned, were always wider than those of today. The legs of the chairs were sometimes carved out and the feet were connected by means of wooden planks.[26] Stools were used in those days. Usually covered with leather or cloth, they could be interwoven with cane also. *Mundas* of reed and *pidis* or seats made a suitable wood are also referred to in contemporary literature. Tables were not in much use except by the merchants of the West Coast. *Khatta* or bedstead, the most common article of furniture in those days, was used by the rich and the poor alike. It was used by the poor as a couch to sit, and recline upon during day time and served the purpose of a cot at night. These bedsteads woven with cords or braids of cotton or silk according to the owner's means had their legs often painted or lacquered. The aristocracy were very particular about their bedsteads which were lavishly ornamented with gold, silver or even with jewels and diamonds.[27]

Fairs and Festivals[28]

Both the communities, Hindus and Muslims, had a large number of festivals which they celebrated with great enthusiasm during medieval times. There was general uniformity in their observance for the most part, throughout the country. But they enjoyed degrees of popularity and were celebrated with certain local variations. Decorations, illuminations, fire-works, splendid processions, abundant display of gold, silver, pearls, diamonds, and jewels, observed by Muslims in India in the celebrations of their festivals, were the natural consequence of their contact with the Hindu culture. The enlightened rulers like Akbar and Jahāngīr adopted some of the Hindu festivals and gave them a place in their court calendar. Humāyūn adopted *tulā dān* or the weighing ceremony of the Hindus Akbar went further and associated *Holi, Dasehra,* and *Vasant Panchami,* with court celebrations. Jahāngīr and, to a certain extent, Shāh Jahān continued the tradition. Aurangzib followed a reverse course. He banned most of the Hindu and Persian festivals in the court, making it Islāmic as far as he could in Hindu surroundings.

Holi, one of the ancient festivals of the Hindus, was the most popular day of rejoicing, music and feast, as it is today. Colour throwing was a lively part of the celebrations.[29]

Akbar observed the festival of *Rakshā Bandhan,* and had a *rākhī* tied on his wrist. It became the custom for the courtiers and others to adorn the emperor's wrist with beautiful strings of silk, bejewelled with rubies and pearls and gems of great value. Jahāngīr, who called it '*Nighadasht*', ordered: 'Hindu *amins* and the head of the caste should fasten *rakhis* on my arm."

On the occasion of the Dasehra festival royal elephants and horses were washed, groomed, and caparisoned to be arrayed for inspection by the Emperor. *Diwālī* or *Dīpāwalī* was observed in much the same manner, as it is today; fire-works were discharged and sweets and other presents were exchanged. Gambling was considered auspicious on this day and people kept awake the whole night trying one another's luck at dice. Akbar was interested in the festive aspect of the celebrations, while Jahāngīr preferred gambling. Sometimes the latter ordered his attendants to play the games in his presence for two or three nights. In the time of the later Mughuls, it appears, the permission of the Governor was necessary to hold the *Diwālī* fair for which a poll-tax was sometimes imposed.[30] Akbar also took part in the celebrations of *Govardhan Pūjā* and several cows, properly washed and ornamented, were brought before him for his review.[31] Both solar and lunar eclipses were observed with all sanctity by the Hindus who kept a fast for 24 hours before the actual eclipse and passed the day in prayers. A bath in the Ganges on this occasion was regarded as of special merit and large numbers resorted to Hardwar, Kashi and Prayag.

Śivarātri[32] or the festival of Lord Śiva was observed with all solemnity during Mughul times. Akbar participated in the meeting of the principal *jogis* of the Empire held that night and ate and drank with them. Jahāngīr also refers to this festival. *Rāmnavamī* and *Janmāshṭamī* were the two other important Hindu festivals referred to by Abu-'l-Fazl in the *Āin-i-Akbarī*.[33]

Muharram, Id-i-Milad, Shab-i-Barat, Id-ul-Fitr, and *Id-ul-Zuha,* are some of the important Muslims festivals which were observed with all solemnity during Mughul times. The Mughul Emperors, though Sunnī in belief, put no restrictions on the osbervance of Muharram. Aurangzīb however, stopped the practice of Muharram processions throughout his dominions. But though the tazia processions were never given up and Muharram assemblies, mourning and distribution of charity continued to be practised all over the country, sometimes Muharram celebrations were marred by riots between the Sunnīs and Shiahs in which numerous lives were lost.[34] On the occasion of the festivals of *Id-i-Milad* or the feast of Prophet's nativity, a meeting of the Sayyids, scholars and saints was arranged in the Palace at Āgra. Shāh Jahān took special interest in this festival and used to give away large sums in charity. Equally popular was the festival of *Shab-i-Barat* or the night of the Prophet's ascent to Heaven. The Muslims, during Mughul days, illuminated their houses and shops and displayed fire-works. Jahāngīr and Shāh Jahān were very particular about this festival and observed it regularly with great pomp and show. The palaces, government buildings, public gardens, reservoirs etc. were all illuminated on this occasion and the King would distribute money among the poor. The two Ids, *Id-ul-Fitr,* and the *Id-ul-Zuha,* were the two most important festivals of the Muslims. The *Id-ul-Fitr* which comes after the long drawn-out part of *Ramzan* was proclaimed by firing of guns and blowing of trumpets. Friends and relatives exchanged dainty dishes and visits and wished each other good luck. It was customary to call on elders and superiors to offer greetings. In the afternoon Muslims assembled in the *Idgah* to offer prayers. *Id-ul-Zuha* was observed with ceremonious display during Mughul times. Preparations were made both in the capital and in the provinces well in advance. The Emperor rode in procession and sometimes even took up his quarters at the *Idgah*. The sacrifice of a camel would be performed in his presence with due ceremonies. The people could afford it performed the same ceremony at their homes by solemnly killing a ram or a goat in memory of the ram offered for Ismā'īl. They also cooked stew, sweetmeats and griddle cakes and offered *fatiha* in the name of their deceased relatives.

Some of the other Muslim festivals referred to in the contemporary literature are *Bara Wafat, Akhiri Chahar Shamba,* etc.

There were a few festivals like the *Nauroz* (birthday celebrations of the ruling monarch), *Meena* or Fancy Bazar and the *Ab-i-Pashan* which assumed more or less national character. *Nauroz*[35] was easily the greatest national festival during Mughul times and its celebrations lasted for full 19 days. It was borrowed from the Persians and was observed on the first *Farwardis,* the first month of the Persian Year (20th or 21st of March). In India, it marked the advent of spring. Grand preparations for the festival were made months ahead at the imperial cities, bazars, and porticoes; the public and private audience halls were profusely decorated with costly stuffs such as satin, velvet, clothes of gold, etc. The common people whitewashed their entrances and decorated the doors of their houses with green branches. The people from neighbouring towns would flock to the capital and indulge in all sorts of merry-making. Restrictions on gambling were also relaxed and people were allowed free access to the presence of the King once a week. The King and the court celebrated this festival in a right royal manner. Special kinds of coins called '*nisars*' were struck by the Mughul Emperors from Jahāngīr onwards for distribution among the people or for offering tribute to the King on the occasion of certain festivities such as New Year's day, or the anniversary of their coronations. During these 19 days "wine flowed in rivulets, verse and ode flew in hundreds, gaiety and merriment ruled everything." Singers and musicians flocked to the court from all quarters particularly from Persia. *Nautch* girls with their wonderful and attractive performances thrilled the hearts of all those present. Several European travellers have given a picturesque description of the lavish display of wealth and magnificence on this occasion. Manrique, perhaps copying from somewhere or depending on hearsay, gives a detailed account of the decorations of the Imperial Palace at Āgra.[36] The nobles, too, adorned their palaces with jewels, pearls, diamonds, and their richest treasures and greatest rarities, so that, to quote Nizām-ud-dīn, the author of the *Tabqāt-i-Akbarī,* "the spectators on seeing them were filled with wonder and admiration." This main function usually took place in the *Dīwān-i-Ām* which was richly decorated with velvets, gold cloth, and European curtains and screens, and the royal tent was fixed there in the middle beautified with diamonds, pearls, rubies and fruits of gold. It was surrounded all round by the tents of the nobles. The nobles presented the King with rare and precious gifts on this occasion and the King bestowed on them *jāgīrs,* robes of honour, stipends and titles and promotion in rank.

Birthday of the ruling monarch provided another opportunity for rejoicings. Akbar introduced the custom of observing both his lunar and solar birthdays. The royal palaces and the courts were decorated on this occasion as on the occasion of *Nauroz,* and the elephants and horses, bedecked in rich trappings and glittering robes, were brought before the Emperor for review. The King paid a visit to his mother to receive her blessings. Presents were offered, feasts were given and bonfires lighted. Humāyūn was the first Mughul ruler to adopt the custom of weighing the emperor against certain precious metals and commodities on this occasion.[37] Akbar observed it twice a year both on his solar and lunar birthday anniversaries. The practice was continued by Jahāngīr and with slight alterations by Shāh Jahān. Aurangzīb, however, reverted to the old custom of having himself weighed only once a year and even this was dispensed with in his 51st year (March, 1670). But he allowed it in the case of his sons on their recovery from illness on the specific condition that the money and articles should be distributed among the poor.[38] The princes and their sons were also weighed on their solar anniversaries. The weighing commenced at the age of 2 years against one commodity, and one was added each year, till the number reached generally 7 or 8 but in no case was it to exceed 12. These commodities were later on distributed among the Brāhmans, *fakirs* and other deserving persons. After the ceremony, the King ascended the throne and received presents which, according to Thevenot, were valued at millions of rupees.[39] The king would announce increase in the *manṣabs* of some and bestwoed gifts and *jāgīrs*.

Humāyūn was the first Mughul Emperor to introduce what later came to be known as *Meena Bazar*. The first of this kind was held on boats near the King's palace after the customary mystic feast.[40] Akbar who continued the festival in a modified form exalted such days as *Khushroz* or joyful days. Shāh Jahān arranged such a *bazar* on the occasion of every festival. It invariably followed the *Nauroz* celebrations. The stalls in the specially constructed *bazar* were distributed among nobles to be arranged by their wives or daughters who acted as traders. If we are to believe Badāūnī, stalls in the *Meena Bazar* were sometimes conducted by nobles themselves.[41] The King with princesses and ladies of the royal household would pay visits to the *bazar* to make his bargain, frequently disputing the value of a *dām*. After the women's *bazar, a bazar* for men was held; there the merchants brought their merchandise from all parts of the world.

A festival similar to *Holi,* called *Ab-i-Pashan* by Jahāngīr and *Id-i-Gulabi* (rose water festival) by Lahori, the author of *Pādshānāma,* was celerbated at the Mughul court at the commencement of the rainy season. The princes and the prominent nobles took part in the festival and sprinkled rose water on each other.

Sports, Games and Pastimes[42]

Leaving aside twentieth century amusements like cinema-going, and outdoor games like hockey, cricket, football, tennis, etc. that have come to us through contact with the West, the pastimes in vogue during Mughul times were similar to those commonly found today. The difference, if any, lies in details only. Chess, *chaupar,* and playing cards were the most popular indoor games and were enjoyed by the rich and the poor alike. The various types of tiger play, games of *guṭis* and the games of sheep and goats were favourites with the rural population. Abu-'l-Fazl has given some details about these games in *Āin-i-Akbari*.[43] The Mughul pack of cards consisted of 12 suits of 12 cards each making a total of 144 with different kinds of kings and followers. The names of all the suits were in Sanskrit till the time of Akbar who renamed the last seven suits and reconstituted Dhanpati, the fifth. As distinguished from our present day cards, they were all in pictures; the highest represented the King, the second highest, a *vazīr* and the rest were followers from one to ten. The game was quite popular with the Mughul Emperors many of whom were expert players.

The game of chess[44] was equally popular with the kings, nobles and the commoners alike. Akbar is said to have played the game of living chess with slave girls as pieces moving on the chequered pavement of the *Pachisi* court at Fathepur Sīkrī. Sometimes international matches were held and bets offered. Khān-i-Khānān was deputed by Jahāngīr to combat Shāh Shafi of Persia.

The game of *chaupar* was quite popular among the people, but no ready-made tables for the game were available in those days. The Mughuls, it appears, were not familiar with the game as it existed in India till the time of Akbar who framed special rules and regulations.[45] It was a favouraite game of Zib-un-Nisā, the eldest daughter of Aurangzīb, who spent most of her spare time in playing *chaupar* with her girl friends. *Āīn* refers to another game called *Chandal Mahal* which was, in fact, a modified *chaupar*, designed to increase the number of players to 16 with 64 pieces divided equally among them. *Nard* or *backgammon* was introduced into India by the Muslims while *Pachisi* was an ancient Hindu game enjoyed frequently by Akbar. The boards of this game were marked out on a marble square in a quadrangle in the Āgra Fort and Fathepur Sīkrī. The games of *Guṭis*—*do guṭi, tre guṭi, nao guṭi*, and *bāra guṭi*—were popular with the rural as well as the urban population. *Mughul pathan, lam turki, bhag chal, bhag chakar, chhabis guṭi, bhag chal* and *bheri bakri* were its popular variations.[46]

Of the outdoor diversions, hunting, animal fights and *Chaugan* were the privilege of the few, while *Ishq-bazi*, wrestling, etc. were enjoyed by one and all. It is regrettable that no reference to *kabaddi* is traceable in contemporary records. But the game must have been played in the villages, as it is even today. Of all the Mughul Emperors Akbar liked *Chaugan* (Polo) most and even invented illuminated balls which made the playing of game on dark nights possible. The most famous of the *chaugan* playing fields were at Fathepur Sīkrī and Āgra. The game of hockey, too, is referred to in contemporary records.[47] Wrestling and boxing were a favourite pastime during the Mughul Age. In Vijayanagara even women took part in wrestling contests.[48] Akbar was very much fond of boxing and kept a large number of Persian and Turani boxers at the court. Horse-racing was a source of entertainment prevalent among the high class Mughul nobles. Martial sports like archery and swordsmanship had a special fascination for the people; matches and contests were held and rewards offered.

Hunting was one of the best means of amusement and recreation during the Mughul times and was indulged in by the king, nobles and the commoners. The costly and dangerous expeditions were the privilege of the few and the quarry consisted of elephants, lions, tigers, buffaloes and wild goats. Lion hunting was exclusively reserved for the king. Elephant hunting, too, could not be indulged in without the special permission of the king. Akbar invented a special kind of hunting called '*qamargha hunt*'[49] which became very popular with the Mughul kings, who took lively interest in the game. Shooting of birds was a common hobby and a source of entertainment for the rich and the poor.

Fishing was in vogue during the Mughul times both as a recreation and as a profession. The use of nets for catching fish was not totally unknown but professional fishermen did not have recourse to it. A special type of net called *safira* (or *bhanwar jal* in Hindi) was used.

Animal fight was one of the popular amusements and recreations of the age. The people had to content themselves with the less expensive fighting of goats, rams, cocks, stags, antelopes, dogs and bulls to entertain their friends. Young boys favoured fight among *bulbuls* and sometimes quails. The kings and the nobles amused themselves with costly and dangerous combats between elephants, tigers, deer, cheetas, boars, leopards, bulls and other wild beats. Cock-fighting was very common among the higher middle class. *Ishq-bazi* or pigeon flying was primarily a sport of common folk. Nobles, too, enjoyed it and brought excellent pigeons from foreign countries like Turan and Irān to be trained for the game.

Among other pastimes reference may be made to *mushairas*, magic shows, acrobatics and dramatic performances, *Ramlīlā* or theatrical representation of scenes from the *Rāmāyaṇa* were common during the Hindu festival of *Dasehra* and even Muslims witnessed this show.[50] "The visits to periodical fairs and seats of pilgrimage", to quote Sir Jadunath Sarkar, "were the sole joy of the Indian village population and men and women were passionately eager to undertake them."[51]

Mathura, Allahābād, Banaras, Nasik and Madura were the main religious centres of the Hindus while Ajmer, Gulbarga, Nizām-ud-dīn Auliya and Burhanpur were the seats of Muslim pilgrimage.

Customs and Ceremonies

From the few and scattered references in the contemporary literature, it is evident that both the communities, Hindus and Muslims, observed their rites and ceremonies[52] in much the same manner as they do today. Of the 16 principal ceremonies prescribed by Hindu law-givers, only 6 important ones, *viz. Jāta karma* (birth ceremony), *Nāma-karaṇa* (name-giving ceremony), *Chūḍākaraṇa* (hair-cutting ceremony), *Upanayana* (initiation), and *Vivāha* (marriage) and certain funeral rites were observed by majority of the Hindus. Abu-'l-Fazl[53] describes the birth ceremony, when honey stirred in *ghee* is put into the mouth of the infant by means of a gold ring. Tulsīdās and Sūrdās refer to the performance of *Nāndimukh Śrāddha*[54] just after the birth when offerings of gold, cows, plates and jewels were made to the Brāhmans. A cord made of *durbā* grass interwoven with mango leaves was usually hung over the main door as a mark of festivity. The *Nāmakaraṇa* ceremony was usually performed after the period of confinement lasting forty days was over.[55] The ceremony of *Annaprāśana,* it appears, was performed when the child was 6 months old. *Khīr,* honey and *ghee,* according to the poet Sūrḍas, would be placed before the child whose father helped him to take it after due ceremonies.[56] The *Muṇdan* or the hair-cutting ceremony was celebrated with due rites not earlier than the age of three leaving one lock on the top of the head. The ears of the child were also bored usually on that day. The *Upanayana* or the sacred thread ceremony was performed before the age of eight when a special function was held and a large number of Brāhmans were invited.[57] Being thus invested with the sacred thread, the boys began his studies in right earnest. The ceremony of *Samāvartana* was performed when the student returned home after the completion of his studies.[58]

The craving for a male child was quite intense among Muhammadans. Manucci relates in detail the rejoicings which followed the birth of a son in a rich family.[59] It was customary to pour honey into the infant's mouth immediately after birth and to press his mother's breast so that "a drop of milk comes out". *Azan,* or the Muslim call to prayer was sounded in the ears of the infant. The naming ceremony was performed on the very day of his birth when the grandfather would give the name. Manucci refers to great celebrations on the *Chhathi* day. It was customary, after bathing the child, to cover him with a shirt made of any article of dress worn by some ancient worthy. The *Aqiqah* rites were usually performed on the seventh day which consisted of a sacrifice of two goats for a boy and one for a girl. The first shaving of the child was also done on this day. Abu-'l-Fazl specially alludes to a Turkish custom adopted by the Mughuls. When a child began to walk, it was usual for the father or the grandfather to strike it with his turban so that it might fall down. The *Bismillah* or more properly the *maktab* ceremony was performed when a boy was four years, four months and four days old. Circumcision or *Sunnat* ceremony was performed with great pomp and show. Akbar prohibited this rite before the age of 12 and even then left it to the boy's option.

Early marriages were in vogue in both the communities. It is, however, almost certain that the actual consummation did not take place before the age of puberty. Inter-caste marriages were out of fashion among Hindus. No such restrictions existed among the Muslims who had complete freedom of choice barring a few closer relations. Akbar, however, did not like marriages between near and dear ones. The marriage rites and ceremonies of Hindus and Muslims were observed in much the same manner as today. Dowry system seems to have been quite harsh and many a poor father had not the means to procure wedding outfits for their daughters. Tukārām could get his daughter married only through the contribution of the villagers.[60] Huge dowries have been referred to by Muhammad Jayasi, Tulsīdās and Sūrdās. Mughul kings, too, used to accept huge dowries. Akbar was, no doubt, against this custom but he made no effort to check this evil practice.

Greater stress was laid upon the funeral ceremonies by the Hindus to whom the value of next world is higher than that of the present one. The most important ones were cremation, *Udakarma, Aśaucha, Asthi Sanchayana, Śāntikarma,* and *Sapiṇḍīkaraṇa.* Abu-'l-Fazl enumerates certain classes to whom the privilege of burning was denied. Inhumation (burial, preferably water burial) was, however, resorted to, as prescribed by the scriptures, in the case of small children and ascetics. Abu-'l-Fazl has referred to a curious custom which was sometimes followed in Bengal. A person in a dying condition would be carried to a nearby river where the lower half of his body would be immersed in water at the moment of his death.[61] Gurū Nānak refers to the Indian custom of tearing the top of a letter when announcing the death of a relative. The generality of the Hindus, it appears, followed the prescribed rules which forbid certain things during the period of defilement such as the cutting of the hair and beard, study of the Vedas, offering to the deities, etc. The positive rules which enjoin, for a period of three days, continence, sleeping on the ground, living on begged or purchased food, eating only in the day time, were also observed.[62] Gaudy dresses were avoided and the women covered their heads with white *dopāṭṭās* as a sign of mourning. *Sañchayana,* or the ceremony of collection of bones and ashes took place after an interval varying according to different castes. The bones after being washed with milk were thrown into a river, preferably the Ganges. The period of mourning ended on the 13th day when some offerings were made to the heir of the deceased by the relatives. *Śrāddha,* which Abu-'l-Fazl describes as the charity given in the name of the deceased, was observed usually on the anniversary of the deceased's death. Its significance and mode of performance has been described at length in the *Āīn.*[63]

Like those of the Hindus, the Muslim funeral customs have not changed much since the days of the Mughuls. The *Yasin* chapter of the *Qur'ān* was read by the sick bed of the dying person and his face was usually turned towards Meeca. *Sharbat* or holy water from Zamzam well at Mecca, if available, might be poured down his throat to "facilitate exit of the vital spark." Death was announced by using certain euphemism, specially in the case of great men; for example, "Emperor Bābur departed from the fleeting world for the everlasting abode in paradise". In case of the death of a prince or a dear one to the Emperor, the *vakil* of the deceased would appear before the king with a blue handkerchief tied around his arm.[64] The body, covered with flowers and heavily perfumed, was carried in a befitting manner and decorum, according to the deceased's position in life, to the burial ground. If he was a noble, his insignia of rank, flags, elephants, cavalry, etc. accompanied it. The period of mourning lasted for 40 days, according to Manucci. The Hindu custom of getting oneself shaved after the death of a dear one seems to have been followed by Muhammadans also. Dainty dishes and gaudy dresses were avoided during this period. The mourning ended on the 40th day when the relatives visited the grave and distributed food, clothes and money to the poor and the needy in the name of the deceased.

Social Etiquettes and Manners[65]

Hindus and Muhammadans differed in their mode of greeting friends, relatives and superiors. Manucci describes five kinds of salutations prevalent among the Hindus in Mughul days. 'Rām Rām' was the most popular form of greeting among equals. A person of higher status, a governor, minister, or a general was greeted by raising the folded hands above the head.[66] The younger would greet an elder by bowing down, touching his or her feet and raising the hand to his head. He would even prostrate himself before his teacher. The Rājā or King was also received in the same manner by all classes except the Brāhmans who would only raise their folded hands. Gurū Nānak, the founder of the Sikh religion, is said to have advised his followers to return the salutation with the words *"Sat Kartār"*[67] (the true Creator).

'*Salām*' was the usual salutation among all classes of Muhammadans, among whom it was obligatory to greet each other with the words '*al-Salām alekum*', the other responding '*wa-lekum al Salām*'. Friends would greet each other by raising the right hand to the forehead and would even embrace or grasp each other's hands in token of love.[68] High personages were greeted by raising the right hand to the forehead and bending the body forward. *Kurnish* and *taslim* have been mentioned by Abu-'l-Fazl as the recognised modes of salutation to the King. *Kurnish* consisted in placing the palm of the right hand on the forehead and bending down the head.[69] While offering *taslim*, the person placed the back of his right hand on the ground, raised it slowly till he stood erect, when he put the palm of his hand on the top of his head. After raising the hand from the ground, it was usual to place it on the breast before taking it to the forehead. Akbar issued orders that the *taslim* should be repeated thrice. He also introduced another salutation called '*Sijdah*' or prostration before the King. But as it was objected to by the orthodox as man-worship, he forbade it in the *Darbār-i-Ām* but allowed it in private assemblies.[70] This custom was, however, discontinued during the reign of Shāh Jahān who introduced instead *Zaminbos* or the practice of kissing the ground. This, also, was given up and the customary *taslim* was restored with the addition that it had to be observed not less than four times. Aurangzīb completely did away with these so-called pretensions to idolatry and ordered that the usual mode of salutation *'Salām alekum'* be observed.[71]

Mode of Travelling and Conveyance[72]

Modern technical devices being unknown, means of transport in those days were confined to human carriers, beasts of burden, and wheeled traffic on land and boats on rivers and small sailing ships in the coastal seas. The ox was the conveyance of the poor in villages and even in towns. Instead of a saddle, they put on a soft cushion. Horses, ponies, mules, and even donkeys were used for riding purposes. In sandy places, like Rājasthān and Sind, camels were employed to cover long distances. The swiftest camels came from Ajmer. The traditional *bail gāri* or the bullock-drawn cart was much more in use then. Drawn by 2 or 3 oxen, it could cover 20 miles a day. The rich used highly decorated chariots[71] which were covered like the rooms of a house, their windows adorned with gilded leather or silk hangings, their mattresses made of silk quilts. Sometimes a beautiful canopy was used as a protection against the sun. The nobles preferred to use white oxen to drive their carriages. Akbar preferred to drive in a two-horse chariot "wherein he would sit cross-legged upon a couch covered with scarlet rugs".[74] An English couch presented to Jahāngīr by the East India Company was also used as a model by local craftsmen. Elephants with beautiful *howdahs* were quite often used as conveyance by kings and nobles. Princesses, too, moved about on elephants. Bernier refers to the trip of Roshanārā Begam seated in a golden *howdah* on a Pegu elephant. During Akbar's time there were 101 elephants in the royal stables for King's use. They were known as *Khas* elephants. Abu-'l-Fazl gives a detailed list of the trappings of the elephants and other animals in the *Āin-i-Akbarī*.[75]

Mules were particularly liked for travelling on uneven ground. For the poor a saddle and a rope or a chain sufficed as the equipment for riding a mule. The rich used a larger number of accessories including a *palan* (pack saddle), a *shaltang* (shawl strap) *palastang* (blanket strap), a *sardoz* (common head stall), a curry comb, a hair glove etc. Horses were preferred to other beasts for their swiftness, impressive look and comfortable ride. Horses were imported from Iraq-i-Arab, Iraq-i-Ajam, Turkey, Badakhshān, Tībet etc. The nobles and wealthy, however, preferred to travel in palanquins which were covered all over with cloth. In case of rain, wax cloth was placed all over the palanquin.

Doli and *dolā* were ordinary types of palanquins. The former was specially hired for women to cover short distances. It is still customary to carry home the bride in a *doli* which is covered with a red cloth.[76] In Bengal the rich used *Sukhāsan* or *Sukhpal,* a crescent-shaped litter covered with camlet or scarlet cloth. *Chandol* was perhaps the most luxurious litter, closed or covered like the room of a house. The roof of the palanquin was covered with a piece of thick silk. It was tastefully decorated with plates of carved silver while others had been painted with flowers or other curiosities.[77] The nobles also used elephant and camel litters. In summer *khas tatties* (screens made of the fragrant *khas* grass) were fixed on all its four sides.

Ships and boats were the principal means of water transport. Some of these ships could accommodate 200 persons. Each ship had a number of cabins which were hired out to passengers. There was a fleet of 300 to 400 sea-going ships plying on the eastern cost of Bengal and Orissa.[78] Boats and crafts were used as a means of conveyance on rivers. There were different kinds of boats for purposes of war, carriage, and swift sailing. Larger boats could even carry an elephant. The boats made for the royalty were highly artistic. Abu-'l-Fazl refers to the "wonderfully fashioned boats with delightful quarters and decks and gardens." In the coastal regions various kinds of brigantines or fustas were used for crossing rivers. Some people used coracles or round basket boats covered with hide for the same purpose. In the Coromandel Coast there was in use a type of boat called *masala.*[79]

Postal System

Indian postal system during Mughul times did not cater to the needs of the common man. There was no regular provision for the carrying of public mail. There were, however, excellent arrangements for carrying king's mail. There were two kinds of couriers, horse and foot, posted at regular intervals. Bābur had a tower built at every 9th *kuroh.* At every 18th *kuroh* (13th or 14th mile) were kept ready 6 post-horses for carrying the mail.[80] Sher Shāh's *sarais* also served as stations of *dāk chaukis.* Two government horses were kept ready in each *sarai* for carrying persons and despatches.[81] Akbar improved upon

Sher Shāh's system and established throughtout his dominions 2 horses and several Mewars every 5th *kuroh*. Whenever a royal *farmān* or a letter from a nobleman reached a *chauki,* it was immediately conveyed to the next *chauki* by a rider. According to Firishta, 50 *kurohs* were thus covered in 24 hours. Akbar had in his employment, for an emergency, 4,000 runners some of whom would cover a distance of 700 miles in 10 days. Runners had been posted in the villages 4 to 5 *kurohs* apart and they took their turn of duty day and night. Aurangzīb issued strict orders that postal runners were to cover one *jaribi kuroh*[82] in one *gāri*. It took 12 days for a runner to reach Delhi from Ahmadābād. The Mughuls did not practise the ancient custom of sending letters through pigeons on any large scale. The *Āin*,. however, refers to a special variety of pigeons known as *rath* pigeons which were trained to carry letters to a great distance. There were no regular arrangements for private post. It was either entrusted to these agencies or in some cases despatched through special messengers. Sometimes a touring acquaintance would take the letter for a friend or relative of the sender. Special measures were adopted for the security of the royal letters sent abroad to the Emperors or principal ministers. Letters were enclosed in a large hollow cylinder of bamboo with an opening at one end and about 2 inches long. After putting in the letter, this opening was sealed. Thus the letter was carried neat and clean unaffected by rain or dust.[83]

Position of Women

There had been definite deterioration in the position of women in the centuries that followed the Vedic Age. But in all these periods there was no seclusion of women. With the advent of Islām new social forces affected Hindu society. Strict veilng of women was the common practice among the Muhammadans in their native lands. Naturally in a foreign country like India, greater stress was laid upon it. Even a liberal king like Akbar had to issue strict orders that "if a young woman was found running about the streets and bazars of the town and while so doing did not veil herself or allowed herself to be unveiled.....she was to go to the quarters of the prostitutes and take up the profession."[84] Hindus adopted *purdah* as a protective measure to save the honour of their womenfolk and to maintain the purity of their social order. The tendency to imitate the ruling class was another factor which operated in favour of introducing *purdah* among Hindu families.

Seculsion thus became a sign of respect and was strictly observed among the high class families of both the communities. Eunuchs were freely employed as a means of communication between the male and female members of a royal or noble's family. Even male doctors were not allowed to face the ailing ladies of the noble and princely families. The ladies would stir out of their houses very rarely and that, too, in covered palanquins, surrounded on all sides by servants and eunuchs. If, for any reason, a Muslim lady of rank discarded *purdah* even for a temporary period, the consequences for her were disastrous. Amir Khān, the Governor of Kabul, felt no scruple in renouncing his wife when her *purdah* was broken in an attempt to save her life by leaping from the back of the elephant who had run amuck.[85]

Purdah was, however, less rigorously observed in Rājput families. There the women, trained in all the arts of warfare, would frequently take part in hunting parties, and other expeditions. Barring notable Muslim families there, South India did not adopt *purdah*. No such coercive *purdah* system was observed among the Hindu middle class, and certainly not among the Hindu masses. Hindu ladies could move out of doors with little or no restrictions.[86] Unlike Muslim women they did not cover themselves from head to foot. It was enough to have a sheet or *dopāṭṭā* to cover their heads. Women of the lower stratum of our society such as peasant and working classes were entirely free from the bondage of *purdah*. They were expected to help their husbands in all "external pursuits and internal economy."

The birth of a daughter was considered inauspicious. A Rājput was often heard to say: "accused to the day when a woman child is born to me." A wife who unfortunately happened to give birth to girls in succession was despised and even sometimes divorced.[87]

Even in the royal family the difference was clear and well marked. Only women rejoiced and feasted on the birth of a daughter while the whole court took part in the celebrations, if a prince was born.[88] The deplorable custom of infanticide was luckily confined to a very minor section of the less cultured Rājput families. The custom in those days did not allow, for whatever reasons, girls to remain in the parents' home for more than 6 to 8 years after their birth. "A father", according to Mukundarāma, "who could get his daughter married in her ninth year was considered lucky and worthy of the favours of God."[89] The rigidity of the custom, together with the celebration of marriage at a very tender age, left no room, whatsoever, for either the bride or bridegroom to have time to think of a mate of their own choice. The custom left it solely to the discretion of their parents or nearest relations and friends to arrange the match. Dowry was demanded and sometimes parents disregarded the suitability of the match and cared primarily for a rich dowry. In some castes and localities the bridegroom had to pay money to the bride's guardians.[90] Sometimes for the sake of wealth, a young man would marry a woman older than himself. The evil grew so much that Akbar issued orders that if a woman "happened to be older by 12 years than her husband, the marriage should be considered as illegal and annulled."[91] Akbar tried in vain to bring home to the people that the consent of the bride and bridegroom as well as the permission of the parents was essential before the confirmation of the engagement.[92] There seems to have been greater liberty at least to girls belonging to high class Rājput families to choose a husband. Sometimes a romantic lady would fix the price of her hand. Tārābāi, the daughter of Rāo Surthan, promised to marry the youth who would recover her father's domain Todah, from the Pāthāns. Jaimal, the brother of Prithvi Raj, won her, Karam Devī, the beautiful daughter of the Mohil chieftain, renounced her betrothal with the heir of the Rāo of Mandor and chose to be the bride of Sādhu, heir of Pugal, whose admiration she had won.[93]

Monogamy seems to have been the rule among the lower stratum of society in both the communities during the Mughul period. In spite of the decision of the '*Ulema* in the *Ibādat Khānā*, that a man might marry any number of wives by *mutah* but only four by *nikah*, Akbar had issued definite orders that a man of ordinary means should not possess more than one wife unless the first proved to be barren.[94] He considered it highly injurious to a man's health to keep more than one wife. Polygamy was the privilege of the rich Muhammadans most of whom kept 3 or 4 wives at a time. Hindus, with the exception of a small number of princes and very wealthy persons, strictly restricted themselves to monogamy as enjoined by their social custom. In the extreme case if a wife proved to be barren, they had the liberty to marry another with the consent of the Brāhmans.[94a]

The girl was brought up under parental supervision and was married without her consent. When married, she was under the control of her mother-in-law whose commands must be carried out. If she failed to come up to her standard, she might be divorced in a

Muhammadan family, and her life would become miserable in a Hindu home. But when grown up and away from the domineering influence of her mother-in-law, she had a large share in the management of her household. She was to prove herself a devoted wife who would not take meals until her husband had dined.[94b] The position of women with regard to her husband was that of a dependent, in honourable subordination, at least as long as mutual relations remained cordial. Jahāngīr writes in the *Tuzuk:* "It is a maxim of the Hindus that no good deed can be performed by men in the social state without the partnership or presence of the wife whom they have styled the half of men." Both would give way to accommodate each other, though the last word was that of the husband. But with all this, the ladies belonging to high and respectable old families, especially Rājputānīs, were reluctant to compromise when their self-respect was at stake. Tod relates how Rājā Jai Singh of Amber once cut jokes with his wife, the princess of Haroti, about the simplicity of her dress and contrasted it with the robes of the belles of his own capital. Greatly annoyed, the princess spoke in words which clearly bring out the true sex relations prevalent among high Rājput families. "Mutual respect is the guardian not only of happiness but of virtue, and if again she was insulted he would find that 'the daughter of Kotaḥ' could use a sword more effectively than the prince of Amber the scissors."[95] It appears most of the Hindus led a happy domestic life. The woman adored her husband with passionate reverence and in return her husband rendered her all tenderness and protection.

Divorce and remarriages, common among Muslims, were prohibited to Hindu women. Widow remarriage, except for the lower caste people, had completely disappeared in Hindu society during the medieval age. *Sati* was the prevalent practice in spite of the efforts of the Mughuls to check it. Even the betrothed girls had to commit *sati* on the funeral pyre of their would-be-husbands. Those widows who would not burn themselves with their husbands were harshly treated by the society; they were not allowed to wear their hair long or to put on ornaments. These unfortunate widows had to put up with their parents who treated them no better than ordinary maids, hated and despised by even their family as being afraid of death.[96] Whatever might have been the position of a woman as a girl, bride and widow, she certainly occupied a most respectable position in society as a mother. There are numerous instances, in the contemporary records, of Mughul kings who would travel some stages to receive their mothers. They would perform *kurnish, sijdah* and *taslim* when entering their presence.[97] On his birthday, the Mughul Emperor, accompanied by princes and nobles, would necessarily pay a visit to his mother to receive her felicitations. It is interesting to recall that the first lady of the realm was not the Empress (except in cases of Nūr Jahān and Mumtāz Mahall) but the royal mother or royal sister.[98] Perhaps no people showed greater regard for their mothers than the Rājputs. This is best illustrated by the ever recurring phrase "make thy mother's milk resplendent". Rānā Saṅgrām Singh II of Mewar had made it a principle to pay his respects to his mother every morning before taking his meals.[98a] At the command of his mother, 16 years old Patta put the saffron robe and died fighting during the famous assault of Chitor by Akbar.[99]

A Muslim woman inherited a definite share of her husband's or father's property with absolute right to dispose of it. Unlike her Hindu sister, she retained the right after marriage. *Mahr* or antenuptial settlement was the another safeguard whereas a Hindu lady had no right to the property of her husband's parents. A Hindu lady was entitled to maintenance besides movable property like ornaments, jewellery, costly apparel, etc. Thus from legal point of view, women were reduced to a position of dependency in every sphere of life. Caste and seclusion brought about her social, political and intellectual stultification. They confined themselves to household work excepting the women belonging to agricultural and labouring classes who helped their men-folk in their home industries, agriculture, breeding of animals, spinning, weaving, tailoring, etc. Some of them even kept shops. Many others, especially Muhammadans and Bengalis, took up dancing and singing as a profession. Some acted as midwives, while the more educated adopted teaching as a profession.[100]

In spite of their strict seclusion, however, some Mughul ladies were writers of distinction and administrators of rare merit. Gulbadan Begam, the author of the *Humāyūn-nāma,* and Jahān Ārā, the biographer of *Shibyah* and *Munisal Arwah* hold an enviable position among the literary figures of that age. Mīrā Bāi, Salimā Sultānā, Nūr Jahān, Sitn-un-Nisā, the tutoress of Jahān Ārā, and Zib-un-Nisā, the eldest daughter of Aurangzib, were poetesses of distinction. Rāmabhadrāmbā, the author of *Raghunāthābhyudayam,* Madhurāvanī, translator in verse of *Andhra-Rāmāyaṇa,* Tirumalambā, author of *Varadāmbikāpariṇayam,* and Mohanāṅgī, author of the love poem *Marīchiparinayam* are well-known Sanskrit poetesses of the period. In Mahārāshṭra Aka Bāi and Kena Bāi, disciples of Rāmdās Svāmī, were considered important literary figures. In the administrative sphere, we might mention the names of the Chandel princess of Gondwana, Rānī Durgāvatī, Chānd Bibi of Ahmadnagar and Makhduma-u-Jahān, who ruled Deccan as a regent on behalf of Nizām Shāh of the Bahmanī family. Sāhibjī, the daughter of 'Alī Mardān, was the actual ruler of Kabul during her husband's viceroyalty and, after his death, ruled over the turbulent Afghāns without any serious opposition.[101] Nūr Jahān was the real power behind Jahāngīr's throne. Tārābāi Mohite was the supreme guiding force in Mahārāshṭra after the death of her husband Rāja Rām. She displayed such marvellous capacity and administrative ability in encountering the Mughul onslaught that threatened to engulf the Marāṭhā State that all the efforts of the Emperor Aurangzīb failed miserably. Sir Jadunath Sarkar rightly observes: "Her administrative genius and strength of character saved the nation in that awful crisis."

Education

The system of education in medieval times was still at a rudimentary stage. Primary schools in the modern sense of the word, probably did not exist. *Tols* or schools attached to temples, Hindu or Buddhist, and maintained by grants or endowments made for that specific purpose, were to be found throughout the country. The teachers there would not only solicit contributions to raise the building but also to feed their pupils. No fee was paid as to give instruction free is enjoined by the sacred scriptures of the Brāhmans. John Marshall, who visited India in the later 17th century writes: "Hindus never teach their children for money; those they teach, they give them victuals, too, besides their learning which is estimated as a gift."[102] *Maktabs* or the Muslim primary institutions, usually attached to a mosque, were common sight during the Mughul period. The traveller, Della Valle, probably refers to them when he writes that in Jahāngīr's time there were private schools in every town and village.[103]

There was no printed primer, but the children were made to write the letters of the alphabet and figures on wooden boards or on the dust of the ground with their fingers. Usually the students had their lessons under the shade of a tree. Combined letters were practised and difficult words selected from a standard book like the *Qur'ān* were dictated. Great importance was attached to calligraphy and students were instructed to imitate and practise the style of the best calligraphists of the day.

As soon as the boys could read and write, grammar, followed by the text of the *Qur'ān*, was invariably introduced in every *Maktab*.[104] Every child had to learn it by rote. There is definite evidence of the fact that most of the boys could read even if they did not understand the text. There is little evidence about the course of instructions in vogue in Hindu institutions. Growse, however, thinks that *Rāmāyaṇa* formed the chief text in the primary schools.[105] But as the *Rāmāyaṇa* was put in Hindi by Tulsī Dās at the end of Akbar's reign, that could not obviously have been a text book till the end of the 16th century. According to Bernier, however, the Puraṇas were taken up after learning the alphabet. The teaching of elementary mathematics went side by side with literacy. After finishing *Qur'ān,* Muslim students took lessons in Gulistān, Bostān and poems of Firdausi, while the Sanskrit scholars studied the Purāṇas, Upanishads and Śāstras and sometiems the Vedas.[106] At Banaras there were in existence various colleges for specialisation in different subjects such as the Vedas, grammar, poetry, Vedānta, logic, law and astronomy.

The teachers were held in high respect. The pupils would touch their feet and speak only with permission. A teacher who could lecture without the help of books was very much respected and remembered for his knowledge. Badāūnī specially mentions one Shaikh 'Abdullah of Badaon, who never felt the "necessity of referring to a book for the purpose of solving those questions and obscure subtleties, for whatever he had once seen, he had on the tip of his tongue."[107]

The chief centres of learning or universities, if we may call them so, were at places where the renowned scholars had made their abode. Hindus preferred shrines and sacred places where pilgrim traffic supplied a subsidiary source of income to the teachers residing there, and thus, free from the worries of livelihood, they pursued their studies undisturbed. Banaras, Nadia, Mithilā, Mathurā, Tirhut, Paithan, Karhad, Thatta, Multan and Sirhind were the famous seats of Hindu learning. Dharmādhikārī, Sera Bhaṭṭa and Mounī were the learned families which figured prominently at Banaras for more than three centuries (1500-

1800). Rājā Jai Singh also founded a college there for the education of the princes. There were other seminaries where famous Paṇḍits interpreted and expounded the fundamentals of Hindu religion and philosophy. Nadia, in Bengal, was, after Banaras, the greatest centre of Hindu learning in the country during the Mughul days. In Navadvipa alone there were 4,000 pupils and 600 teachers in 1680. Vāsudeva Sārvabhauma (1450-1525), the great scholar of the 16th century, was the founder of the famous Nadia school of *Nyāya* which even outrivalled Mithilā. Raghunātha Śiromaṇi was also the founder of a school of logic at Banaras. Raghunandana created a school of Smriti in the 16th century along with that of logic at Nadia. Mithila retained its importance as a centre of learning during the Mughul times. In fact a student of this university performed *digvijaya* at the instance of Akbar, who was so pleased that he gave him the whole town of Mithilā as a gift. Madurā was famous as a centre of studies in Indian philosophy. There were over 10,000 students in its several colleges which specialised in the different branches of Indian philosophy. Thatta had about 400 colleges according to Hamilton. The students there specialised in theology, philology and politics.[108] Multan was famous as a centre of specialisation in astronomy, astrology, mathematics and medicine.[109] Sirhind had a famous school of medicine, most probably Āyurvedic. It supplied doctors to the whole Empire.[110]

Āgra, Delhi, Lahore, Jaunpur, Gujarāt, Sialkot and Ahmadābād were some of the main centres of Muslim learning. Akbar, Shāh Jahān and Jahān Ārā built *madrasahs* at Āgra. Akbar even invited a scholar, Chalpi Beg, from Shirāz to teach there.[111] Some of the renowned scholars like Sayyid Shāh Mīr of Samānā took their abode there and attracted students from far and wide.[112] The traveller Peter Mundy refers to a College of Jesuits at Āgra. At Delhi there were a number of *madrasahs,* important among them being Humāyūn's *madrasah* built in honour of Zain-ud-Dīn Khafi[113] and Māham Anaga's *madrasah* known as Khair-ul-Manzil, opposite the western gate of Purānā Qilāh, called Madrasah-i-Begam by Badāūnī.[114] It was a residential *madrasah;* students resided there in the rooms of both the storeys and classes were held in the hall. Shāh Jahān built a magnificicent *madrasah* called *Darul Baqa* on the southern side of the Jāmi Masjid.[115] Madrasah-i-Rahimiyya known after the name of 'Abdur Rahim, father of Waliullah, was built during Aurangzib's time.

Jaunpur and Gujarāt were the two other centres where learned scholars had taken up their residence. Jaunpur, rightly called the 'Shiraz of India', kept up its importance throughout the Mughul period and attracted students from far and wide. Mukundarāma, the author of the poem *Chaṇḍī-maṅgala,* refers to the existence of several *maktabs* in Gujarāt.[116] The Madarsah Faiz Ṣafa in Naharwara Paṭtan (Gujarāt) and Langar-i-Duwazda Imam in Ahmadābād (now called *Bara Imam ka Kotla*) were famous centres of learning. Aurangzīb instructed the *diwāns* of Gujarāt to appoint every year teachers at the cost of the state and to pay stipends to students, according to the recommendations of the *Sadr* of the province and attestation of the teacher.[117]

Lahore's importance as a centre of learning dates from the time of Aurangzīb when the reputation of its scholars "attracted many a pupil from far and wide."[118] Kāshmīr, with its pleasant and refreshing climate, was a place of retreat for scholars, some of whom such as Abu Talib Kamil, Mulla Shāh Badakshi completed their works there. Among other centres of learning, Gwālior, Sialkot, Ambala and Thaneswar may be mentioned.

Duration of Courses, Texts and Certificates

The courses of study usually varied from 10-16 years for graduation. Some more years were required for doctorate after studying under a renowned scholar. No regular examinations were held in those days. A good mastery of certain specified courses, of which the teacher was the sole judge, was sufficient for promotion to the next standard. It was not surprising to see a pupil being promoted to the next standard within 6 months. No regular degrees were awarded. To have studied in a reputed institution or under a renowned teacher was the greatest qualification one could have. There are, however, instances of diplomas being awarded by great scholars of theology to the pupils conferring upon them the authority to give instructions therein.

Some sort of diploma or degree was awarded in some of the Hindu institutions, as for example, in the University of Mithilā. Raghunātha, a student of the Nadia University was deputed to "exact from Mithila, a charter to confer degrees". An unusual type of examination called *Salākā-parīkshā* marked the termination of the graduation course in Mithilā. A candidate was expected to explain correctly that page of the manuscript which was pierced last by a needle run through it.[119] *Chhurikā-bandhanam* resembled our present day convocation which was marked by the tying of a dagger to the dress of the pupil as a token of his graduation.[120] Some renowned scholars earned the titles of *Sārvabhauma, Akbariya Kālidās, Pratyagra Patañjali,* etc. The post-collegiate studies were invariably completed under a specialist. It was not easy to get one-self admitted as the scholars were reluctant to have more than a limited number of students. It was with great difficulty that Mullah Shāh Badakhshi agreed to take Jahān Ārā as his pupil. Badāūnī was proud to have had the privilege to study under Mīr Sayyid Jalāl, the saint. For still higher studies eager scholars visited the chief places of Muslim learning in Western and Central Asia such as Mecca, Medina, Basra, Kofa, Yemen, Cairo, Nishapur (Īrān), Baghdād, Hijāz, Khurāsān, etc.

Courses of Study

Very little information about the curriculum then in vogue is available. The courses of study in Muslim institutions usually comprised grammar, rhetoric, logic, theology, metaphysics, literature and jurisprudence. Astronomy, mathematics and medicine were included under Hindu influence. The Arabic curriculum included besides grammar, syntax, rhetoric, philosophy, logic, scholasticism, tafsir, fich, Hadis, etc. The Persian texts included *Ruqqat-i-Abu-'l-Fazl,* Letters of Chandra Bhān Brāhman, and Mulla Munir, Insha-i-Yusūfi, Insha-ī-Madho Rām, Lilāvatī translated by Faizi, Shaikh Nasr-ī-Zahuri's work, Zafar-nāma-i-Kangra by Raja Husain; Akbar-nāma of Abu-'l-Fazl, Iqbal-nāma-i-Jahāngiri, Zafar-nāma of Sharafuddin 'Alī Yazdi, Tārīkh-i-Firūz Shāhī, Razm-nāma, Firdausi's Shāh-nāma, Poems of Amir Khusrav, Mulla Jami's works, Nizāmi's works, Diwāns of Hafiz, Khaqani, Anwari, Shams-i-Tabriz, Qasaid of Badr-i-Chach, Urfi and Faizi, Bahar-i-Danish of Inayatullah, Anwar-i-Suhali of Husain Waiz, etc.[121]

The subjects of study in Hindu institutions included grammar, logic, philosophy, history, poetry, mathematics, astronomy, astrology, medicine, and veterinary science. Physics and Chemistry were studied but were regarded as a part of the science of Mathematics. Hindus, especially Brāhmans, were interested in philosophy and mathematics which were in vogue in India from ancient times.

Very little attention was however paid to geography in schools and colleges. Aurangzib heaped abuses on his tutor for wasting time on the subtleties of Arabic metaphysics to the neglect of practical subjects such as geography and politics. People were ignorant of the geographical position of the neighbouring countries. A map of the globe was so rare a thing that Sir Thomas Roe included it among the presents he offered to the Governor of Surat.

Women's Education

Women's education was not completely ignored, though regular separate school seems to have existed for imparting education to girls who had their lessons usually from their parents. Girls in their childhood attended schools along with boys and learnt the *Qur'ān* (if they were Muhammadans) and one or two other lessons by rote. The rich appointed tutors to teach their daughters at home. The daughters of Rājput chiefs and some Bengali *zamindārs* were usually able and write. Special care was taken for the education of Mughul princesses, almost all of whom daily read the *Qur'ān* and occasionally corresponded with their relatives. Some of them even composed verses. The average Mughul princess received but a limited education.[122] Her regular studies came to an end with her marriage which usually took place at an early age. Gulbadan Begam's *Humāyūn-nāma,* too, abounds with spelling mistakes and clumsy sentences. Even the poems of Zīb-un-Nisā and Zinat-un-Nisā do not rise so high in poetic excellence as those of contemporary male authors.

There is, however, little doubt about the literacy of the average middle class woman who had sufficient knowledge of either Hindi, Persian or the native provincial language to enable her to study the religious scriptures.[122a] The knowledge of Sanskrit was widespread in the South. A Malayalam work *Chandrotsavan* gives us an idea about the general reading of educated women in the South and this includes, *Śakuntalam, Mālavikāgnimitram* and other Sanskrit dramas. A well-known work of the period entitld *Mahilāmṛiduvani* gives us a list of no less than 35 women all of importance, "not minor poets poetesses who have left their mark on the literary sphere". Special stress was laid on the education of widows, some of whom, as for example Haṭi Vidyālaṅkāra became teachers. We may well concur with Mukundarāma's view that "there is evidence to show that women belonging to the lower ranks of society, such as house-maids, were illiterate, but there is nothing to discountenance female education."[123]

Libraries

Quite a large number of libraries existed during the Mughul times. Every *madrasah* usually possessed a library, big or small, attached to it. We might refer here to the libraries attached to the *madrasah* called Shams-i-Burhani at Ahmadābād, Madrasah Faiz Safa, Shaikh Ibrahim's *madrasah* at Kutiana in Kathiawar (1689) and Sultan Ahmad Khatwi's *madrasah* at Sarkahaiz (Ahmadābād). The biggest was, however, the Imperial Library which contained the King's collection of books. All the Mughul Emperors[124] from Bābur to Aurangzīb were men of literary taste; they were eager to collect and preserve rare books and valued presents of scholarly books from learned authors. As in every other sphere, Akbar introduced reforms in the management, classification and storage of books which had by that time increased enormously.[125] The Mughul princesses Salimā Sultānā, and Zīb-un-Nisā, possessed libraries of their own.[126]

The example of the royalty was followed by nobles and courtiers who had their own libraries. 'Abdur-Rahīm Khān Khānān kept a staff of 95 persons to look after his huge collection of books.[127] Shaikh Faizī had about 4,600 books in his library. Mahmūd Gawān, Vazīr of Muhammad Shāh Bahmanī, left a huge library containing 35,000 volumes.

Mahārājā Chhika Deva, Rājā of Mysore 1672-1704, collected in his library very rare Sanskrit and historical works which were unfortuantely subsequently destroyed by Tipu Sultān.[128] *Mahārājā* Sawāi Jai Singh possessed an unrivalled library containing all the astronomical treatises available in India. He procured books even from Europe.[129] There were big libraries at the famous seats of Hindu learning such as Banaras, Tirhut, Mithilā, Nadia, etc. These libraries stocked huge collection of rare, authentic and ancient works on philosophy, medicine, religion, history and many other sciences. Bernier saw a large hall at Banaras entirely filled with these manuscripts.[130] The Brahmans of Kāshmīr had a sufficient stock of books which they regularly studied.[131] Many of these libraries were later on destroyed by the Muhammadans.

—*P.N. Chopra*

References

1. This chapter is mainly based on the author's *Society and Culture* during the *Mughal Age,* Second Edition, Agra, 1963, and *Social Life Under the Mughals,* Agra, 1963. (The picture is only a broad and general outline, as it is not possible to give details of local variations in a vast country like India—Editor).

2. *Bāburnāma* (trans. Beveridge), p. 519. For details refer to Chopra's *Society and Cutlrue during the Mughal Age,* op. cit., pp. 1.3.

3. *Ain,* I, trans. Blochmann (1873), pp. 88-90.

4. Monserrate, S.J., The Commentary of Trans. from Latin by J.S. Hoyland, annotated by S.N. Banerji, 1922, p. 198.

4a. Turbans were not used by the Hindus in Eastern and Southern India, though some put them on in imitation of the Muslims—Editor.

5. *Ain,* I, (1873), *op. cit.,* pp. 75-77.

6. Saletore, B.A., *Social and Political Life in Vijayanagar Empire,* Vol. II, p. 302.

7. *Padumavati* of Malik Muhammad Jayasi, translation by Grierson, p. 569.

7a. *For ornaments refer to Ovington, J., A Voyage in the Year 1689,* London, 1696, p. 320; Manucci, op. cit., III; p. 40; Ain, III (ed. J.N. Sarkar), p. 343; Ain, II, pp. 314-16; Mandelslo, op. cit., p. 50; Thevenot, Monsieur de Travels of, Into the Levant, Trans. English, 1686, pt. III, chapter XX, quoted in Chopra, *Society and Culture during the Mughal Age, op. cit.,* pp. 25-31.

8. For details refer to Chopra, *op. cit., Society and Culture during the Mughal Age,* pp. 32-54.

9. Mandelslo Albert, Book III, by Adam Olearious, Second Edition, London, 1669, p. 64. Della Valle, Pietro, *The Travels of a Noble Roman into East Indies and Arbian Deserta,* London, 1664, p. 409; Tavernier, John Baptista, *The Six Voyages of, through Turkey Into Persia and the East Indies,* London, 1678, p. 124.

10. *Iqbalnāma-i-Jahangīrī,* trans. Urdu by Maulavi Abalswala Muhammad Zakriya, Osmania, 1928, p. 105.

11. *Tuzūk-i-Babari,* trans. Rogers and Beveridge, I, p. 419.

12. Ain *I, (1873),* op. cit., *p. 59.*

13. A.N. (trans.), *op. cit.,* I, p. 208. Faluda is "a jelly strained from boiled wheat, and eaten with the expressed juice of fruits and ice to which cream is also sometiems added."

14. Purchas, 'Hakluyt Posthumus' or *Purchas and His Pilgrims*, Vol. IV, p. 41.

15. Mandelslo, *op. cit.*, p. 69.

16. Dasgupta, J.N., *Bengal in the 16th Century*, p. 181. Many other Bengali texts refer to Bengali food in great detail. Cf. *History of Medieval Bengal* (in Bengali) by R.C. Majumdar, pp. 318-23.

17. *Ain*, I, trans. Blochmann (1873), p. 58.

18. Ibid., *pp. 58-59.*

19. *Tuzūk-ī-Jahangīrī*, trans. Rogers & Beveridge, I, p. 374.

20. Manucci, I. p. 175.

21. Storey, C.A., *Persian Literature—A Biographical Survey*, London, 1927-39, II. Fasc. III, p. 460.

22. For a detailed treatment of the subject refer to P.N. Chopra, *Social Life Under the Mughals*, pp. 86-122.

23. Havell, E.B., *Indian Architecture*, London, 1913, pp. 153, 171; Percy Brown, *Indian Architecture—The Islamic Period*, Bombay, pp. 100, 127-130. 132; Fergusson, James, *History of Indian and Eastern Architecture*, II, p. 170, etc.

24. Pelsaert, Francisco, The Remonstrantie of translated from the Dutch by W.H. Moreland & P. Geyl, Cambridge, 1925, pp. 66-67.

24a. For a contemporary account of the houses of the various classes of people refer to Bernier, *Travels in the Mughal Empire*, English trans. by A. Constable, revised by V.S. Smith, Oxford, 1934, pp, 247, 285; Mandelslo, *op. cit.*, p. 54; Pelsaert, *op. cit.*, pp. 66-67; Sen, S.N. *Indian Travels of Thevenot & Careri*, published by National Archives of India, 1949, pp. 22, 163; Khulasat, *India of Aurangzib* by J.N. Sarkar, p. 34; Travernier, J. Baptista, *The Six Voyages of, through Turkey Into Persia and the East Indies*, London, 1678, pt. I; *Ain* (Sarkar) III, p. 352; Manucci, III, p. 41.

25. Bernier, *op. cit.*, p. 247. Also see Chopra, *Social Life under the Mughals*, pp. 117-19; and Mahalingam, *Administration and Social Life Under Vijayanagar*, p. 268; Roe, Sir Thomas, *The Embassy to the Court of the Great Mogul* (1615-19) edited by William Foster. London, 1899, p. 65.

26. Abdul Aziz. *Thrones, Chairs and Seats used by the Indian Mughals*, p. 182.

27. Dasgupta, *op. cit.*, p. 298; Mahalingam, *op. cit.*, pp. 289-90.

28. For a deailed account of these festivals refer to Chopra, *Society and Culture during the Mughal Age*, pp. 83-107.

29. *Ain,* III (Sarkar), p. 319; *Tuzūk-i-Jahangīrī* (R & B), I, p. 246.

30. Macauliffe, M.A., *The Sikh Religion,* Indroduction, pp. lxxi-lxxvi.

31. *Ain*, I, (1873), p. 216.

32. *Ibid.*, p. 210; *Tuzuk* (R & B), I. p. 367.

33. *Ain,* III, (Sarkar), pp. 350-52.

34. *Khafi Khan, Muntakhab-ul-Lubab,* II, p. 214; Sarkar, *History of Aurangzib,* III, p. 91.

35. For details about *Nauroz* refer to Roe's Embassy, pp. 142-44; Mandelslo, *op. cit.,* p. 41; Bernier, *op. cit.,* pp. 272-73; Monserrate, S.J., *The Commentary of,* Trans. by J.S. Hoyland, Oxford University Press, 1922, pp. 175-76.

36. Manrique, F.S., Travels of ed. by Luard & Hosten, Vol. II, pp. 195-200.

37. *Qanun-i-Humayuni* by Khwandamir trans. into English by Beni Prasad, 1940, p. 76.

38. Sarkar, J.N. *History of Aurangzib,* III, pp. 85-86.

39. Thevenot, Monsieur de, Travels of into the Levant, in three parts, translated into English, 1686, pt. III, chapter XXVI, p. 47.

40. *Humayūnnāma* by Gulbadan Begum, trans. into English by A.S. Beveridge, London, 1902, p. 126.

41. Badauni, *op. cit.*, II, p. 322, Tr. II, p. 331.

42. For detailed treatment of the subject and sources refer to P.N. Chopra, *Society and Culture during the Mughal Age, op. cit.*, pp. 55-82.

43. *Aīn-i-Akbari* I. (edition 1939), pp. 318-19. Also see *Baburnāma* trans. into English by A.S. Beveridge, 1921, p. 584.

44. Mandelslo, *op. cit.,* p. 66; Manuscci, II, *op. cit.,* p. 460; Badauni, *Muntakhabut-Tawarikh,* trans. Vol. II by W.H. Lowe, pp. 18, 324, etc.

45. A.N. II, p. 368. Tr. II, p. 534.

46. For details see Chopra, *op. cit.*, pp. 62-65.

47. Majumdar, A.K., *The Chaulukyas of Gujarat,* p. 359; Mazumdar, B.P., *Socio-Economic History of Northern India,* p. 254.

48. Saletore, *op. cit.*, II, p. 420.

49. *Qamargha* is a Turkish word denoting a great battle in which a large number of wild animals are driven into enclosure and killed. Being a Turkish game, it must have been in vogue during the regimes of Bābur and Humayūn but no documentary evidence is traceable.

50. Quoted from *Chaitanya Bhagavata* in "Indian Culture", Vol. X, 1943, p. 121.

51. Sarkar, J.N., *Aurangzib*, Vol. V, pp. 471-73.

52. For a detailed treatment of this subject refer to P.N. Chopra, *Social Life During the Mughal Age, op. cit.*, pp. 1-51.

53. Abu-'l-Fazl, *Ain-i-Akbari*, Vol. III, trans, by H.S. Jarrett, revised by Sir Jadunath Sarkar, 1948, p. 317.

54. *Nandimukh Sraddha* is a commemorative offering to the Manes prelimianry to any joyous occasion such as initiation, marriage, etc. in which nine balls of meat are offered to the deceased father, grandfather, great grandfather, to the maternal grandfather and to the mother, paternal grandmother and paternal great grandmother. Pandey, R.B., *Hindu Samskaras*, Banaras, 1949, p. 123. Also see Atkins, A.G., *The Ramayana of Tulsidas*, English translation, Vol. I, p. 246.

55. Macauliffe, M.A. *The Sikh Religion*, Oxford, 1909, Vol. I, p. 242.

56. Dass, Shyam Sunder, *Hindi Shabd Sagar*, Vol. I, Prayag, 1916, p. 291.

57. *Tuzūk-ī-Jahangiri*, trans. Rogers & H. Beveridge, Vol. I, p. 357.

58. Majumdar, R.C. *History of Bengal*, Vol. I, p. 600.

59. Manucci, N.V., *Storia Do Mogor* or *Mughal India*, trans. William Irvine, Vol. III, p. 150.

60. J.R.A.S. (Bombay), III, p. 15. Also see Macauliffe, *op. cit.*, I, p. 145, Jayasi's *Padumavati* (Urdu), pp. 148-49; Growse, *Ramayana of Tulsidas*, p. 159, etc.

61. *Ain*, III (Sarkar), op. cit., p. 354.

62. *Ibid.*, p. 356.

63. *Ibid.*, p. 307.

64. *Maasir ul Umra*, I, trans, Beveridge, p. 123.

65. Refer to P.N. Chopra, *Social Life Under the Mughals*, pp. 52-69 for details.

66. Manucci, *op. cit.*, III, p. 38.

67. Macauliffe, *op. cit.*, I, p. 49.

68. Mandelslo, *op. cit.*

69. *Ain*, I, trans. Blochmann, revised by D.C. Philliott, 1939, p. 166.

70. *Ibid.*, p. 167 and f.n. 1.

71. *Maasir-i-Alamgiri*, p. 98.

72. For details refer to Chopra, *Social Life Under the Mughals, op. cit.*, pp. 123-40.

73. Sen, S.N., *Travels of Thevenot & Careri*, p. 73.
74. Hoyland, J.S., The Commentary of Father Monserrate, translated by S.N. Banerji, Oxford University Press, 1922, p. 199.
75. *Ain, op. cit.*, I. pp. 161-62.
76. Sen, op. cit., p. 72; Das, H.H. Norris Embassy to Aurangzib, Calcutta, 1902, p. 162.
77. For details refer to Chopra, *Social Life Under the Mughals*, pp. 132-33.
78. Balakrishna, *Commercial Relations between England and India* (1600-1757), pp. 279-81.
79. Mahalingam, T.V., *Economic Life in Vijayanagar, op. cit.*, p. 148.
80. B.N. (Beveridge), p. 626.
81. Qanungo, K.R., *Sher Shah*, p.392.
82. One Jaribi equalled 25 *dhara* and one *dhara* amounted to 42 fingers.
83. Ovington, *op. cit.*, p. 250.
84. Badauni, II, pp. 391-92, Tr. II, pp. 404-6.
85. Sarkar, J.N., *Studies in Mughal India*, p. 118.
86. Della Valle, Pietro—*The Travels of a Noble Roman into East Indies and Arabian Deserta*, London, 1664, p. 434; Mandelslo, *op. cit.*, p. 51.
87. *Akbarnāma* III, p. 58 & 260; Tr. III, p. 83 & 378.
88. Manucci, *op. cit.*, p. 343.
89. Author of the poem *Chandi* composed in the 16th century. Translated into English by J.N. Dasgupta under the title "Bengal in the 16th century", Calcutta, 1914, p. 178.
90. Manucci, *op. cit.*, III, p. 55.
91. Badauni, II, p. 39, Tr. II, p. 405.
92. *Ain*, I, (1873), p. 227.
93. Tod, Col. James, *Annals & Antiquities of Rajasthan*, edited by W. Crookes, Vol. II, pp. 731-32.
94. Badauni, *op. cit.*, II, p. 356; Tr. II, p. 367. Also *Ain*, I, (1873), p. 277.

94a. But in Bengal, a section of Brahmans, called Kulins, had normally many wives, whose number sometimes exceded even fifty (Editors).

94b. Manucci, *op. cit.*, III, p. 155.

95. Tod, *op. cit..* II, pp. 728-30.
96. Manucci, *op. cit.*, II, p. 60; Thevenot, *op. cit.*, chapter XLIX, p. 84.

97. A.N., I, p. 90, Tr. I, p. 231, *Tuzuk* (trans. R. & B), I, p. 78.
98. Sarkar, J.N., *Aurangzib, op. cit.*, III, p. 57.
98a. Tod, *op. cit.*, I, p. 479.
99. *Ibid.*, p. 326.
100. Badauni, II, pp. 301-2, Tr. II, p 311; Manucci, II, pp. 330-31.
101. Sarkar, J.N., *Studies in Mughal India,* pp. 114-17.
102. John Marshall in India, notes and observations in Bengal (1668-72), edited by Sir Shafaat Ahmad Khan, Oxford, 1927, p. 386.
103. Della, Valle (ed. Edward Grey), II, pp. 227-28.
104. Badauni, III, p. 28, Tr. III, p. 48.
105. Growse, F.S. *Prologue to the Ramayana of Tulsi Das,* ASB (1876), pp. 22-23.
106. Bernier (1891), pp. 335-36.
107. Badauni, III, p. 56, Tr. III, p. 73.
108. Hamilton, Alexander, *A New Account of East Indies (1688-1723),* Vol. I, p. 127.
109. Maasir-i-Alamgiri, E & D. Vol. VII, p. 184.
110. Monserrate, *op. cit.*, p. 102.
111. Nadvi, Abul Hasan, *Hindostan ki Qadimi Islami Darsgahan,* p. 29.
112. Badauni, III, p. 119; Tr. III, pp. 174-75.
113. *Ibid.*, I, p. 471, Tr. I, p. 471.
114. *Ibid.*, II, p. 60, Tr. II, p. 62.
115. Nadvi, *op. cit.*, p. 22.
116. Dasgupta, *op. cit.*, p. 91.
117. Mirat-i-Ahmadi, Calcutta Review, October 1940, p. 311.
118. Manucci, *op. cit.*, II, p. 424.
119. Mookerji, R.K., *Ancient Indian Education,* p. 598.
120. Altekar, A.S., *Education in Ancient India,* pp. 292-93.
121. Refer to Appendix A. in Chopra, *Society and Culture. During the Mughal Age,* pp. 172-73 for details. This list has been compiled from Chahar Chaman, Shibli Numani, Shir ul Ajam, III, (1922), pp. 149-50, Latif, Dr. Sayyid Abdulla, *Adliat-i-Farsi Main Hinduon ka Hissa. Anjaman-i-Taraqqi-i-Urdu* Delhi, 1924, pp. 239-42, Nadvi, A.H., *Hindostan ki Qadimi Islami Darsgahan.* pp. 120-24.
122. *Tuzuk* (R & B), II, p. 277; E.D. VII, p. 162.

122a. *This seems to be very doubtful* (Editor).

123. Dasgupta, *op. cit.*, p. 180. So far as Bengal is concerned we have positive evidence that female education was at its lowest ebb in the eighteenth and the first half of the 19th century and there was a superstitious belief that a woman who reads or writes becomes a widow (Editor).

124. For sources refer to Chopra, *Society & Culture in Mughal Age*, p. 168, f.n. 1 & 2.

125. *Ain*, op. cit. I, p. 10.

126. *Maasir-i-Alamgiri*, trans. Urdu by Talab pp. 387, 394. Also see Magan Lall, Dewan of Zeb un Nīsa, BORS, Jan. 1927.

127. *Maasir-i-Rahimi*, III, pp. 1680, 1696.

128. Margaret, Macricol, edited, *Poems by Indian Women*, Heritage of India Series, p. 26.

129. Kaye, G., *Astronomical Observatories of Jai Singh*.

130. Bernier, *Travels, op. cit.*, p. 335.

131. *Iqbalnāma-i-Jahangīrī* translated in Urdu by Maulavi Abalswala Muhammad Zakriya, Osmania, 1928, p. 107.

8

Some Forms of Special Education

Female Education: Mohammedan women used to observe *'puradh'* system. Therefore, they could not attend Maktabs or Madrasahs like male students, regularly. Some girls of a locality assembling in company would go to the Maktabs attached to mosque for the sake of education, their main purpose being to learn simply reading and writing only. There was no universal system of woman education prevalent during that period. Whatever woman education was there, it was confined only to urban areas. There was no separate provision for the education of the girls of general masses. It is no wonder then that they remained comparatively educationally backward. During Moghul period also, education of women-folk was prevalent in some form or the other. The daughters of royal family and those of nobles were educated privately at home. It is also conjectured that the girls of middle class Hindu families must have been receiving elementary education with boys or at home privately. The curriculum for girls was mainly the study of religious books and Home Science. Some princesses were proficient in literature and music. The daughter of Emperor Babar named Gulbadan Begum had written *Humāyūnāma;* Sultānā Rizia was a learned and able lady. She was expert in military, art or warfare, politics and administration. Sultana Salima, Nūr Jahan, Mumtaz Mahal and Jananara Begum had thoroughly studied literature and arts. From amongst these, Nūr Jahan was a very capable empress who would look to the administrative duties for her husband. Zeb-un-Nisa, the daughter of Aurangzeb, was a born poetess of Arabic and Persian languages. *Diwan-i-Makhafi* is her immortal poetic work.

Fine Arts and Handicrafts: The major part of Mohammedan rule in India passed through warfare and political chaos and uncertainties; but such times were interspersed by peaceful intervals. It was during these intervals when literature, arts and architecture made appreciable progress. The Mohammedans adopted popular Hindu handicrafts in the sphere of crafts of a general nature. Some of the handicrafts reached the culminating point in artistic beauty. Ivory-work, jewellery, embroidery, enamelling, muslin, ship-building, manufacture of chariots and ammunitions of war etc. were the main industries which were followed both for art and learning livelihood. Royal courts and feudal aristocracy extended sufficient patronage to these industries which produced a very wholesome effect upon their further growth. The training method in these industries was hereditary and traditional *i.e.* apprentices were trained at home or in the workshops from generation to generation. There were no technical schools for them like modern times. "Technical training or vocational knowledge was diffused by the system of apprenticeship. There were thousands of *Kārkhānās* or workshops wherein boys were that often apprenticed with the artisan to the trade for receiving instruction in particular arts and crafts.

From the viewpoint of fine arts, Mohammedan period can very well be called the 'golden age' in the history of India. As a matter of fact, most of the rulers and emperors were easeloving and epicurean in taste and spent their lives in pompous luxuries. Such circumstances were quite conducive to the progress and patronage of fine arts. Consequently, music and painting flourished well during this period. The royal courts sheltered musicians and painters of high and exceptional accomplishments. The paintings of Moghul period are still regarded as objects of wonder and admiration in the world. Art of dancing also received ample patronage in the courts. This art was popular among the general masses also. Expert teachers were kept to give training in the arts of music and dancing. The Mohammedan rulers were exceptionally fond of constructing buildings. Hence architecture attained a high level of advancement. The Taj Mahal at Agra and other wonderful massive buildings at different places are still reminding people of the glory that India once was.

Military Education: The Mohammedans had to remain engaged in constant warfare in order to establish and stabilize their empire in India. Hence military art flourished well during this age. This art was very popular in India during the reign of early Sultans. Princes were given military training from the early period of their life. It is unquestionably an admitted fact that military skill of the

Mohammedans was superior to that of the contemporary Hindus. Though as regards physical strength and individual skill, the Hindu soldiers were not, in any way, inferior to the Muslim soldiers, yet the Mohammedan military art was remarkable of its own kind. Art of warfare made still more progress during Moghul period.

Military education for the princes included mainly, riding the horse, handling of lance, bow and sword, art of besieging and other soldierly feats. The military curriculum for the ordinary soldiers was more or less identical with that of the princes.

Progress of Literature: 'Literature is the mirror of society'; according to this saying, we can very well imagine the educational condition of medieval times through contemporary literature. Literary productions of that age are eloquent testimony to the fact that education was widely spread and it was of a high standard.

Indeed, Persian literature progressed considerably under the benign patronage of the courts. Amir Khusrau who had lived in the courts of the rulers of Khilji and Tughlug dynasties, was an eminent poet. His compositions are read with interest and liking even today. Another poet named Mir Hassan Dehlawi was patronised by Mohammad Tughluq for his superb poetic talents. He composed *Diwan* and wrote memoirs of Sheikh Nizamuddin Aulia. The works of these great poets have found admirers even outside the country. During 13th century, history, poetry, and fiction made progress with lone strides.

The court historians produced ample historical literature. The *Tarikh-i-Firozshahi* written by Ziauddin Barni, *Tarikh-i-Firozshahi* by Shamash Shiraj Afif and *Tarikh-i-Mubarakshahi* written by Yahia Bin Abdullah are some of the important historical productions.

In many cases, these Mohammedan litterateurs were also erudite scholars of Sanskrit literature. Albiruni who came to India in 10th. Century, was an eminent scholar of Sanskrit. He translated Sanskrit works on philosophy and astronomy into Arabic. His work '*Tarikh-i-Hind*' throws sufficient light on Indian culture. During 14th. century, Firozshah got a famous Sanskrit volume dealing with philosophy, Tantra and science of Omens translated into Persian and named it *Dalail Firozshahi*. During the regin of Sikander Lodi also a Sanskrit work on Medical Science was traslated into Persian.

Progress of literature reached its zenith during Moghul period. Babar himself was a profound scholar of Arabic, Persian and Turkish languages as well as superb poet. He has written memoirs in Turkish. The adoption of a policy of religious tolerance by most of the Moghul emperors created a congenial atmosphere for the unprecedented growth and progress of literature and arts of higher order. During the term of Akbar's reign both Persian and Hindi made simultaneous progress in a great measure. A new language 'Urdu' had emerge and some compositions had been made in it also.

Some historical works were also produced during Akbar's reign. Some of the important productions of the period are *Tarikhi-i Alafi* by Mullah Daood. *Ain-i-Akbari* and *Akbaranamah* by Abul Fazl and *Muntakhabut Tavarikh* by Badauni. Abul Fazl was pre-eminently the greatest writer, poet, historian, administrator and logician of the period. Many Sanskrit volumes were also translated into Persian language through the orders of Akbar. Badauni translated some chapters from the *Ramayana* and *Mahabharata* into Persian. Hazi Ibrahim Sarhindi translated the Atharva Veda. Faizi also translated *Lilavati*—a famous work on Arithmetic into Persian. Gizali and Faizi were the famous poets of Persian language.

Hindi Literature and ancient Indian system of education were also making progress along with Persian literature and Islamic system of education. Reference to it will be made at proper place. Thus production of literature (Prose and Poetry), history and philosophic literature is an unmistakable proof of the fact that contemporary system of education was capable of producing eminent scholars, poets, literary celebrities and historians.

Teacher-taught Relationship: During medieval period, teacher was held in high respect and enjoyed a unique position in society under Islamic system of education. "Their integrity was absolutely unshakable. They occupied a high position in society, and though their emoluments were small, they commanded universal respect and confidence,[3] Pupils, would revere their teachers and serve them. Teachers themselves regarded pupils as their own sons and thus followed the ideal of ancient Indian educational system. Children reading in Maktabls could come in contact with the teacher only when they went to Maktabs during the day, but in some Madrasahs where there was hostel arrangement, teachers and pupils resided under the same roof and reaped the advantages of closest contact. A teacher was never seriously confronted with the problem of discipline. Pupils were habitually humble and obedient owing to the high honour and prestige of teachers in the society. Service of teachers was deemed as the sacred duty of pupils. The belief was prevalent that true knowledge could be attained only through the blessings of the preceptor. It is, indeed, very deplorable that the ideal of service and reverence due to a teacher was not followed so conscientiously as it was done in ancient times. The spirit of sacrifice for teachers was more or less on the decline. Reference to the slighting treatment meted out to Mullah Shah Saleh, the teacher of Aurangzeb by the pupil has already been made. The Emperor had refused to interview his teacher and when at last he called him, he was behaved very severely and was ordered to live in secret asylum forever.

Hostels: There was no hostel-arrangement for the students of Maktabs. Hostels were provided in Madrasahs alone. Big *jagiris* or estates were attached to these Madrashs and hostels for the purpose of meeting daily expenditure incurred on their maintenance. Some benevolent citizens would construct hostels in order to earn name and social prestige. Allāma Shibli, giving a description of a hostel wrote that within the premises of the institution there was a hospital and a *Mazabata* or pond. At the time of opening of the Madrasah, 240 students were admitted to the hostel. They were provided with room, carpet, food, oil, paper and pen by the Madrasah. Students would get sweets and fruits with their daily food and they were given one golden coin (*Asharfi*) each per month. Jaffar also, giving an account of a Madrasah constructed by Firozshah Tughluq, writes: "The Madrasah was a very commodious building embellished with lofty domes and situated in an extensive garden adorned with alleys and avenues, and all that human art combined with nature could contribute to make the place fit for meditation. An adjacent tank mirrored in its shiny and placid breast, the high and massive house of study standing on its brink. What a charming sight was it when the Madrasah hummed with hundreds of busy students, walking its clean and smooth floors, diverting themselves on the side of the tank, or listening in attentive masses to the learned lectures of the professors from their respective seats!"[4] Jaffar mentions of another Madrasah Known as Firozshahi Madrasah. "It was a superb and spacious mansion situated within well planned gardens, containing separate apartments for the reception and entertainment of foreign celebrities, who paid it frequent visits. It was a residential college with suitable provision for poor students and professors, who resided there in constant intellectual communion. It had a mosque and a reservoir attached to it. The mosque was famous for its bounty, which was enjoyed by the professor as well as students who lived there."[5] Similarly Ibn-Batuta also describes about another big and beautiful Madrasah with 300 rooms for the residence of the students. They daily studied the Quran and were provided with daily allowance for food and annual allowance for clothes. Referring to another institution of Higher learning he had observed that he had stayed there for sixteen days and marvelled at the beautiful and costly diet for students. They were provided with four kinds of food daily, *viz.* chickens, loaves, *'Polao'* and *'Korma'* (special meat dishes) and a plate of sweets. Ibn-Batuta during the course of his travels used to reside in those hostels. According to his opinion, Madrasahs and hostels of that sort ware scattered throughout the country at that time.

It is, however, evident that the hostel life of this period was much more convenient an comfortable than that in the Ashramas or Viharas of ancient vedic or Buddhist age. The hard mode of living was not so strictly prescribed. The ideal of student-teacher relationship had also altered. Things which were entirely forbidden in ancient times for the students for example, carpet, *korma,* oil and sweets, were freely provided to them during the medieval period. In ancient times, the Ashramas were situated in the forests away from the haunts of mankind where students were taught the lesson of self-dependence and strict discipline. But under the Islamic system of education, the hostels were usually situated amidst the town where all the means of comfort of the students were provided conveniently by the their guardians. Observance of strict discipline and a hard *modus vivendi* had begun to slacken during this period.

Analysis of Merits and Demerits: Muslim education in India, with all its glory and setbacks, persisted for a period of a little more than six hundred years. Though some Maktabls still exist here and there and fulfil the need of Mohammedan religious. education to some extent; yet they are of no importance from the viewpoint of the provision of practical education—a significant aspect of modern education. The Islamic system of education possessed some special qualities which helped its survival through ages and amidst innumerable vicisitudes—political and social. The state and rulers contributed to its growth and protection. An education system brought into being by a ruling class could not survive long with the fall of empire in an ancient and civilized country like India; yet it has left an indelible mark on Indian life and we find its glimpses in our daily life at all places. Here are some special characteristics of it as follows:-

Merits

(i) *Harmonisation of Secular and Religious Education*:One of the most salient features of Islamic system of education is, its co-ordination between secular and religious education. Islam does not believe in the principle of metempsychosis and the conception of another world. Hence it attaches much importance to materialism and mundane glory. The result was that Muslim educationists laid emphasis on secular aspect of education. In addition to that, they realized the essentiality of religious fanaticism and bigotry. Hence education had necessarily to be influenced by religion. At times, the religious preachers established the importance and indispensability of education for practical life. Mohammad, the famous Prophet preached that acquisition of knowledge was essential for every true Muslim and had recommended for all his followers to 'seek knowledge from the cradle to the grave.' Firozshah Tughlug, Akbar and Aurangzeb especially emphasised secular education. There was always the need of *Kazi, Vazir* (Judge, Counsellor) and army commander for state administration. Appointments to these posts was made from amongst the students who had finished academic career. Besides, provision of education in arts and crafts, architecture, agriculture, medicine and commerce and such other subjects of practical utility defined the essential aim of education to be a harmonisation between secular and religious education. The contemporary educational system sought to effect co-ordination between the two kinds of education by providing for secular education in Maktabs side by side with the study of the Quran and Hadis and chanting the religious prayers.

(ii) *Objectivity*:Education was not meant only for the sake of education; but on the other hand, it was subservient to the practical aspect of life. The philosophic nihilism had no appeal for the Muslims. They were staunch believers in the theory of action and hence thought it their prime duty to load every moment of their life with the ore of practical deeds in this present life. Education as such, aimed at preparing students for the practical aspects of life. Emperor Aurangzeb made intrepid efforts to make the education of princes more practical and vital in character. According to his views, education in the art of administration, history, geography, civics as well as military art was far more useful and practical for princes than mere theoretical learning of words.

(iii) *Indispensability of Education*:Under the Islamic system, education was considered to be indispensable for life; for according to the dictates of the Holy Quran, only that person who has acquired knowledge, is the real devotee and worshipper of God. Muhammad preached his followers to "acquire knowledge because he who acquires it in the way of the Lord, performs an act of piety, who speaks of it, praises the Lord, who seeks it adores. God..........who imparts it to its fitting objects, performs an act of devotion to God. Knowledge enables its possessor to distinguish what is forbidden from what is not; it lights the way to heaven, it is our friend in the desert, our society in solitude, our companion where benefit of friends, it guides us to happiness...........With knowledge the servant of God rises to the heights of godness."[6]

The religious background, therefore, enhanced the indispensability and universality of education. It was, again, thought to be essential even to attain material prosperity. That is why many religious-minded citizens, emperors and princes deemed it their sacred duty to educate the masses. The students also took a keen interest in learning and regarded the acquisition of knowledge as important. According to the preachings of the Prophet Muhammad it was the belief amongst the Muslim students that "To the student, who goes forth in quest of knowledge, God will allot a high place in the mansions of bliss; every step he takes is blessed and every lesson he receives, has its reward".

(iv) *Evolution of History and Belles:Lettres*—Another important feature of Islamic education was that polite literature and history made appreciably good progress during the period. Heretofore, the tendency to produce true historical works had not evolved under the ancient Indian educational system. Whatever little history we get, it is in the form of legendary and mythological tales. We get very little of a true and authentic account of historical events in chronological order before the advent of the Mohammedans. *Raj-Tarangini* written by Kalhan can be placed in the category of history. But, the Muslim rulers, as has been pointed out, wrote history in the form of memoirs and extended patronage to famous historians in their courts. *Belles-Lettres* of the period owned its existence especially to the epicurean taste and high aesthetic sense of the Mohammedans. Therefore, different aspects of literature such as prose, verse, fiction and poetry were included in the curricula of contemporary education.

(v) *Mutual Contact between Students and Teachers*:Like ancient Indian system of education, it is a special feature of the Islamic educational system that it effects a very close personal contact between the teacher and pupil. Teachers of Maktabs and Madrashas paid individual attention to the students. Every student proceeded with his lesson independently according to his level of intelligence and capacity. It should, however, be remembered that there was no class system during that period. Consequently, able and intelligent students got ample opportunities to display their worth.

Demerits

Despite the above-mentioned merits, Islamic education was not immune from certain glaring defects. The system sometimes received rude shocks at the hands of occasional wars and other political disturbances; but, as has been indicated above, some emperors like Shah Akbar and Aurangzeb, having improved the situation organised education on a new pattern. But Muslim system of education was dealt fatal blows, in course of time, by a series of historical occurrences, *i.e.* downfall of Moghul Empire, invasions of Nadir Shah and Ahmad Abdali and rise of the Marathas and the establishment of British empire in India. The roots of ancient Indian system of education had gone deep into the soil of the country. It, therefore, survived even fierce and persistent efforts of Muslim rulers to extirpate its root and branch. But it was not so in the case of Islamic education; it could not pervade and suffuse Indian life so thoroughly and deeply. Consequently, it is no matter of surprise, that it submitted even to only a few political unpheavals.

The following are the main defects of the Islamic system of education:-

(i) *Too much emphasis on Secular Aspect*:The system emphasised materialism more than spiritual aspect of education owing to the radical principles underlying the Mohammedan religion. Spiritualism was, therefore, neglected to a great extent. Though religious education formed an integral part of primary curriculum and the study of the Quran was compulsory, yet it could not attain that mark of spiritualism which had been done by ancient Indian educational system. The sole aim of education was confined only to social recognition and seeking for posts under the State. The materialistic avarice did not let students probe the depths of life which was a unique aspect of ancient Indian education. In a way, this system of Education was only a temporary phase according to the demands of circumstances. It could not evolve in the form of universal law of life.

(ii) *Ephemeral Nature of Institutions*:Another defect of Mohammedan system of education was that the Maktabs and Madrasahs had a very short term of life and would generally collapse owing to scarcity of funds for their maintenance, or the withdrawal of sate patronage only to serve as the dwelling places of birds and wild animals.

(iii) *Domination of Persian and Arabic*:From the very elementary stage, children were taught the Persian alphabet in Maktabs. The medium of instruction in Madrasahs was Persian. Persian, being the State language, was compulsorily to be studied. Even the Hindus acquired knowledge of Persian with a view to obtaining State service. Consequently, provincial languages could not develop. Akbar tried to promote the cause of Hindi side by side with Persian, but

this policy could not be translated into practice. Aurangzeb condemned the practice of wasting time in cramming words and grammar of Persian and Arabic. He, for his part, encouraged the teaching and composition in regional languages especially Urdu. In fact, the scene was entirely dominated by Persian and Arabic.

(iv) *Lack of Universality of Education:*Education has been regarded as compulsory accordingly to the tenets of Mohammedan religion and it was the common belief that "the seeker of knowledge will be greeted in Heaven with a welcome from the angles." In spite of that, surprisingly enough, it could not be universal. Education mostly remained confined to urban areas only, i.e. the main colonies of the Muslims, and consequently mass education was utterly neglected. In fact, the state had not established any organised and regular body like the Department of Education aiming at educating the masses and disseminating educational principles among them. The rulers as well as wealthy nobles had established Maktabs and Madrasahas, being prompted by religious and charitable sentiment or motives of social prestige and wide-spread repute. But the institutions would usually collapse after the death of the founders. Further, on account of religious fanaticism of most of the Mohammedan rulers, education of Hindu masses always lay under a cloud. Barring a few exceptions like Akbar, they provided mostly for the education of the Muslims. Aurangzeb, being blinded by extreme bigotry, went even to the length of demolishing Hindu shrines, universities and other educational centres and encouraged Islamic religion and education by constructing Muslim religious and educational institutions on their ruins. Thus, only a particular class was benefited by this system of education.

(v) *Negligence of Women-Education*—Women remained generally deprived of education owing to strict *Pardah* system. No doubt, princesses and other girls belonging to royal families as well as daughters of wealthy nobles received education inside their own palaces, and some of them were profoundly learned persons; but there was no proper arrangement for the girls of the general masses. Only

a few girls would learn mere reading and writing in the local mosque with boys. According to some writers this neglect of female education was due to the adversity of circumstances and not due to any inherent defect in the system.[7]

(vi) *Indiscrepancy between Reading and Writing:* According to Islamic system of education, the child would first learn the reading of letters and words and it was followed by writing. This did not bring about harmonious development in the child and thus much of the valuable time was wasted uselessly. Akbar amended this system by prescribing simultaneous learning of reading and writing and *farmāns* or State mandates to this effect were issued throughout the empire. Nevertheless, the defect could not entirely be remedied.

(vii) *Other Defects:* Besides the above-mentioned limitations of the Islamic education, there were other glaring defects also, such as, comparatively lack of 'Svadhyaya' (self study) and that of originality through the habit of cramming in students, inclination towards luxury and comfort on the part of students, severe mode of corporal punishment and the engendering in pupils a tendency to indulge in vain controversies.

Despite all these drawbacks inherent in the Islamic system of education, it has its own speciality *i.e.* that of placing a new ideal of life before the Muslim community by uniting them together. The credit of strengthening the hands of Mohammedan culture can rightly be claimed by their system of education. The educational system not only helped the Indian Muslim masses in keeping their relations intact with other Muslim countries of Asia, and Middle East, but also succeeded in infusing a spirit of harmony and fraternal sentiments among the Hindu converts.

References

1. Jaffar: *Education in Muslim India*. p. 4.
2. Jaffar '*Education in Muslim India*'. p. 12-13.
3. Jaffar: Education in Muslim India, p. 4.

4. Jaffar: *Education in Muslim India.*

5. Jaffar: *Education in Muslim India*, p. 51 (1936 Edn.)

6. Amir Ali: *Spirit of Islam*, ch. IX, p. 360.

7. "In India daughters of Islam could not rise to the standard of perfection their preceptors had attained in *belles-lettres,* yet when allowance is made for the age they lived in and the circumstances that obtained then, it will be evident that they had made a fair advance in the sphere of intellect, and it will be wrong to suppose that their education was neglected." Jaffar: *Education in Muslim India,* p. 8.

9

Mughal Education

Education and Literature

In Mughul India there was nothing like the modern system of education established and maintained by the State. But primary and secondary education of some sort existed. The rulers themselves, as well as many of the grandees, encouraged such education by grants of lands or money to moques, monasteries and individual saints and scholars. Thus almost every mosque had a *maktab* attached to it, where the boys and girls of the neighbourhood received elementary education. Hindu Sanskritic and vernacular schools also continued to function for the benefit of students in the urban as well as rural areas.

The Mughul rulers of India were patrons of education. It is stated, on the authority of the *Tawārīkh* of Sayyid Maqbar 'Ālī, a minister' of Bābur, that one of the duties of the Public Works Department (*Shukrat-i-Ām*) of that ruler's time was the building of schools and colleges. Humayūn, though indolent and addicted to opium, had a passion for study, his favourite subjects being geography and astronomy; and his fondness for books was so great that he always "carried a select library with him". He caused a *madrāsā* to be established at Delhi and changed the pleasure-house built by Sher Snāh in the *Purāna Qil'ā* into a library. "Akbar's reign marks a new epoch for the system introduced for imparting education in schools and colleges". He built colleges at Fatehpur Sīkri, Āgra and other places. With a view to improving the state of Muslim education, he effected certain changes in its curriculum, which it would be unreasonable to say produced no effect at all. As a matter of fact, Abul Fazl, referring to its good results, writes that "all nations have schools for the education of youths; but Hindustān is particularly famous for its seminaries". Prompted by his policy of religious toleration, Akbar arranged in later years for the education of Hindus in *madrāsās*. Jahāngir, possessed of some literary teste and well-read in Persian as well as Turki, issued a regulation to the effect that on the death of a rich man or traveller without any heir, his property would escheat to the crown and be utilised for building and repairing *madrāsās*, monasteries, etc. It is recorded in the *Ta'rīkh-ī-Jan-Jahān* that, soon after his accession to the throne, Jahāngīr "repaired even those *madrāsās* that had for thirty years been the dwelling-places of birds and beasts, and filled them with students and professors" Shāh Jahān, though more interested in magnificent buildings than in anything else, was educated in his early youth in Turki, spent a part of the night in his own studies, and encouraged learning by granting rewards and stipends to scholars. He founded one college at Delhi and repaired the college named *Dār-ul-Baqū* (abode of Eternity), which had been almost in ruins. In Dārā Shukoh the Mughul imperial family possessed one of the greatest scholars that India has ever produced. Well-versed in Arabic, Persian and Sanskrit, he was the author of some famous works, including Persian translations of the *Upanishads*, the *Bhagavat Gītā* and the *Yoga Vāsishṭha Rāmāyaṇa;* a calender of Muslin saints; and several works on Sūfī philosophy. Looking at the grave of this unlucky person, Sir William Sleeman rightly thought that had he lived to occupy the throne, the nature of education, and there with the destiny of India, would have been different. Aurangzeb, though highly educated, did nothing substantial to promote learning in general, though he extended every encouragement to Muslim education, and founded, according to Keene, "numerous colleges and schools".

Female education of some sort existed during the Mughul period. The daughters of the imperial household, and of rich nobles, were given tuition in their houses, and we may assume that the daughters of the middle-class people among the Hindus received primary education along with the boys in the schools and that some of them were conversant with religious literature. The Auxiliary Committee of the Indian Statutory Commission rightly observed in September, 1929, that there is "nothing inherent either in the Hindu in or in the Muslim religion which militates against the education of women. In fact, there were in India even in early days many examples of women possessings wide knowledge, particularly of sacred and classical literature". In Akbar's time "regular training was given to the ladies of the royal household". Some of the ladies so instructed distinguished themselves in the sphere of literature. Thus Bāhur's daughter, Gulbadan Begam, authoress of the *Humāyūnāmāh*, Humāyūn's niece, Salimā Sultānā, authoress of several Persian poems, Nūr Jahān, Mumtāz Mahal, Jahāanārā Began and Zeb-un-Nisā are highly educated ladies, well-read in Persian and Arabic literature. Besides being a fine Arabic and Persian scholar, Zeb-un-Nisā was an expert in calligraphy and had a rich library.

As we have already noted, the Tīmūrīd rulers of India were patrons of literature and gave a considerable impetus to its development in different branches. Many scholars flourished and wrote interesting and important works under the patronage of Akbar. One of Akbar's contemporaries, Mādhavāchārya, a Bengali poet of Triveni and author of *Chandī-mangal*, bestows high praise on the Emperor as a patron of letters.

The Persain literature of Akbar's reign may be considered under three heads: (i) historical works, (ii) translations, and (iii) poetry and verse. The well-known historical works of the reign are the *Ta'rīkh-i-'Alfi* of Mullā Dāūd, the *'Āīn-i-Akbarī* and *Akbarnāmāh* of Abul Fazl, the *Muntakhab-ut-Tawārīkh* of Badāūnī, the *Tabaquāt-i-Akbari* of Nizām-ud-dīn Ahmad, the *Akbarnāmāh* of Faizī Sarhindī, and the *Ma-'āsir-i-Rahīmī* of 'Abdul Bāqī, compiled under the patronage of 'Abdur Rahīm Khān-i-Khānān. The most accomplished writer (in Persian) of the reign was Abul Fazl, a man of letters, a poet, an essayist, a critic, and a historian. By order of the Emperor, many books in Sanskrit and other languages were translated into Persian. Different sections of the *Mahābhārata* were translated into that language by several Muslim scholars and were compiled under the title of *Razm-Nāmāh*. After labouring for four years, Badāūnī completed the translation of the *Rāmāyaṇa* in A.D. 1589. Hājī Ibrāhīm Sarhindī translated into Persian the *Atharva Veda;* Faizī the *Libābatī,* a work on mathematics; Mukammal Khān Gujarātī the *Tajak*, a treatise on astronomy; 'Abdur Rahīm Khān-i-Khānān the *Wāqiāt-i-Bāburī;* and Maulānā Shāh Muhammad Shāhābādī translated the *History of Kāshmīr*. Some Greek and Arabic works were also translated into Persian. A number of famous poets or versifiers produced works of merit under the patronage of Akbar. The most famous among the verse-writers was Ghizalī. Next in importance to him was Faizī, a brother of Abul Fazl. Other prominent poets were Muhammad Husain Nazirī of Nishāpur, who wrote *ghazals* of great merit, and Sayyid Jamāluddīn Urfī of Sirāj, the most famous writer of *Qasidāas* in his days.

Jahāngīr, possessed of an excellent literary taste, also extended his patronage to scholars. His autobiography is second only to that of Bābur in matter and style. Among the learned men who adorned his court, of whom the *Iqbālnāmāh-i-Jahāngīrī* has given a comprehensive list, we may mention here the names of Ghiyāz Beg, Naqib Khān, Mu'tamid Khān, Niāmatullah and 'Abdul Haqq Dihlawī. Some historical works were written during Jahāngīr's reign, the most important of these being the *Ma'āsir-i-Jahāngīrī,* the *Iqbālnāmah-i-Jaḥāngīrī* and the *Zubd-ut-Tauārīkh.* Shāh Jahān followed his predecessors in patronising learned men. Besides many poets and theologians, there flourished in his court some famous writers of history like 'Abdul Hamīd Lāhorī, author of the *Pādshāh-nāmāh.* Amīnāī Qazwīnī, author of another *Pādshāhnāmāh,* Ināyat Khān, author of the *Shāh-Jahānnāmāh,* and Muhammad Sālih, author of *'Amal-i-Sālih,* all of whom are important authorities on the history of Shāh Jahān's reign. The scholarly works of Prince Dārā Shukoh, to which reference has already been made, are masterpieces of Persian literature. A zealous Sunnī, Aurangzeb was a critical scholar of Muslim theology and jurisprudence. He had no taste for poetry. Though opposed to the writing of histories of his reign, so that the *Muntakhab-ul-Lubāb* of Khāfi Khān had to be written in secrecy, there are some well known works of this kind, such as the *'Ālamgīrnāmāh* by Mīrzā Muhammad Kāzim, the *Ma'āsir-i-Ālamgīrī* of Muhammad Sāqi, the *Khulāsat-ut-Tawārīkh* of Sujan Rāi Khatri, the *Nuskha-i-Dilkushā* of Bhīmsen and the *Fatūhāt-i-Ālamgīrī* of Ishwar Dās.

The peace and order secured by Akbar, and the cosmopolitan ideas of the religious movements of the period, preached by a band of saintly teachers in a language "understanded of the people", stimulated the genius of the latter, which unfolded itself in manifold petals. The sixteenth and seventeenth centuries consequently became "the Augustan age of Hindustani literature". The first writer of note after 1526 was Malik Muhammad Jayasī, who in 1540 wrote "the fine philosophic epic entitled the *Padmāvat,* which gives the story of Padminī, the queen of Mewār, in an allegorical setting". Akbar's keen interest in, and patronage of, Hindī poetry gave a great stimulus to Hindi literature. Among the courtiers of the Emperor, Bīrbal, who received from him the title of Kavi Priya, was a famous poet. Rājā

Mān Singh also wrote verses in Hindi and was a patron of learning. The most distinguished writer among Akbar's ministers was 'Abdur Rahīm Khān-i-Khānān, whose *dohās* are even now read with interest and admiration all over Northern India. Narahari, whom the Emperor gave the title of Mahāpātra, Harināth and Ganj were also noted writers of his court.

The greater part of the poetical literature of the time was religious, marked by an exposition of either Krishna worship or the Rāma cult. Many writers of the former faith flourished in the Brajabhūmi, corresponding roughly to the Jumnā valley, where it developed remarkably. Among the eight disciples of Vallabhāchārya and his son Bithal Nāth, grouped under the name of "*Astachāp*", the most notable was Surdās, "the blind bard of Āgra", who, writing in *Brajabhāshā*, described in his *Sursāgar* the sports of Krishna's early life, and composed many verses on the charm of Krishna and his beloved Rādhā. The other important poets of this school were Nand Dās, author of the *Rās-panchadhyāyi*, Vithal Nāth, author of the *Chaurāsī Vaishnava ki vārtā* in prose, Paramānanda Dās, Kumbhan Dās, and Ras Khān (a Muslim disciple of Vitchal Nāth), author of *Premavārtikā*. Among the writers of the Rāma cult, the most illustrious was Tulsī Dās (A.D. 1532-1623), who lived in Benares "unapproachable and alone in his niche in the temple of Fame". He was not merely a poet of a high order, but a spiritual teacher of the people of Hindustān, where his name has become a household word and his memory is worshipped by millions. The most famous of his works, known as *Rāmcharitamānasa*, or "The Pool of Rāma's Life", has been justly described by Sir George Grierson as "the one Bible of a hundred millions of people" of Hindustan. Growse also observed in his translation of the *Rāmāyaṇa* of Tulsī Dās that "his book is in every-one's hands, from the court to the cottage, and is read and heard and appreciated alike by every class of the Hindu community, whether high or low, rich or poor, young or old". This period was also marked by "the first attempts to systematise art of poetry itself", made by the writers like Keshava Dās (A.D. 1580), a Sāndhya Brāhmaṇa of Orchā, Sundar Senāpati and the Tripāthī brothers, who flourished during the reign of Shāh Jahān.

In Bengal, this period was remarkable for a brilliant outburst of the Vaishṇava literature. Its various branches, such as the *Karchās* or notes, the *padas* and songs, and the biographies of Chaitanya Deva, have not only saturated the minds of the people of Bengal with feelings of love and liberalism, but have also survived as a mirror of the social life of the province during that age. The most prominent Vaishṇava writers were Kṛishṇadās Kavirāj (born in A.D. 1517 of a Vaidya family of Jhāmālpur in Burdwān), the author of the most important biography of Chaitanya, bearing the title of *Chaitanyacharitāmitra;* Brindāvan Dās (born in A.D. 1507), the author of *Chaitanya Bhāgavata*, which besides being a standard work on the life of Chaitanya Deva, is a storehouse of information concerning the Bengali society of his time; Jayānanda (born in A.D. 1513), the author of *Chaitanya Maṇgal,* a biographical work giving some fresh information about Chaitanya Deva's life; Trilochan Dās (born in A.D. 1523 at Kowgrām, a village situated thirty miles to the north of Burdwān), the author of a very popular biography of Chaitanya Deva also known as *Chaitanya Mangal;* and Narahari Chakravarty, the author of *Bhaktiratnākar,* a voluminous biography of Chaitanya Deva, written in fifteen chapters and considered to be next in importance only to the work of Kṛishṇadās Kavirāj. This period also saw the production of numerous translations of the great epics and the *Bhāgavata,* and books in praise of Chandī Devī and Manasā Devī. The most important of these works were the *Mahābhārata* of Kāsirām Dās and the *Kavikankan Chandi* of Mukundarām Chakravarti, which enjoys to this day as much popularity in Bengal as the famous book of Tulsī Das in upper India. Mukundarām's work depicts a graphic picture of the social and economic conditions of the people of Bengal of his time, and it is for this that Prof. Cowell has described him as "the Crabbe of Bengal", and Dr. Grierson considers his poetry "as coming from the heart, and not from the school, and as full of passages adorned with true poetry and descriptive power".

The Emperors' fondness for books led to the foundation of libraries, which were stocked with numerous valuable manuscript works. Akbar's library had enormous collections, which were properly classified under different sections. The art of calligraphy reached a high state of excellence. Among the famous penmen of Akbar's court, of whom the '*Āin-i-Akbarī* has preserved a list, the most distinguished was Muhammad Husain of Kāshmir, who got the title of *Zarrinqalam* (Gold-pen).

The growth of Hindi literature received a setback during the reign of Aurangzeb, owing to the stoppage of court patronage. Not much

Urdu poetry also was written in Northern India during this period; but some famous writers of Urdu verse flourished in the Deccan.

Literary activity did not entirely cease even in the troubled days of later Mughul rule. Men of lettes were patronished by Emperors like Bahādur Shāh and Muhammad Shāh, *Subahdārs* like Murshid Qulī Jāfar Khān and 'Ālīvardī Khān, and zamindārs like Rājā Kṛshṇachandra of Nadiā, Asadullāh of Birbhūm and some others. The literature of this period, with the exception of the devotional songs of Rāmprasād, was often of a low tone and a vitiated taste. Female education, both among the Hindus and the Muslims, was not unknown to the age. The two daughters of Jan Muhammad, a covnerted Hindu and father of the well-known Kokī Jiu, were "sent to school and attained some proficiency in letters". Kokī Jiu "excelled her brothers in handwriting and composition". In Bengal, we find several instances of educated ladies; for example, the wives of Rājā Navskṛshṇa of Sobhābāzār (in Calcutta) were famous for their capacity to read, and Ānandamayī of East Bengal was a poetess of no mean repute.

10

Education During the Reign of Akbar

Moreland writes that during the reign of Akbar there was not a system of popular education and there were no useful foundations and endowments established for that purpose. However, this view does not hold water. There was no department of education which was under state control. Education was dependent on private initiative and arrangements. The Emperors and many of the nobles gave grants of land or money to mosques, monasteries, and saints and scholars to impart education to the children. Sir J. N. Sarkar observes: "This, however, was recognised as a religious and not a political duty, nor were the recipients of these favours bound to maintain schools with money." There was a maktab or school attached to every mosque, where the Mullah taught the children. Keay writes that the maktab signifies a primary school attached to a mosque where the Mullah taught them Quran which they must learn by rote for devotional purposes and sometimes there was teaching, elementary reading, writing and ciphering, while the madrasah is a school or college for higher learning.

The Mughal rulers of India patronished education. Babur was an accomplished scholar of Arabic, Persian and Turki. He composed several Turki poems. His Memoirs written in Turki are of high literary grace and quality. Dr. N.N. Law has wirtten on the basis of Tawrikh of Sayyid Maqbar Ali, a minister of Babur, "that the Public Works Department (Shuhrat-i-Am) of the time, which contiuned through the reigns of the with that of conducting postal service, the publication of a Gazette and the building of schools and colleges." Humayun was greatly interested in the study of books and held discussions with the scholars on literary topics. He also composed verses. He was interested in the study of astronomy and geography and had a select library. Jauhar, the author of the *Tazkirat-ul-Qaqiat* (Private Memoirs of Humayun) was his servant. Dr. N.N. Law writes that Humayun founded a madrasah at Delhi and transformed the pleasure-house erected by Sher Shah in the Purana Qilah into a library.

Dr. N.N. Law writes," Akbar's reign marks a new epoch for the system introduced for imparting education in schools and colleges." Akbar was the first Muslim ruler to transform the stereoytyped character of the Islamic institutions. The subjects which were taught in the Muslim madrasahs did not broaden the vision and widen the knowledge which is necessary for an Indian who was predominantly Hindu. Therefore, Akbar made changes in the curriculum. According to Abul Fazl, he laid emphasis that "Everybody ought to read books on morals, arithmetic, the notation peculiar to arithmetic, agriculture, mensuration, geometry, astronomy, physiogonomy, household matters, the rules of government, medicine, logic, the tabii (physical sciences), riyazi (science that treats of quantity) and Ilahi (theology), science and history, all of which may be equally required."

Akbar ordered that in the schools for Sanskrit learning, Vyakaran, Nyaya, Vedanta and commentary of Patanjali should be taught. Akbar emphasised, as Abul Fazl maintains that "No one should be allowed to neglect these subjects which the present time requires" Moreover, he tried to simplify the system of imparting education and the changes affected by him produced good results. Abul Fazl writes: "All civilised nations have schools for the education of youths; but Hindustan is particulary famous for its seminaries." Edwardes maintains: "It seems more reasonable to assume that Akbar intended merely to indicate those subjects which, in his opinion, might most profitably be studied. The character of the programme lends support to this view; for scientific subjects preponderate, and son Dara Shikoh, was a great scholar of Arabic, Persian and the order in which they appear, indicates a preference for those of practical utility such as would naturally be favoured by a man of Akbar's tastes."

Akbar built colleges at Fatehpur Sikri, Agra and other places. Keay maintains that in accordance with the policy of religious toleration, he arranged in the later years of his reign the education of the children of Hindus in the Muslim madrasahs. Dr. N.N. Law maintains that the example of the Emperor was followed by private benefactors; a madrasah was built by Maham Anaga, Akbar's nurse, near the western gate of Purana Qilah; another was built by Khwaja Muin, in which Mirza Muflis, one of the many learned men attracted to Akbar's court, taught pupils for three years.

Akbar did not effect changes in the curriculum and the method of instructions of the traditional theological madrashas. Akbar appointed the chief sadrs in 1580, who were of liberal views, incharge of education. The Muslim madrashas remained the places of orthodox learning.

Jahangir was also a patron of education but not as great as his father was. He was taught by teachers like Maulana Mir Kalam Muhaddis and Abdul Rahim Mirza. He knew Persian and Turki well. According to Dr. N. N. Law, he promulgated a regulation in his dominions that "whenever a well to-do man or a rich traveller died without any heir, his property would escheat to the Crown and be utilised for building and repairing madrasahs, monasteries, etc." According to the *Tarikh-i-Jan-Jahan,* Jahangir "repaired even those madrasahs that had for thirty years been the dwelling places of birds and beasts, and filled them with students and professors."

Shah Jahan also patronished education like his predecessors. He was educated in Turki, which language he wrote and spoke fluently. Sir J. N. Sarker writes that he spent some time at night for his own studies. Dr. N.N. Law writes that he encouraged scholars by rewards and stipends. He laid the foundation of an Imperial College at Delhi near the Jami Masjid and repaired a college named Dar-ul-Baqa (Abode of Eternity) which was in ruins. Like Akbar, he was greatly impressed by Sufism and tried to conciliate the discordant elements in the State, His succeeding Mughal Emperors, was entrusted among other duties, Sanskrit and had keen interest in philosophical and religious studies. At his behest, the *Upnishads,* the *Bhagwat Gita,* and the *Yoga Vashistha* and *Ramayana* were traslated into Persian. He wrote *Safinat-ul-Auliya,* a biography of the saints of Islam, *Sakinat-ul-Auliya,* an account of saint Mian Mir and his disciples and the *Majma-ul Baharain,* which, according to Dr. N. N. Law, is "a treatise on the technical terms of Hindu Pantheism and their equivalents in Sufi phraseology." His works on Sufism are the *Nadir-ul-Nukat,* the *Hasonat-ul-Arifin* and the *Risalah-i-Haqnuma.*

Being an orthodox Sunni, Aurangzeb destroyed Hindu temples and schools and encouraged the education of Mohammedans only. Keene writes that he "founded numberless colleges and schools." At his behest, the *Fatwa-i-Alamgiri,* a digest of Islamic laws was compiled under the supervision of Mulla Nizam.

Aurangzeb's interest in education caused the establishment of many madrasahs by private benefactors and the development of Sialkot as a seat of learning. Aurangzeb was well educated. He knew Turki and was highly proficient in Persian and Arabic. He learnt the Quran and Hadis by heart and was well-versed in Muslim theology. He added many theological volumes to the library. Bernier tells the tale of the rebuke of Aurangzeb to his tutor of youthful days which clearly indicates that Aurangzeb was dissatisfied with the character of education given to princes and young nobles of that period. "Were you not aware," he cries in the course of his indictment, "that it is during the period of infancy, when the memory is commonly so retentive, that the mind may receive a thousand wise precepts, and be easily furnished with such valuable instructions as will elevate it with lofty conceptions, and render the individual capable of glorious deeds?" And again, towards the end of his outburst, "Answer me, sycophant, ought you not to have instructed me one point at least, so essential to be known as a King, namely on the reciprocal duties between the sovereign and his subjects"?

Bigoted and of narrow outlook he might have been in many ways, Aurangzeb fully realised that the education imparted to the children in the maktabs and madrasahs was too formal and scholastic and that "the formation of character on the basis of a broad humanism and high ideals was far more valuable than the teaching of grammar and the discussion of dry, metaphysical trivialities." It is true that in the madrasahs, sometimes science, literature and history were taught. The last-named subject was always in the favour of the Muslims. It is also true that the maktabs remained while the other Mohammedan institutions decayed. In the maktabs, the teaching continued to the days of the British supremacy. The main defect "yet at its best," writes Edwardes, "the Mughal educational system did little to develop the character and fit the pupil for his vocation in life; and such a demand for the wider extension of scholastic facilities as might have existed from the general population was stifled by the poverty of the country and the rapacity of the public officials. The defects of the system, the spasmodic nature of the encouragement given to education, which was an inevitable result of despotic rule, must not, however, blind up to the fact that Mughul rulers did try according to their own ideas and limitations, to foster the establishment of scholastic institutions, and that two of the greatest of them appear in the records left by contemporary writers to have advocated some of the very reforms which are being sought by the leading educationalists of the present day."

During the Mughal period, there were no maktabs and madrasahs where the girls were educated as it was not considered apt to educate the girls. In Akbar's time, writes Dr. N.N. Law, "regular training was given to the ladies of the royal household." Gulbadan Begum, a daughter of Babur, was a learned lady and is the author of *Humayunnama,* which records the events of Humayun's reign. Salima Sultana (Salima Begum), daughter of Humayun's other sister Gulrukh. Maham Anaga, Nurjahan, Mumtaz Mahal, Jahanara Begum and Zeb-un-Nisa were all educated and keenly interested in art and literature. Most of the lady tutors in Muslim royal families and families of nobles came from Persia and the growth of Persian influence in court circles might be attributed to them. Monserrate writes that Akbar bestowed "great care and attention to the education of the princesses, who were kept vigorously excluded from the sight of men. They are taught to read and write, and are trained in other ways by matrons." But large number of Muslim women, even amongst middle classes, did not receive liberal education.

References

Tuzuk-i-Baturi by Babur, tanslated by Mrs. Beveridge, 2 Vols. Luzac, London, 1921.

2. *Tarikh-i-Rashidi* by Mirza Haider, English translation by Elias and Ross (1895).
3. *Humayunnama* by Gulbadan Begum. Translated and ediled by Mrs. Beveridge. Calcutta, 1902.
4. *Tarikh-i-Ferishta* by Mohamed Kasim Ferishta. English translation by Col. Briggs History of the Rise of the Mohomedan Power in India till the year 1612 A.D., Longmans, London, 1829.
5. *Humayunnama* by Khwandamir.

6. *Tazkirat-ul-Wakiat* by Jauhar.
7. *Tabakat-i-Akbari* by Nizam-ud-din Ahmad.
8. *Tarikh-i-Sher Shahi* by Abbas Khan Sherwani.
9. *Makhzan-i-Afghana* by Niamat Ullah.
10. *Tarikh-i-Daudi* by Abdullah.
11. *Tarikh-i-Badayuni* by Abdul Qadir Badayuni.
12. *Akbarnama* by Abul Fazl, translated into English by Henry Beveridge.
13. *Ain-i-Akbari* by Abul Fazl translated from the Persian by Blochman, Vol. I, Calcutta, 1873, Vol. II, 1891 and H.S. Jarett, Vol. III, 1894.
14. *Tuzuk-i-Jahangiri.*
15. *Tatimma-i-Waqiat-i-Jahangiri* by Muhammad Hadi.
16. *Iqbalnama-i-Jahangiri* by Motamid Khan.
17. *Ma'asir-i-Jahangiri* by Kamgar Khan.
18. *Padshahnama* by Kazwini.
19. *Tuhfat-us-Salatani* by Amir Salih.
20. *Amil-i-Salih* by Muhammad Salih Kambu.
21. *Alamgirnama* by Mirza Muhammad Kazim.
22. *Ma'asir-i-Alamgiri* by Muhammad Saki Mustaid Khan.
23. *Zafar-Nama* by Akil Khan Razi.

11

Important Centres of Education

The Mohammedans, at their arrival in India, established their colonies at places. These establishments eventually developed into big towns. In course of time, these towns became the important centres of Islamic education and culture. Primary education was imparted in the Maktabs attached to mosques. The mosques were usually situated in most of the towns, villages and *Mohallahs*. Primary education, therefore, evolved from Maktabs. Nearly in all parts of the country, the mosques had been constructed. Higher education was conducted in the Madrashas. The Madrasahs were established in towns where the muslim population was in majority and where some muslim administrator would reside. Generally every town had one or more Madrasahs. Any town, would however, grow into famous educational centre by virtue of being the capital seat of some Muslim ruler, or the native town of some subedar or chief or possessing religious importance (being *Dargah or Khangah* etc.). Thus Agra, Fatehpur Sikri, Delhi, Jaunpur, Lahore, Ajmer, Bihar, Lucknow, Firozabad, Jullunder, Multan and Bijapur etc. were important centres of Muslim education and culture. A brief account of some of the famous centres will be given as follows.

Agra: Agra had been founded by Sikander Lodi. "In course of time a splendid city sprang upon the selected site and took the name of Agra, which played a prominant part in shaping the destinies of India in her future history. Once founded, the new capital launched upon a career which was characterised by a rich afflorenscence of learning and literature. It became a radiant centre of Islamic culture and civilization."[1] Sikander Lodi developed it into a famous educational centre and to this end established hundreds of Madrasahs. "Men of learning and erudition from Arabia, Persia, and Bokhara

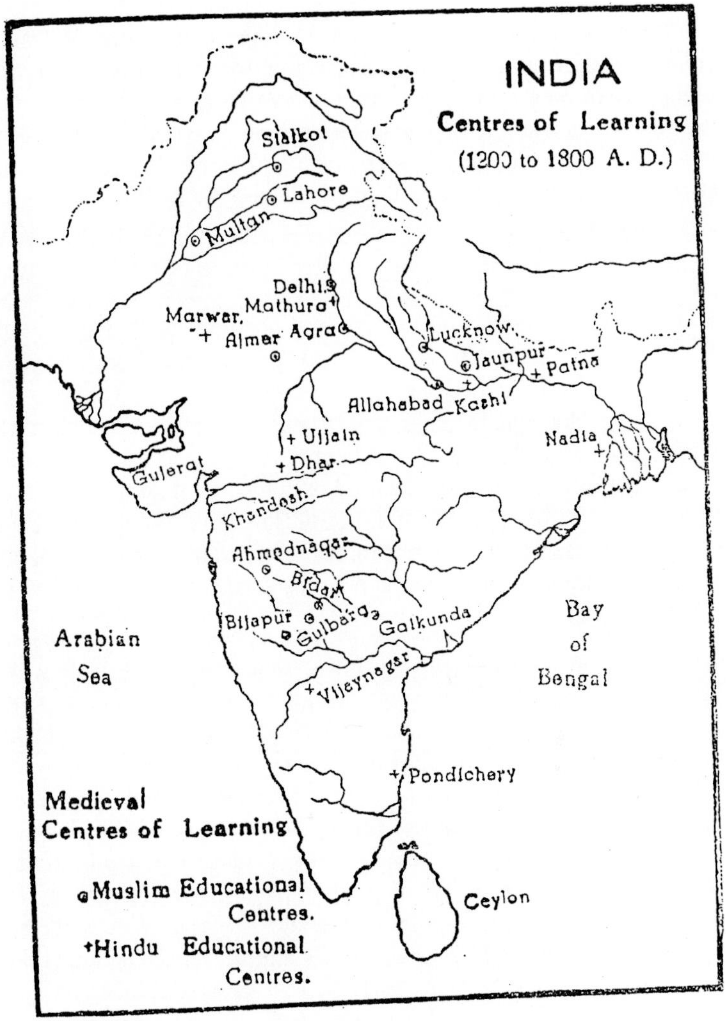

poured into it in ever-increasing numbers at the prospect of receiving better patronage from the ruler of India, who was remarkable for his munificence............The result was that in course of time Agra grew into a great university-city, containing several schools and colleges, where people flocked from far and wide for higher education."[2] After Sikander Lodi, Babar too established some Madrasahs at Agra. During the reign of Akbar, Agra became an important centre of Islamic education and culture as well as arts and crafts. Several scholars, philosophers, poets and artists came to Agra from different parts of the country. The emperor himself participated in learned disputations with the scholars and philosophers. Akbar established many Madrasahs at Agra and Fatehpur Sikari, a town founded by the Emperor himself at a distance of a few miles from Agra. In these Madrasahs, higher education was imparted in the subjects such as literature, arithmetic philosophy, medicine, agriculture, astronomy and commerce. There was proper arrangement for the lodging and boarding of students coming from Central Asia for the sake of education. The period of Akbar's reign can aptly be called the 'golden age' of the progress of Agra. After Akbar, his son Jahangir and grandson emperor Shahjahan also established some Madrasahs at Agra. Aurangzeb too gave much encouragement to the promotion of primary and religious education. With the downfall of the Moghul Empir, the glory of Agra also began to fade away. In modern times too, some of the Maktabs are dragging on their miserable existence in some mosques.

Delhi: Delhi has remained an important centre of the Islamic system of education from the very beginning. In fact, it continued to be the metropolis of *Sultans* and Moghul Emperors too contributed much to its glory and magnificence. Nasiruddin had established Nasiria Madrasah under the leadership of Minhaj-i-Shiraj. Afterwards, Delhi remained an important centre of culture and education during the reigns of other rulers of slave dynasty. During the period of Allahuddin Khilji Delhi became the rendezvous of many a scholar and philosopher. According to Farishta, at that time 43 eminent religious preachers who were profound scholars of religion and law, taught in those Madrasahs which were established by Allahuddin Khilji at Delhi. The importance of Delhi as educational centre increased all the more during the reign of Firoz Tugluq. He found 30 new Madrasahs and got older ones repaired. He made provision for the education of his slaves also. After that, Delhi reached the climax of its progress during Moghul reign and became pre-eminent by an important educational centre in northern India. Humayun had founded a Madrasah for the purpose of conducting education in asronomy and geography. Akbar also brought many a Madrasah into being at Delhi and Mahamnaga, his nurse had also founded a big Madrasah in 1561 at the metropolis. Badauni had received education in this very Madrasah. Jahangir got older Madrasahs of Delhi repaired. Shahjahan, for his part, had founded a Madrasah near Jumma Masjid. Aurangzeb too continued his educational efforts. After him, Ghazi-ud-Din established a Madrasah there. With the collapse of the Moghul Empire, and invasions of Nadir Shah and Ahmed Shah Abdali, the glory of Delhi faded, and thus with the destruction of other educational centres of northern India, importance of Delhi as Muslim educational centre dwindled. For a long time Delhi continued to enjoy the status of an eminent educational centre disseminating Islamic culture throughout the country.

Jaunpur: Jaunpur had been a very important centre of Muslim education. During the reign of Sultans, it was an important centre of Islamic education. Many Madrasahs and Maktabs sprang up during. the period of Firozshah's reign. Jaunpur had grown in fame and importance from the viewpoint of arts, literature and learning of highest order. That is why it was called *Shiraj-i-Hind.* Sharkis founded many Madrasahs at Jaunpur. During fifteenth century Ibrahim Sharki made large contributions to the growth of education. He had attached *Jagirs* to these institutions and encouraged capable students by awarding them *Jagirs* and appointing them to higher ranks in the state. Shershah Suri had been a student of this place. Jaunpur was an important and special education centre of history, philosophy, politics and military training. It continued to enjoy fame for its handicrafts and architecture for centuries, and remained an important educational centre till the last days of Moghal Empire. The University town of Jaunpur lost much of its glory due to the political chaos that followed the downfall of Mughul Empire. The Subedar or Governor of Jaunpur could no longer maintain and patronise the magnificent system of education there and like many other educational centres the glory of this seat of learning also faded away. One historian has lamented the downfall of such towns in the following words.

"Like Jaunpur many a great Muslim University had now ceased to exist, leaving behind only a memory of its former glory. The days are past when the Indian Musalman Universities, as also those of Damascus, Baghdad, Nishapur, Cairo, Kairawan, Seville, Cordova were thronged by thousands of students, when a professor had often hundreds of hearers, and when vast estates set apart for the purpose maintained both students and professors."[3]

Bidar: Another important educational centre was Bidar. Mahmud Gavan had established there a big Madrasah with vast and rich library well-stocked with thousands of books. In course of time, it was destroyed by Aurangzeb. Before Mahmud, many Maktabs and Madrasahs had been founded there by Allahuddin Ahmed. Owing to the development of Bidar into an important educational centre the standard of education in Bahamani Empire had risen considerably. Here Arabic and Persian learning was spread through the rural Maktabs. These Maktabs were attached to mosques and big land grants had been sanctioned by the State for their maintenance. 'There was not even a single hamlet which did not contain at least a Maktab'. The educational system followed in these institutions was uniform the aim of which was as much the propagation of religious doctrines and principles of Mohammedan rulers as the expansion of education and literature. Its remnants are visible even today.[4]

Besides these important seats of learning, Bijapur, Golconda, Malwa, Khandesh, Multan, Gujerat, Lucknow, Sialkot and Bengal were other centres of educational importance at different times during the medieval period.

Conclusion: Thus in a long and chronicled history of about 700 years we find that Muslim education had considerably been spread in India. The Islamic education not only slaked the intellectual thirst of the people but also solved their economic problems. The most important aim which was fulfilled through Muslim education was the propagation of Mohammedan religious principles. From the viewpoint of administration, it was essential on the part of the rulers to acquaint their subjects with their religion, civilization and language. Moreover, it became almost indispensable to imbue the Hindu converts with Islamic religion to the core through religious education so that they might forget their former religion.

But, it is, nonetheless, true that Islamic education, as is evident from the accounts given by Babar and Bernier, could not grow into popularity. That is why the Muslim system of education could not enter into the depths of the life of masses as ancient Hindu education had done. The Islamic education, despite State patronage could not affect Indian soul, whereas ancient education spread throughout the country even without any patronage of whatsoever description. Not only that, the ancient Indian system of education co-existed with Islamic education during medieval age in spite of the absence of state patronage. The Mohammedan institutions could not attain to that universal fame which had been the unique privilege of the Buddist Universities, whose fame did not remain confined only in India but had travelled to China, Japan, Tibet and East Indies. As had been indicated above, most of the Muslim centres of education enjoyed only local repute. But on the other hand, there were educational centres like Jaunpur, Agra and Delhi which had established some high educational traditions.

References

1. Jaffar: "Muslim Education in India" p. 57.
2. *Ibid.* pp. 57-58.
3. N.N. Law: *Promotion of learning in India,* pp. 104-105.
4. J.M. Sen: *History of Elementary Education in India;* p. 27. H.I.E. 8.